INTRODUCTION TO THE COMMON LAW

VOLUME I

French

I0041661

DR. PATRICK B. GRIFFIN

Published in 2017 by
English Language Solutions for Law and Business Ltd

Layout design by Gough Typesetting Services, Dublin

ISBN: 978-1-911404-01-9 (ePub)
ISBN: 978-1-911404-10-1 (Print)

Copyright 2017: Patrick B Griffin

CONTENTS

Each book is broken-up into 10 chapters and each chapter is divided into five parts:

- Part 1 allows the student to increase his/her knowledge of a specific area of law and to develop his/her technical vocabulary.
- Part 2 concentrates on the area of grammar revision.
- Part 3 allows the student to work on his/her listening and speaking skills.
- Part 4 encourages the student to work on his/her translation skills and is made up of translation exercises focused on the theme of each chapter.
- Part 5 allows the student to access more in-depth information on the theme under discussion in each specific chapter.

If possible each chapter/course segment should be completed over a one-week period in order to achieve maximum benefit.

We believe that Mylegalenglish books can have a major impact on the ability of students to use and understand legal English. However, to ensure positive results, it is necessary that students apply the system relied on in the books and actively make use of the book's interactive character, discussed immediately below.

Mylegalenglish books have an interactive content that can be accessed on Mylegalenglish channels located on YouTube.com:

- Part 1 of each Mylegalenglish book has both a vocabulary pronunciation support (with a separate channel for each language version) and a presentation video:
  - Language pronunciation videos are located on Mylegalenglish Youtube channel – *Mylegalenglish* **French** *vocabulary support* – **(insert appropriate language to find the video of your choice: Chinese, French, Italian, Japanese, Polish, Portuguese, Russian, Spanish, Turkish**);
  - Presentation videos are located on Mylegalenglish Youtube channel – *Mylegalenglish Videos* **Introduction to the Common Law Vol 1**.
- Part 3 of each Mylegalenglish book allows students to work on listening and speaking skills with the help of recorded conversations. Conversation videos for each chapter are located on Mylegalenglish YouTube channel – *Mylegalenglish* **Introduction to the Common Law Vol 1** – *Conversations*.

To access the Mylegalenglish channel of your choice:

- search **Youtube.com**;
- on the *left hand* column (2/3 down the screen) click on **"Browse channels"**;
- then in the search box write in the name of the *Mylegalenglish channel* you wish to access, for example *Mylegalenglish French vocabulary support* and press return
- then on the *right side* of the screen immediately below the *search box* click on **"Filter"**;
- then go to the column headed **"Type"** and click on **"Channel"** (second option on the list);
- then click on the Mylegalengish channel (identifiable by the Mylegalenglish logo);
- finally click on **"Created playlists"** and choose the playlist for the book or chapter that you are using.

NOTE TO TEACHERS

As regards teachers with a non-legal background, one is not expected to have a complete understanding of all the legal terminology. The meaning of legal words and their equivalent in the students' own language *should be a source of class discussion and in this regard there are no absolute meanings*. Legal terms are used to describe concepts not necessarily having defined limits or having exact legal equivalents in the students' legal system. These books represent the first step of a *fabulous learning process* and full appreciation of all the legal terminology will in most cases require further study by students with teachers specialized in the area of law. Our courses serve as a gateway to introduce students to the legal English applicable in a specific area and should they wish to facilitate subsequent law studies in English. In this regard, the role of the language teacher is to offer linguistic support and *not to be an expert in law*.

Chapter one

LEGAL PRACTICE IN COMMON LAW COUNTRIES

PART 1 – TEXT 1 – INFORMATION

To facilitate understanding of both the text and the technical English contained in Part 1 and Part 5 of each Chapter, it is recommended that the student access the video presentation available on the relevant Mylegalenglish learning Channel (see instructions at the beginning of the book).

The organization of the common law legal practice

Law firms in common law countries such as the United States and United Kingdom are **frequently** very large, with some of the bigger firms employing hundreds if not thousands of people. In reality such firms are legal **factories,** many being global in character and **reach**. These firms, described as **full-service firms**, offer legal **advice** above all in the area of commercial law. **Alongside** these firms are also found smaller **stand-alone law firms** or **sole practitioners**.

Legal structure of law firms

Law firms can be structured in a number of different ways.
- *Sole practitioner* A sole practitioner is a single lawyer working alone and thus effectively (s)he is the law firm.
- *General partnership* This is the traditional legal structure for common law firms. The firm is made up of **partners** that own the business collectively and each has **joint and several liability** toward the other(s). Each lawyer is taxed directly on any profits taken from the business. The popularity of the general partnership structure has been overtaken in recent years by new business forms that offer the partners in a law firm the benefit of limited liability.
- *Limited liability partnership/limited liability company* Limited liability partnerships (LLPs) in the United Kingdom or limited liability companies (LLCs) in the United States are structured like general partnerships. However, unlike general partnerships, LLPs and LLCs are treated as separate corporate entities, granting the lawyers who work for them limited liability. Nonetheless, unlike an ordinary company, no corporate tax is **levied** on the profits made by either LLPs or LLCs and thus, partners are only taxed once on the income or **dividend** that they receive from the business's profits.

Management and employment structure of a law firm

A law firm is organized around its partners. However, there are many different types of people working in law firms.

- *Partners* Law firms are run and **managed** by their partners. The partners can be compared to the **directors** of a company, with one partner elected as managing partner, the equivalent of a **Chief Executive Officer (CEO)**. Many firms are organized pursuant to a **tier system** with very senior partners being classed in the first or second **tiers** and the more junior recently elected partners placed in lower tiers.

- *Special counsel/of counsel* Just under partner level, some law firms have a position referred to as of counsel or special counsel. This position is sometimes offered to senior associates who, although valuable to a firm, are thought to be lacking some of the necessary **attributes** to allow them to be considered for election to partner. Alternatively, of counsel positions are sometimes offered to well-known academics, whose reputation in a particular field of law is sufficiently valuable that the firm benefits from having the person's name on its **notepaper** or **stationery**.

- *Associates* Associates are the **rank and file** members of a law firm. They can be broken up into two **categories**: junior and senior associates. Normally, after working in a firm as a lawyer for a period of two to three years, a successful junior associate will be **promoted** to senior associate. Thereafter, senior associates are expected to put in long hours of **billable** work, in the hope of being chosen to become junior partner.

- *Support staff* Law firms, especially large full-service firms, tend to employ many people under the heading of support staff. For example, there are **paralegals,** whose role is to carry out work of a semi-legal nature, such as research work and **filing** of documents. **Personal assistants (PAs)** and general secretarial staff carry out the secretarial duties in an office. Personal assistants of senior partners organize their partner's appointment **diary, book** their tickets when they need to travel **abroad,** etc. The work they do is considered important and they are often quite well paid. Lower down on the secretarial scale are typists, especially night-time typists who often work on a short-term contract basis. Finally, there are the day and night receptionists, office administrative staff, human resources and **IT personnel,** all managed by the office manager. The office manager is only an administrative manager and a lawyer does not normally hold the position.

VOCABULARY

Law firm – *cabinet d'avocats*
Firm – *entreprise/firme*
Frequently – *fréquemment/souvent*
Factory – *usine*

Reach (to) – *atteindre*
Reach – *portée*
Full-service firm – *cabinet offrant une expertise juridique multidisciplinaire*
Advice – *conseil*
Alongside – *à côté de*
Stand alone firms – *cabinets indépendants (non affiliés à un réseau)*
Sole-practitioner – *avocat travaillant seul et pour son propre compte*
General partnership – *société en nom collectif*
Sole proprietorship – *entreprise individuelle dans laquelle un avocat (= sole practitioner) travaille seul pour son propre compte*
Partner – *associé*
Partnership (to go into) – *s'associer*
Joint and several liability – *être responsable conjointement et solidairement*
Limited liability company – *société à responsabilité limitée* (liabilities – *passif;* limited liability – *responsabilité limitée*)
Levy (to) – *taxer*
Dividend – *dividende*
Limited liability partnership – *société à responsabilité limitée*
Manage (to) – *gérer/diriger*
Directors – *administrateurs*
Chief Executive Officer (CEO) – *Président-Directeur Général (PDG)*
Tier system – *hiérarchie composée d'échelons (niveaux/grades) au sein des associés*
Tier – *échelon*
Special counsel/of counsel – *conseiller expert auprès des associés, parfois un universitaire de renom*
Attributes – *qualités*
Notepaper/stationery – *papier à en-tête*
Associates – *collaborateurs*
Rank and file – *subordonnés*
Category – *catégorie*
Promote (to) – *promouvoir*
Billable – *facturable*
Support staff – *personnel administratif*
Paralegals – *assistants juridiques*
File (to) a document – *1. déposer un document auprès d'une autorité administrative 2. classer un document dans un dossier*
Personal assistant (PA) – *assistant personnel*
Diary – *emploi du temps/agenda*
Book (to) – *réserver*
Abroad – *à l'étranger*
IT Personnel – *personnel responsable des technologies de l'information*

PART 1 – TEXT 1 – EXERCISES

1. Vocabulary test

Fill in the missing words using the vocabulary in Text 1

 a) A law firm that offers its clients a complete service covering many different areas of law is called a _____ law firm.

 b) A lawyer can practice by himself as a _____ or work in _____ with other lawyers.

 c) Partners in a general partnership have _____ liability toward each other; however, if they form a company they will benefit from _____ liability.

 d) The most important people in a law firm are the _____, who are led by the _____ partner.

 e) In order to improve its reputation, a law firm can decide to appoint a leading academic as _____.

 f) Paralegals and secretaries are referred to as the _____ staff in a law firm and are managed by the office _____.

 g) I have just got a job as a paralegal with a large US law firm and I will be responsible for _____ documents and doing _____.

 h) Associates can be divided into _____ associates and _____ associates; the former hope to be appointed as partner and consequently work very hard.

 i) The managing partner's personal assistant is very important and is responsible for organising the managing partner's _____, as well as _____ his/her airplane tickets.

 j) The senior partner in a law firm can be compared to the _____ of a company and his partners carry out a role similar to the _____ of a company.

2. Vocabulary test

Write sentences with the following pairs of words. Your sentence should demonstrate your knowledge of the relationship between the words

 a) Notepaper/of counsel
 b) Senior associate/junior partner
 c) CEO/partner
 d) Support staff/office manager
 e) Paralegal/research
 f) Joint and severable liability/partner

3. Knowledge test

Each of the following statements is false; do you know why? Write a sentence stating why it is false

 a) Partners in a law firm always have unlimited liability.
 b) A sole-proprietorship is also called a full-service law firm.
 c) The associates in a law firm are like the directors of a company.

d)   Paralegals are also called junior associates.
e)   Partners make up the rank and file members of a law firm.

Access answers at the end of the book.

PART 1 – TEXT 2 – MORE INFORMATION

The organization of the common law legal practice

In the common law world, a **law firm** is **primarily** a business, the function of which is to offer its clients legal **advice**. A law firm is made up of one or more lawyers and in common law countries a lawyer is considered as much a businessman as someone exercising a **profession**. Consequently, they are simply viewed as **service providers** and are not given any official title[1]. As they are profit orientated businesses, law firms **seek economies of scale** and this explains why Anglo-Saxon law firms are amongst the largest in the world, with some of the larger firms employing thousands of lawyers. In reality such firms are legal **factories,** many being global in character and **reach**. Indeed, Anglo-Saxon firms were among the first to realize that, with the development of global businesses, globalized law firms were necessary to offer complementary global advice.

However, this is not to say that smaller firms do not also exist in the Anglo-Saxon world. Some lawyers work alone and are referred to as **sole practitioners**. There are also **stand-alone firms**, which are not integrated into any national or international group or network of firms. Smaller firms specializing in one specific field referred to as **boutique** law firms also exist. These firms focus on particular areas of law, for example intellectual property law, labour law, tax law or mergers and acquisitions. Larger firms sometimes referred to as **full-service firms** offer legal advice in many areas, but generally concentrate on the area of commercial law. Given the significance of the **outcome** of any eventual **trial**, criminal law is normally practiced by firms specializing only in this area. Large firms do, however, work in the area of corporate criminal law, dealing with what is known as **white-collar crime**.

Legal structure of law firms

Law firms can be structured in a number of different ways. For example a firm, depending on its size and area of activity, can take many different forms.

• *Sole practitioner* A sole practitioner is a single lawyer working alone and thus he/she is effectively the law firm. In such firms, the lawyer has **unlimited liability** towards his/her clients for any **losses** that **occur** as a result of an error on his/her part. Sole practitioners can either specialize in one specific area or be a **jack-of-all-trades**, dealing with whatever legal problem a client may have. Attempting to practice in a **wide variety** of **areas** can be **stressful** and such practitioners are often found in **rural** areas. Sole practitioners are taxed directly on their income and thus are only taxed once on the money they make.

---

[1] For example, a lawyer in France is referred to by the term *maître.*

- *General partnership* A general partnership is the traditional legal structure for common law firms made up of a number of different lawyers. Under this legal form, all the **partners** in the firm own the business equally and each has **joint and several liability** toward the other partners. As in the case of a sole practitioner, the firm's partners are taxed directly on the profits they take from the partnership.
- *Limited liability partnership/limited liability company* A limited liability partnership (LLP, UK) or limited liability company (LLC, US) operates as a type of separate entity formed by the lawyers making-up the firm. An LLP/LLC grants lawyers **limited liability** in the same way as does a limited liability company. Thus, a partner is not considered to be jointly and severally liable as regards the **acts** of other partners, as is the case in a traditional general partnership. However, unlike a company, partners are not subject to double taxation on the firm's **earnings**, as the partnership is not treated as a separate legal entity for tax purposes. Consequently, partners are only required to pay income tax on the profits or **dividends** they receive from the business, i.e. on their share of the company's profits.

Management and employment structure of a law firm

Law firms are traditionally organized around a partnership structure. However, there are many different types of people working in a law firm, each having their own important contribution to make. It is proposed to consider each of these groups in order of importance.

- *Partners* Law firms are run and **managed** by their partners. The partners in a firm can be divided into those who find the work, sometimes referred to as *rainmakers* and those who then actually perform the work; these two types of partners are sometimes referred to as finders (rainmakers, i.e. those who find clients) and **grinders** (service partners and associates who do the work). Many partners fall somewhere in between these two groups. Partners are responsible for everything that occurs in the firm and can be likened or compared to the **directors** of a company, with one partner elected as managing partner, the equivalent of a **Chief Executive Officer (CEO)**. In order to be elected partner in a law firm, it is normally necessary to have worked in the firm as an associate for a minimum of five years. However, sometimes lawyers are **headhunted** from other law firms and are offered a partnership as part of their recruitment **deal;** such partners are sometimes referred to as lateral partners or lateral hires. If the firm takes the form of a general partnership, the partners are joint-owners of the firm and, as we have already seen, have joint and several liability toward each other. It is for this reason that partnerships can be dangerous from a financial point of view and one is advised to consider carefully the financial position of a firm, before agreeing to become a partner. At partner level, many law firms operate on the principle of *you eat what you kill*, i.e. you are paid directly on the basis of the money that you bring into the firm. As a result there can be great disparity between partner incomes, which can in turn create ill feeling. For this reason, some firms **put in place** a system allowing for a more **even** or balanced division of profits. Partnership structures are normally organized around a **tier system** and senior partners are also referred to as **top tier** partners, while more junior partners will be placed in a **lower tier**, i.e. lower tier partners. The higher the tier, the greater the share in the profits of the firm enjoyed by the partner in question. Partners can also be divided into **equity partners/full partners** and **non-equity partners**. An equity partner is part-owner in the firm, i.e., (s)he has **equity** in the firm and thus shares directly in its profits and its losses. Non-equity partners, also called paid partners, have no actual ownership in the firm. Obviously, it is much easier to remove a non-equity partner than an equity partner and thus one has security of tenure as equity partner. However, a non-equity partner has less exposure to any debts attaching to the firm, which can be important in times of economic downturn.

- *Special counsel/of counsel* Just under partner level, some law firms have a position referred to as **of counsel**. Lawyers who work as of counsel can have different profiles. The position is sometimes offered to senior associates who, although valuable to a firm, are considered as lacking the necessary **attributes** to allow them to become partner in the firm. The advantage of being appointed of counsel is that a lawyer remains an employee of the firm and consequently is not expected to put in the long hours required from junior partners. Alternatively, of counsel positions are offered to well-known academics, whose reputation in a particular field of law is considered so valuable that the firm benefits from having that person's name on its **notepaper** or **stationery**. Academic of counsel are not normally expected to do much work for the firm and are relied on primarily as a marketing tool. However, they will be expected to advise lawyers of the firm on particularly complicated files and attend **beauty parades**. Finally, retired partners can ask to be made of counsel, so that they can continue to work for the firm at a reduced rhythm.
- *Associates* **Associates** are the **rank and file** members of a law firm. They can be divided into junior and senior associates. Normally after working in a firm as a lawyer for a period of two to three years, a successful junior associate will be **promoted to** senior associate. Such a promotion is a clear sign that the person is potentially partner material. If they are not promoted to senior associate level, junior associates are normally encouraged to leave the firm and find employment elsewhere. Senior associates are expected to put in long hours in the hope of being considered for a position as junior partner. Assessment meetings, referred to as **associate reviews**, are held annually, advising associates as to how they are progressing, underlining their weaknesses and strengths. After a number of years, either a senior associate makes partner, is appointed of counsel or is encouraged to leave the firm. Most firms will not employ a senior

associate on a long-term basis; either (s)he[2] is good enough to make partner or otherwise they will have to leave the firm. US firms refer to this as an **up or out policy**.

- *Support staff* Law firms, especially large full-service firms, tend to employ many people under the heading of **support staff**. There are **paralegals** that carry out work of a semi-legal nature, for example research work and **filing** documents, etc. There are also **personal assistants (PAs)** and general secretarial staff. Being the personal assistant of the managing partner of a large law firm is a relatively important position and some PAs will be paid as much as junior associates and will be considered as important, if not more important, to the firm. Lower down on the secretarial scale are typists, especially night-time typists who normally work on a short-term contract basis. There is also the office's technical administrative staff, such as its human resources department, **IT personnel** and its bookkeepers. The office is managed administratively by an office manager, who normally is not a qualified lawyer.

Internal organization of large full-service international firms – the practice group

As we have seen, large multi-jurisdictional law firms, also referred to as full-service firms, have many different areas of specialization and each of these areas of expertise is often organized around the **practice group** specialized in this area. All the lawyers in a firm are expected to have an area of expertise and a lawyer specialized in the area of intellectual property will become a member of the intellectual property law practice group. The intellectual property practice group is consequently made up of all of the firm's intellectual property lawyers, located in all of its offices throughout the world and so the practice group is a trans-national structure. Large international firms try to organize their business around these practice groups, rather than purely on national grounds. Thus, the London members of a firm's competition law practice group may be in more regular business contact with their Japanese competition law colleagues, than with London colleagues who are part of another practice group. This strategy allows such firms to provide their multinational business clients with an equivalent multinational global legal service. Great effort is made to ensure that these multi-jurisdictional practice groups function as a single unit. Thus, members of a particular practice group are encouraged to meet regularly and to develop pan-national **strategies**, in order to **woo clients**. Frequently, a business looking for a new law firm to represent them in a particular **field** will organize a series of beauty parades, where the members of the practice group(s) involved will make a multi-**jurisdictional** presentation to the client, hoping to demonstrate the extent of their legal know-how and the scope of their global reach.

These large law firms are often referred to as international law firms and young

---

[2] Instead of writing he/she, it is possible to write (s)he or sometimes "they". Alternatively, just "he" or "she" can be used although this is disapproved of in the sometimes *politically correct* (PC) Anglo-Saxon world.

students wishing to work with these firms sometimes mistakenly say that they want to work in the area of international law. Mistakenly because although these firms work in an **international context**, the law they practice is for the most part national domestic law. International law in reality plays only a limited role in the area of international business.

Large common law full-service law firms are big businesses, with some having an **annual turnover** equivalent to large multinational companies. **Revenue driven**, they seek ever increasing **billable hours** from their associates and partners. In **boom times** these firms hire aggressively and frequently offer attractive **pay packets**. However, in times of economic **downturn** they do not hesitate to **cut back on staff**. It is a competitive environment offering a rewarding career to those attracted to the world of international commerce.

Vocabulary

Law firm – *cabinet d'avocats*
Firm – *entreprise/firme/cabinet*
Primarily – *principalement*
Advice – *conseil*
Profession – *métier/profession libérale*
Service provider – *prestataire de service*
Seek (to) – *chercher/rechercher*
Economies of scale – *economies d'échelle*
Factory – *usine*
Reach (to) – *atteindre/parvenir à (*to reach a verdict*)/contacter/joindre (quelqu'un)*
Reach – *influence/portée*
Sole-practitioner – *avocat travaillant seul et pour son propre compte*
Stand alone firms – *cabinets indépendants non affiliés à un réseau national ou international*
Boutique firm – *cabinet d'avocats spécialisé dans un domaine spécifique du droit*
Full-service firm – *cabinet offrant une pleine expertise juridique multidisciplinaire*
Outcome – *issue/résultat*
Trial – *procès*
White collar crime – *délits (crimes) de cols blancs/criminalité des entreprises*
Sole proprietorship – *entreprise individuelle dans laquelle un avocat travaille seul, pour son propre compte*
Unlimited liability – *responsabilité illimitée*
Losses – *pertes*
Occur (to) – *survenir/se produire*
Jack-of-all-trades – *un homme à-tout-faire/touche à tout (ici, généraliste)*
Wide-variety – *grande varieté*
Areas – *domaines*
Stressful – *stressant/dur nerveusement*
Rural – *rural*
General partnership – *société en nom collectif*

Partner – *associé*
Partnership (to go into) – *s'associer*
Joint and several liability – *être responsable solidairement et conjointement*
Limited liability company – *societé à responsabilité limitée*
Limited liability – *responsabilité limitée*
Dividend – *dividende*
Limited liability partnership – *« partnership » à responsabilité limitée*
Acts – *actes*
Earnings – *revenus/gains/bénéfices*
Manage (to) – *gérer/diriger*
Rainmakers – *avocats qui génèrent et attirent une grande partie de l'activité d'un cabinet*
Grinders – *(mot-à-mot) « broyeurs » ; professionnels qui, au sein d'un cabinet, fournissent un travail substantiel et souvent fastidieux – ceux qui abattent le travail*
Directors – *administrateurs*
Chief Executive Officer (CEO) – *Président-Directeur Général (PDG)*
Head-hunted – *recruté* (the person who organizes the recruitment is called a head hunter – *« chasseur de têtes »*)
Deal – *affaire/transaction*
You eat what you kill – *vous mangez ce que vous tuez (littéralement)/être rémunéré en fonction de ses performances*
Put (to) in place – *mettre en place*
Even division of profits – *égale répartition des bénéfices*
Tier system – *hiérarchie composée d'échelons (niveaux/grades) au sein des associés*
Top tier – *échelon supérieur*
Lower tier – *échelon inférieur*
Equity/full partners – *associés détenteurs d'une participation financière dans le capital de l'entreprise*
Non-equity partners – *associés salariés sans participation financière*
To have equity – *détenir une participation financière propre dans le capital de l'entreprise (être actionnaire)*
Special counsel/of counsel – *conseiller expert auprès des associés, parfois un universitaire de renom*
Attributes – *qualités*
Notepaper/stationery – *papier à en-tête*
Beauty parade – *(mot à mot = concours de beauté) réunion de promotion destinée à s'attirer des clients*
Associate – *collaborateur*
Rank and file – *subordonnés*
Promote (to) – *promouvoir*
Associate review – *évaluation du travail du collaborateur*
Up or out policy – *politique d'entreprise qui consiste à ne conserver et ne promouvoir que les collaborateurs dont le rendement est satisfaisant*
Support staff – *personnel administratif*
Paralegals – *assistants juridiques*

File (to) a document – *1) déposer un document/dossier auprès d'une autorité administrative ; 2) classer un document dans un dossier*
Personal assistant (PA) – *assistant personnel*
IT personnel – *personnel compétent en matière de technologies de l'information*
Practice group – *unité (département) transnationale spécialisée dans un domaine juridique particulier*
Competition law – *droit de la concurrence*
Grounds – *fondements/bases*
Strategies – *stratégies*
Woo (to) clients – *attirer/séduire les clients*
Field – *domaine/secteur*
Jurisdiction – *juridiction*
Jurisdiction (of the court) – *compétence (de la cour)*
International context – *cadre/contexte international*
Annual turnover – *chiffre d'affaires annuelles*
Revenue driven – *motivé par les profits/gains*
Billable hours – *heures facturables*
Boom – *essor/expansion*
Pay packet – *montant de la rémunération (à l'origine : enveloppe contenant la paie)*
Downturn – *ralentissement (de l'économie)*
Cut (to) back on staff – *diminuer/réduire les effectifs*

To improve pronunciation and understanding of technical vocabulary, the student is advised to listen to the vocabulary recording on the relevant Mylegalenglish learning channel (see instructions at the beginning of the book).

PART 1 – TEXT 2 – EXERCISES

1. Definitions

Write a sentence defining each of the following terms – one sentence per term

- a) Profession
- b) Sole practitioner
- c) Rainmaker
- d) Non-equity partner
- e) Support staff
- f) Full-service firm
- g) Head hunter
- h) Partnership

2. Sentences

Write sentences with the following pairs of words. Your sentence should if possible demonstrate your knowledge of the relationship between the words

- a) Promote/senior associate
- b) Partner/joint and several liability

c)   Managing partner/law firm
d)   Equity partner/non-equity partner
e)   Beauty parade/client
f)   Full-service law firm/boutique firm
g)   Of-counsel/partner
h)   Billable hours/revenue
i)   Support staff/office manager
j)   Paralegal/junior associate

3. Fill in the missing words

Fill in the missing words using the vocabulary in Text 2

a)   In a general partnership, each partner is _____ liable for his own acts and the acts of other _____.
b)   The managing partner of a law firm can be compared to the _____ of a company, whilst the partners are like a company's _____.
c)   A _____ offers clients a wide variety of legal services, while _____ firms tend to specialize in one specific area of law.
d)   Many large international full-service law firms are organized around _____ groups made up of lawyers working in different _____, thereby offering clients a truly global service.
e)   Law firms sometimes _____ well-respected academics as _____, in order to promote the firm's image.

4. Knowledge test

The following questions may be answered in writing or by way of discussion

a)   Compare the organization and structure of French law firms with Anglo-Saxon law firms.
b)   Would you prefer to work in a large full-service law firm or in a smaller firm? Explain the reasons behind your choice.
c)   Do you feel that the profession of lawyer in Anglo-Saxon countries is too orientated toward profit instead of the quality of the legal service?
d)   Do you consider that French law firms are going to start increasing in size to compete with their Anglo-Saxon counterparts?
e)   What is the future of the legal profession? Do you think that firms are going to continue to increase in size?

Access answers at the end of the book.

PART 2 – QUICK LOOK GRAMMAR REVISION

Capitalization

It is very important in English to know when you should use a capital letter and when you should not.

When should words be capitalized?

As a general rule, the following words should be capitalized.

1. *The first word of a sentence.*
   Example: **E**very day John is working harder and harder. **H**e was very cross because he wanted to see the managing partner and he was not allowed to.
2. *The names of people.*
   Example: I met **F**rank **A**brams, the new client I was talking to you about.
3. *Titles with the names of people.*
   Example: I saw **D**r. Smith yesterday. Is he a doctor of medicine or a doctor of law?
   Note: doctor is not capitalized in the second sentence, as it is not used with the name of someone.
4. *Months, days of the week and holidays.*
   Example: I met the client during **D**ecember, on a **T**uesday, I think. It was **C**hristmas **D**ay.
   Note: seasons (spring, summer, autumn, winter) are not capitalized.
5. *The names of places, streets, cities, states, countries, oceans, rivers, lakes, deserts, mountains.*
   Example: I live in 68 **G**riffin **C**rescent, **C**hicago, **I**llinois, in the **U**nited **S**tates of **A**merica. I have sailed on the **P**acific **O**cean, the **D**anube **R**iver and **L**ake **E**rie. I have visited the **S**ahara **D**esert and climbed **M**ount **E**verest and then went to the **F**ar **E**ast.

   Note:

   I crossed the desert/ I crossed the **S**ahara **D**esert. I live in a city/ I live in **N**ew **Y**ork **C**ity. I climbed the mountain/I climbed **M**ont **B**lanc.

   Note:

   I travelled east and then travelled west/ I travelled to the **F**ar **E**ast and then to **W**estern **E**urope.

6. *The names of schools/universities, businesses, parks, buildings.*
   Example: I went to **H**arvard **U**niversity and later got a job with the law firm of **H**ammond and **H**ammond, the offices of which were located in **T**rump **T**ower, opposite **C**entral **P**ark.

   Note:

   I went to university/ I went to **Y**ale **U**niversity. I got a job with a law firm the offices of which are in a skyscraper opposite the park/ the offices of which are in a skyscraper opposite **S**t. **J**ames's **P**ark.

7. *The names of courses, for example at university.*
   Example: I am studying **C**ompany **L**aw.

   Note:

   I like the area of company law and so decided to take a course entitled **C**ompany **L**aw for **L**awyers.

8. *The names of languages and nationalities.*
   Example: He speaks perfect **E**nglish even though he is **A**merican!

9. *The names of religions.*
   Example: He is a **B**uddhist monk now, but he was born a **C**atholic.

PART 2 – GRAMMAR EXERCISES

1. Capitalization test

Add capital letters where necessary

a) the law firm where i work is very relaxed; every friday there is a dress down³ day.
b) do you know frank smith? He is a partner in strawberry & fields, the well-known law firm.
c) professor smith was appointed of counsel in fake & blake solicitors. he is from boston.
d) the danube river flows into the atlantic ocean or is it the black sea, or maybe it is some other ocean?
e) alaska is just north of canada, and sao paulo is in south america, not far from antarctica.
f) dr smith was called to help a passenger on the plane to new york city but he could not do anything because he is a doctor of law.
g) canada is an english speaking country but many people there speak french.
h) frank had a business meeting in the plaza building in chicago; it is located in the south of the city.
i) james had a meeting in bermuda. it was the wettest july in history and he had a cold when he returned to london city airport.

Access answers at the end of the book.

PART 3 – AUDIO – LISTENING AND SPEAKING

Comprehension

Listen to the following conversation, make notes of all the relevant facts and then answer the questions below. If you have trouble understanding, follow the conversation while also reading the text. Access the conversation on the relevant Mylegalenglish learning channel (see instructions at the beginning of the book).

---

³ Some firms have dress-down days during which it is not necessary to wear a suit and tie at work.

Interview between Charles (a lawyer) and Rachel

Rachel is waiting to meet with Charles and his personal assistant (PA) comes to see her ...

PA – Charles: "Hello Rachel, Charles will see you now. His office is just down the hall, the last door on the left."
Rachel: "Thank you very much."

Rachel knocks on the door of Charles's office
Charles: "Yes, come in please."
Rachel: "Hello, my name is Rachel."
Charles: "Ah yes Rachel, please take a seat. I know I have your CV and application letter somewhere here on my desk. Ah yes here it is under my coffee! So let's see; it says here that you are looking for a training period with our Firm."
Rachel: "Yes, last year I successfully sat the Bar examination and as part of the lawyer qualification process, I have to work with a law firm for a period of eighteen months."
Charles: "OK, first I would like to quickly run through your CV. So you studied in Madrid?"
Rachel: "Yes, I did my first four years in Madrid, before coming to Paris to do a Masters in tax law."
Charles: "Good. We are actually looking for people in the commercial area and in particular for someone to start in the area of tax or revenue law."
Rachel: "Super, I did my Masters in that field, so it is obviously the area in which I actually want to work."
Charles: "What area of tax law are you interested in particularly?"
Rachel: "Well, I am interested in tax law in general but I particularly like the area of taxation and international corporations and the whole question of double taxation. From my CV, you can see that I did a course in this area and got particularly high marks in the subsequent exam."
Bob: "Yes, in general your marks are very good; it is one of the reasons for which we[4] decided to invite you for an interview. How are your languages?"
Rachel: "My English is pretty good. I speak French, Italian and of course Spanish."
Charles: "Would you be able to work in Italian?"
Rachel: "Well my written Italian is not too hot, but my spoken Italian is fine."
Charles: "And how is your written English?"
Rachel: "I probably wouldn't be able to write memos to clients, but I could probably handle e-mails and my spoken English is quite good. I spent a couple of summers in the United States and have managed to stay in contact with friends there. Indeed, I was hoping maybe to be able to spend part of my internship in one of your English speaking offices."
Charles: "We speak English in all of our offices Rachel but I understand what you wish to say and it is sometimes possible for interns to spend part of their training period abroad. However, it is something we tend to reserve for exceptional

---

[4]   Note the use of "we". This is to indicate that a law firm is run on a collegiate basis and that partners ultimately take decisions acting together as one.

candidates and even if we were to offer you a position, we could not promise you anything like that."

Rachel: "Of course I understand."

Charles: "Perhaps the best thing is for you to meet with some of the other partners in our Firm. I will ring Frank Thompson now who heads up the Tax Law Practice Group here in Paris and see if he has a minute to see you. Do you have the time right now?"

Rachel: "Yes, of course."

PART 3 – AUDIO COMPREHENSION – EXERCISES

1. Comprehension

From the notes you have taken, answer the following questions

    a)   Where is Charles Smith's office located in the building?
    b)   In which area of tax law is Rachel particularly interested?
    c)   Would Rachel be able to work in Italian?
    d)   Where has Rachel studied?
    e)   For how long does Rachel have to work with a law firm in order to complete her training experience?
    f)   Where was Rachel's CV located on Charles Smith's desk?

2. Speaking practice

In the following series of conversation couplets, develop suitable responses to the questions asked

    a)   Charles: "What area of law are you interested in?"
           Rachel: "_____."
    b)   Charles: "I know I have your CV and application letter somewhere here on my desk. Ah yes here it is. So let's see, it says here that you are looking for a training period with our firm."
           Rachel: "_____."
    c)   Charles: "How are your languages?"
           Rachel: "_____"
    d)   Charles: "What type of salary would you expect to receive?"
           Rachel: "_____."
    e)   Charles: "And how is your written English? Would you be able to talk and write to clients?"
           Rachel: "_____."
    f)   Charles: "If we were not able to offer you a training period exclusively in the area of tax law, would you still be interested in working with us?"
           Rachel: "_____."
    g)   Charles: "Do you speak any other languages?"
           Rachel: "_____."
    h)   Charles: "In our Firm we pay rather well but expect our associates to work hard and be in the office a good deal of the time. Would this be a problem for you?"
           Rachel: "_____."

i)   Charles: "Would working exclusively in the area of tax law be a problem?"
Rachel: "_____."

j)   Charles: "Have you applied to other law firms apart from ourselves?"
Rachel: "_____."

3. Speaking practice continued ......

Create five other conversation couplets using in each couplet at least one word from the vocabulary found in Part 1, Text 1 or Text 2

4. Speaking practice continued ......

Listen to the suggested replies and repeat

a)   Charles: "What area of law are you interested in?"
Rachel: "Generally I am interested in the area of commercial law, but I particularly like the area of tax law."

b)   Charles: "I know I have your CV and application letter somewhere here on my desk. Ah yes here it is. So let's see. It says here that you are looking for a training period with our firm."
Rachel: "Yes, as part of the qualification process to become a lawyer, I have to complete a training period or an internship of 18 months."

c)   Charles: "How are your languages?"
Rachel: "My English is quite good and I also speak Spanish."

d)   Charles: "What type of salary would you like?"
Rachel: "Well, I would like to be paid a reasonable amount, certainly enough to allow me to pay my bills and have a social life. Perhaps we could use the pay scale established by the Paris Bar as a reference."

e)   Charles: "And how is your written English? Would you be able to talk and write to clients?"
Rachel: "Certainly, I think that I would be able to talk to clients in English and participate in meetings."

f)   Charles: "If we were not able to offer you a training period exclusively in the area of tax law, would you still be interested in working with us?"
Rachel: "Of course. As I mentioned, I am interested above all by the possibility of practicing in the area of commercial law."

g)   Charles: "Do you speak any other languages?"
Rachel: "I studied Spanish for a number of years in school. However, it is some years that I have not had an opportunity to speak in Spanish, so it is probably quite rusty."

h)   Charles: "In our Firm we pay rather well but expect our associates to work rather hard and to be in the office a good deal of the time. Would this be a problem for you?"
Rachel: "No, at this stage of my career I want to work hard and above all learn."

i)   Charles: "Would working exclusively in the area of tax law be a problem?"
     Rachel: "No, not at all, as I said, I like the area of tax law."

j)   Charles: "Have you applied to other law firms apart from our office?"
     Rachel: "Yes, I applied to a good few firms and I am due to do interviews with some of them over the next few weeks."

5. Associated questions

Discuss the following questions

a)   What is the best approach when doing an interview? Should the candidate try to dominate the process or should (s)he allow the interviewer to take the lead? Should a candidate say exactly what (s)he believes or what (s)he thinks the interviewer wants to hear?

b)   Do you think Rachel has done a good interview?

c)   Try and improve on the answers that Rachel has given to the questions asked by Charles.

d)   Organize a series of interviews between and make a list of the type of questions and answers that you can expect in an interview.

PART 4 – TRANSLATION EXERCISES

When carrying out the translations it is not necessary to translate directly word for word; rather the emphasis should be on translating the sense of the text. Language is not directly interchangeable and so direct translations do not always convey the meaning in the text.

Translate the following texts from English to French

A. Boutique law firms

A boutique law firm refers to a firm of lawyers that specializes in a niche area of law. Unlike a general practice or full-service firm that brings together a variety of unrelated practice areas within a single firm, a boutique firm normally only specializes in one specific practice area. Generally boutique firms are small but some can have up to two hundred lawyers, depending on how successful they are. The term boutique refers above all to their specialization rather than their size. Boutique firms tend to specialize in fields such as intellectual property law, competition law or labor law. Frequently these areas require industry-specific knowledge, which non-specialized lawyers might not have. For example, any competition law lawyer worth his salt also probably has a business degree, such as an MBA, as an understanding of economic theory is central to the practice of antitrust law.

B. The story of John Sullivan, founder of the law firm Sullivan, Jenkins and Freehold

The history of Sullivan, Jenkins & Freehold is a story of imagination, determination and hard work. For more than one hundred years, the Firm has had only one ambition, to be the world's largest law firm, to become a truly unique global organization. But before there was a law firm established, there was a man with a dream. John Sullivan was born in the harsh mining environment of Wales at the turn of the century. Winning a scholarship to Oxford University, he supplemented his meagre tuition grant by working in various student bars and even worked as a bouncer for a local dancehall. After qualification, he joined the City[5] law firm of Shearer & Watson, before establishing the firm of Sullivan, Jenkins & Freehold. Initially a boutique firm specialized in banking law, the partnership grew into the world's largest commercial law practice, with offices throughout the world's five continents. On his deathbed, Sullivan was asked the secret to his success. "Hourly billing",[6] he replied sardonically.

C. Business planning for law firms

Business planning for law firms is different from planning for an ordinary industrial or commercial enterprise. Primarily, this is a result of the nature of the services that law firms offer to their clients and the way these services can be marketed. Legal advice is not a homogenized product. Nonetheless there are some similarities. Perhaps the first questions any managing partner of a law firm should ask his partners are:
- What kind of work do they want to do?
- What kind of clients do they want to have?
- How big do they want the firm to eventually be?

It is essential to establish clear answers to these three questions if the law firm is to put in place a coherent and achievable business plan. In this regard certain compromises will have to be made. A firm that wishes to work primarily in social areas such as refugee rights will have to accept that its earning capacity will never be that of a firm working in financial services.

Translate the following texts from French to English

A. Les cabinets d'avocats d'affaires en France

La France compte près de 34 000 avocats ; parmi ceux-ci, 14000 exercent à Paris. De plus en plus d'avocats se spécialisent en droit des affaires. Cet essor est allé de pair avec l'émergence, pour ne pas dire l'invasion, de cabinets anglo-saxons sur le territoire français. C'est vraiment là un marché qui connait une mutation constante. Pour donner un exemple, on a pu constater, au cours des dernières années, une augmentation des fusions, tendance génératrice d'une toujours plus forte concentration des cabinets. Des regroupements de taille se sont produits alors que les cabinets français tentent de faire face à la concurrence anglo-saxonne. En outre, la recherche de rentabilité et des économies d'échelle ont accéléré la cadence de tels regroupements.

---

[5] The "City" is the name given the business and banking district located in the heart of London.
[6] Law firms can either charge by the hour or alternatively agree a price in advance for any work that is to be done.

B. Le métier de juriste

Le juriste d'entreprise est quelqu'un qui a fait des études de droit, sans avoir pour autant nécessairement obtenu le diplôme d'avocat. Son rôle en tant que conseiller juridique est de s'assurer que l'entreprise pour laquelle il travaille est en conformité avec les lois qui régissent ses activités. Il est tenu de suivre avec minutie le déroulement des procédures juridiques engagées contre l'entreprise, de défendre et de protéger les intérêts de cette dernière. Parfois, surtout dans les pays anglophones, ce conseiller juridique est aussi un avocat habilité. Cependant, même si une telle référence est de plus en plus courante, elle n'est pas véritablement nécessaire. Dans le cadre de son travail, ce juriste est tenu d'étudier les textes de lois, ainsi que les textes réglementaires qui s'appliquent au secteur dans lequel son entreprise intervient. Pour bien réussir dans ce métier, il faut être persuasif, convaincant, avoir le sens du relationnel et, cela va de soi, savoir négocier. C'est un métier difficile mais très intéressant.

C. Nouvelles qualifications pour les assistants juridiques (parajuristes)

Le Barreau de Québec mettra bientôt au point un dispositif qui permettra de délivrer un brevet aux assistants juridiques qui dispensent des services au public. La loi qui doit être bientôt adoptée par le gouvernement rendra le Barreau responsable des critères de compétence et de déontologie des assistants juridiques. Le Barreau aura aussi la responsabilité de la mise sur pied du mécanisme relatif à la délivrance de ces certificats et aux règles disciplinaires applicables aux assistants juridiques. En outre, les candidats devront suivre un enseignement universitaire reconnu, réussir un examen d'admission et avoir les « qualités morales » requises pour avoir l'autorisation de pratiquer. Des dispositions extraordinaires seront conçues pour les candidats disposant de « droits acquis », c'est-à-dire plus de trois ans d'expérience à temps plein dans les secteurs homologués au cours des cinq dernières années. Les assistants juridiques expérimentés ou titulaires d'un diplôme universitaire de base attestant d'une formation d'assistance juridique pourront bientôt demander de passer l'examen d'admission d'assistants juridiques au Québec.

Access answers at the end of the book.

PART 5 – ADVANCED READING

Management of law firms – the partner/associate and client/law firm relationship

Central to the success of every law firm is the nature of the relationship it has established:
- between its partners and associates; and more generally
- with its clients.

These two relationships are fundamental to the successful functioning of any firm. Times of economic hardship and recession can put both these relationships under pressure. In such periods, the reaction of many firms is to lay off lawyers and support staff. As we have seen, a typical law firm is structured around its partners as supported by the work of their associates. The ratio of associates to partners in a law firm is referred to as *leverage*. The more associates *per* partner, the more leveraged a firm's business model. Highly leveraged[7] firms take exaggerated profits when there is a lot of work available; however, in an economic downturn they are economically vulnerable as they have more overheads, i.e. the cost of paying the wages of a high numbers of associates and support staff. Thus, when an economic downturn is significant, many law firms immediately modify their business model, as they are no longer able to rely on associate multiplication as a means of profit maximization. In other words they lay off or fire some of their associates.

Another area of legal practice that comes under pressure in an economic downturn is the law firm's relationship with its clients, especially as regards the firm's billing practice. Lawyers can bill for the work they do in a number of ways.
- Hourly billing, recognized as the most profitable billing method.
- Flat rates, whereby a fee is negotiated in advance for the work that is to be done. Flat fees are probably the most popular with clients, as they allow some control over the amount of fees that will be payable.
- Retainer fees, whereby a lawyer is paid a fixed amount to represent a client over a fixed period. The retainer fee is payable whether the lawyer has work to do or not.
- Contingency fees, whereby a lawyer is paid a percentage of the award (s)he helps to generate, as a result of his/her involvement.

Many in the business community consider that lawyers' fees have become excessive, with legal bills sometimes threatening to cost more than the problem the lawyer has been hired to solve. However, lawyers would argue, and with some reason, that higher bills are a natural result of the costs of doing business in a society that increasingly seeks refuge in regulation. More regulation naturally results in higher regulatory compliance costs. To comply with the law one first has to know what the law provides and so one has to hire a lawyer. After all, although often the case, it is not fair to blame the lawyer for the law!

---

[7] Leverage can also be used to refer to a business's debt levels: a heavily leveraged or highly geared business is one that has borrowed a lot of money.

Chapter two

THE PROFESSION OF LAWYER IN COMMON LAW JURISDICTIONS

PART 1 – TEXT 1 – INFORMATION

The different kinds of lawyers in the common law world

Practitioner of law, lawyer, attorney, counsel, solicitor, barrister and **in-house lawyer** are all words used to describe someone qualified to practice law in common law jurisdictions. However, these terms do not all have exactly the same meaning and some, for example barrister and solicitor, are not even used in all common law countries. This can be confusing for the non-Anglophone student. So what does each term mean?

- *Lawyer* The term lawyer is used in common law countries to describe any person **licensed to practice law**. It is a general term and does not tell us what type of lawyer the person is, just that they are qualified to practice law.

- *Attorney* Attorney or attorney at law is also a general term used to define someone qualified to practice law. The term is used primarily in the United States. However, lawyers with specialized qualifications in the area of **patent** law may be referred to as patent attorneys in common law **jurisdictions** other than the United States.

- *Solicitor and barrister* In the United Kingdom and in many other **Commonwealth countries** such as Australia, Canada or India, the **profession** of lawyer is divided into two categories, solicitors and barristers. This distinction does not exist in the United States.
  - Solicitors work mainly in the area of regulatory law and also do much of the work carried out by public notaries in civil law countries, such as France.
  - Barristers are lawyers specialized in **pleading**, above all before the higher courts/jurisdictions. They also issue **legal opinions**, advising clients as to their chances of success, if they were they to bring their case to court. Barristers can also work for companies as employees.

- *In-house lawyer, counsel* The term in-house lawyer describes a lawyer who works as an employee for the legal service of a company. In common law countries in-house lawyers are usually qualified lawyers and not just holders of a university law degree. Counsel is another general term for lawyer, primarily relied on in the United States. Lawyers working for companies in the United States are sometimes also referred to as corporate in-house counsel.

What kind of work does the common law lawyer do?

Common law lawyers carry out a number of important tasks.

- *Conveyancing* **Conveyancing** is the term used to describe the **legal transfer of ownership** or **title to property** from one party to another.
- *Succession law* **Succession law** is the law governing the transfer of property on someone's death. **Probate** makes up part of the law of succession and describes the process **whereby** a lawyer makes application to the appropriate state authorities to have the right to administer the deceased's affairs. Once the state authorities certify the deceased's will, the **executor/executrix** is then **empowered** to distribute the **deceased**'s **estate, pursuant** to its **terms**. Frequently, a lawyer represents the executor in the performance of this task.
- *Advocacy* **Advocacy** involves representing clients in **litigation** before the courts. Although in the United States any lawyer may represent his/her client before the courts, in the United Kingdom and many other common law countries, barristers carry out the role of advocacy, especially before the higher courts. However, in the United Kingdom solicitors do have a **right of audience** before the lower courts. Solicitors carry out all of the preparatory work that is necessary for bringing a court case. (S)he **compiles** a **file** containing all of the documentation that is referred to as the "**brief**" and when the solicitor passes the brief to the barrister, (s)he is said "to **brief**" the barrister. The barrister will then draft the pleadings based on the information in the brief and then actually plead the case. When not pleading before the courts, the other activity of barristers involves **issuing** legal opinions. As we have seen, a legal opinion is set out in a document **drafted** by a barrister, advising his client whether or not they should bring a court case. The legal opinion will contain a(n):
  - definition of the **scope** of a party's legal rights;
  - statement of the law applicable to their case; and
  - estimation of the chances of success of this party, were they to bring a case before the courts.
- *Drafting of contracts* This is one of the main jobs of lawyers specialized in the area of commercial law. As people are **bound** to act **in accordance with** the contracts they sign, it is very important that the contract accurately reflect the client's wishes.
- *Regulatory work* One of the main areas of work for lawyers today is **regulatory work**. Modern society has adopted many laws regulating human activity, for example laws governing the sale of goods, safety and building regulations, **environmental law rules, labor law, competition law** etc. When carrying out their business, people and companies have to ensure that they respect these laws. In those jurisdictions where the profession is divided into barristers and solicitors, solicitors mainly carry out this work.

Practitioner of law – *juriste/avocat*
Lawyer – *avocat*
Attorney/attorney at law – *avocat*
Counsel – *avocat*
Solicitor – *avocat qui remplit des fonctions qui, en France, seraient à la fois celles d'un avocat, d'un conseiller juridique et d'un notaire. En principe un « solicitor » ne peut pas plaider devant les juridictions supérieures*
Barrister – *avocat dont l'activité essentielle est de plaider devant des juridictions supérieures*
In-house lawyer/corporate in-house counsel – *juriste d'entreprise*
Licensed (to be) to practice law – *être habilité à exercer une profession juridique (avocat notamment)*
Patent – *brevet*
Jurisdictions – *juridictions*
Commonwealth countries – *pays du Commonwealth, anciennement membres de l'empire britannique*
Profession – *profession libérale*
Pleading – *plaidoirie*
Legal opinion – *avis juridique rédigé par un barrister*
Convey (to) – *transmettre (ici = transférer un titre de propriété)*
Conveyance – *acte de cession d'un titre de propriété*
Conveyancing – *transfert de propriété*
Legal transfer of ownership – *transfert du titre de propriété*
Title to property – *titre/droit de propriété*
Law of succession – *droit des successions*
Probate – *homologation d'un testament*
Whereby – *par lequel*
Will – *testament*
Executor/executrix – *exécuteur testamentaire*
Empowered (to be) – *être habilité (à)*
Deceased – *personne décédée*
Estate – *patrimoine*
Pursuant to – *selon/conformément à*
Terms – *clauses/dispositions*
Terms of a contract – *clauses contractuelles*
Advocacy – *plaidoirie*
Litigation – *litige/contentieux*
Right of audience – *droit d'apparaître ou de plaider devant une cour*
Compile (to) a file – *réunir/dresser un dossier*
Brief – *dossier (rédigé par le solicitor et transmis au barrister à des fins de plaidoirie)*
Brief (to) – *donner instruction/transmettre un dossier (en vue d'une plaidoirie)*
Issue (to) – *émettre (un avis juridique)*
Draft (to) – *rédiger*
Scope – *portée/étendue/champ d'application*
Bound (to be) (to bind) – *être lié/contraint (juridiquement)*

Binding – *contraignant*
In accordance with – *selon/conformément à*
Regulatory work – *travail réglementaire*
Environmental law – *droit de l'environnement*
Labor/labor law – *droit du travail*

PART 1 – TEXT 1 – EXERCISES

1. Vocabulary test

Fill in the missing words using the vocabulary in Text 1

a) Environmental law and competition law are sometimes referred to as _____ law.
b) Once (s)he has compiled the brief, a solicitor then _____ the barrister.
c) When I qualify, I am going to work as an _____ because I would prefer to work for a company rather than to work for a _____.
d) Once I qualify as a barrister I hope to _____ before the courts and also issue _____.
e) My boss told me that I was very good at _____ contracts; he said he liked my style of writing.
f) I spoke to my father and he said he will contact a _____ to take out _____ of my mother's will in the United Kingdom.
g) I decided to sell my house in New York and contacted an _____ to organize the _____ of the title to the purchaser.
h) According to my solicitor, I am _____ by the terms of the contract; however, in order to be sure he has asked a barrister for a _____.
i) After I became a barrister, the first time I _____ before the courts, I was very nervous as I do not like to speak in public.
j) _____ law deals with relations between employers and employees, while _____ law tries to ensure the existence of an efficient economy without monopolies.

2. Vocabulary test

Write sentences with the following pairs of words. Your sentence should demonstrate your knowledge of the relationship between the words

a) Solicitor/barrister
b) Conveyancing/title
c) Probate/deceased
d) To brief/barrister
e) Regulatory work/contracts
f) Advocacy/barrister

3. Knowledge test

Each of the following statements is false; do you know why? Write a sentence stating why

a) Solicitors are not qualified to plead before the courts.

b)   Attorneys specialize in corporate law work.
c)   If I became a barrister I would only be able to plead before the courts.
d)   In-house counsel is someone who has not qualified as a lawyer.
e)   Conveyancing involves the transfer of land upon someone's death.
f)   A legal opinion is issued by a solicitor indicating to a client whether in the former's view (s)he should bring an action before a court or not.

PART 1 – TEXT 2 – MORE INFORMATION

The different kinds of lawyers in the common law world

Practitioners of law in common law countries are known by a number of different titles, for example **lawyer, attorney, counsel, solicitor, barrister, in-house lawyer**. These terms are not interchangeable and each has a specific meaning. Moreover, they are not used in all common law **jurisdictions** and for the non-English speaker they can be confusing. So what do these terms mean exactly?

- *Lawyer* The term lawyer is used in all common law countries and describes any person **licensed to practice law**. It is a general term and does not **denote** any specialization, **i.e.** it does not tell us what type of lawyer the person is, **merely** that they are qualified to practice law.
- *Attorney* Attorney or *Attorney at law* is a general term used to define a general practitioner of law in the United States. However, outside the United States lawyers specialized in specific areas of law, such as patent law, are sometimes referred to as patent attorneys. The term **Attorney-General** is used in most common law countries to describe the government's chief legal adviser.
- *Solicitor/barrister* In the United Kingdom and in many common law countries such as Australia and Ireland, lawyers are divided into two main categories: solicitors and barristers. These terms are not used in the United States or Canada. Both barristers and solicitors are lawyers but the two professions can be distinguished in the following way.
  - Solicitors do most of the legal work carried out by lawyers apart from pleading before the higher jurisdictions. In the United Kingdom, the **profession** of solicitor is governed by the Law Society of England and Wales. Lawyers in Scotland work under a different system as a result of the fact that the Scottish legal system is partly influenced by the civil law system. Solicitors normally work in **law firms** taking the legal form of **partnerships**.
  - Barristers are specialized in **pleading** before the courts. Barristers can be divided into two categories: **Junior Counsel** or **Senior Counsel**. In the United Kingdom, a senior counsel is referred to as a **Queen's Counsel**, which is generally shortened to QC. Senior counsels are specialized in pleading before the higher jurisdictions or courts, such as the High Court or the Supreme Court. In the United Kingdom and many other common law jurisdictions, barristers are required to wear black **gowns** and **wigs** when pleading before the courts. In the United Kingdom,

the Bar Council is responsible for administrating the profession of barrister. Solicitors have always had the right to plead before lower jurisdictions/courts. However, if they qualify as **solicitor advocate** they can also plead before higher courts, as do barristers. As we have seen, the division between solicitor and barrister does not exist in the United States and, once qualified, all US attorneys are free either to plead in court and/or practice in a more administrative context, like solicitors. Interestingly, though there is no official division in the US between solicitors and barristers, most US lawyers who plead before the courts specialize exclusively in this area and are referred to as **trial lawyers/attorneys**.

- *In-house lawyer (also known as corporate **in-house counsel**)* In-house lawyer is the term used to describe lawyers who work as employees of a company or business. In Anglo-Saxon countries, in-house counsel or lawyers are nearly always qualified lawyers.
- *Related professions* Professions such as ***Notary Public*** or ***Commissioner for Oaths*** also exist in common law countries. One does not have to be a qualified lawyer to be either a Notary Public or a Commissioner for Oaths. Unlike lawyers, the office of Notary Public or Commissioner for Oaths is a public one and they are considered to be public officers, rather than private service providers. Above all their work involves confirming the signature and identity of people making written **sworn statements**, for example in the case of a sworn **affidavit**. If this is done by a notary public instead of by a Commissioner for Oaths, the notary is said to **notarize** the document. They also sign and certify copies as being true copies of the original documents. Documents that are to be used in an international context, i.e. relied on by a court operating in another jurisdiction, must be administered by a Notary Public; while a Commissioner for Oaths administers documents that are to be relied on domestically within the jurisdiction.

What does the common law lawyer do?

In Anglo-Saxon countries lawyers can have varied careers. Many do the traditional legal work of lawyers working in **private practice**. Alternatively, lawyers can **work in-house** for a company, work for government departments or go into politics. A law qualification is also considered a good foundation for a career in journalism, banking or business. Lawyers who work for government departments will frequently become **criminal prosecutors** representing the state or alternatively they will work for **government** or state **agencies**, such as the national **competition**, environmental or telecommunications agencies. After practicing for a number of years, a lawyer can seek to become a **judge**. Unlike in many civil law jurisdictions, there is no specific qualification or training for this position. Instead, a successful lawyer is normally **appointed to the bench**, i.e. nominated as a judge, by the **executive branch**. However, in the United States, some members of the judiciary at state level are elected by popular vote.

The work of lawyers in common law countries can be discussed under a number of headings.

- *Conveyancing* **Conveyancing** is the term used to describe the **legal transfer** of the **ownership** or **title of property** from one party to another. When X sells his house to Y, in legal terms X's title to the property is **conveyed** to Y and the legal formalities necessary to give effect to this transfer, i.e. the **conveyance** of the title, are carried out by a lawyer. In jurisdictions where the profession is divided between barristers and solicitors, solicitors carry out conveyancing. The monopoly enjoyed by solicitors in conveyancing in the United Kingdom, Australia and some other common law countries has been extended to other professions such as surveyors or real estate agents, who can sit exams to qualify as **licensed conveyancers**. Despite the reform, the activity continues to be dominated by solicitors. The work carried out under the heading of conveyancing can be summarized as follows:
  - *taking instruction* from the client for whom they are *acting* When a lawyer is requested to perform a task on behalf of a client, the lawyer is said to take instruction from the client. In a conveyancing transaction, it is recommended that the **vendor** (seller) and **purchaser** (buyer) instruct different lawyers. At the first meeting the lawyer should give the client an overview of the transaction, the different steps involved, the applicable timescale and the taxes and payments that will become due. For example the **stamp duty** that is payable on the transfer of property and the **legal fees** that will be charged;
  - *carrying out* **searches** *against the property being bought* It is the job of the purchaser's solicitor to carry out a search to ensure that the property being purchased is not **encumbered**, i.e. that the property is free of all charges. If free of charges the property is said to be unencumbered;
  - *representing the client at the* **closing**[1] The seller's and vendor's solicitors must both ensure that all the documentation required to allow the sale go through at closing is collected. It is also necessary that the buyer's lawyer establish a **chain of ownership/ title**, whereby the vendor's ownership of the property is beyond doubt;
  - *drafting* the contract for sale In the common law, contracts for the sale of property must be in writing and are referred to as **deeds**;
  - *liaising with the lender bank* When the purchaser is taking out a **loan** guaranteed by a mortgage in order to buy the house, the **mortgagor's** (borrower's) lawyer will be required to liaise with the lending institution to ensure that the **purchase cheque/check** is issued by the **mortgagee** (lender) in time;
  - *payment of taxes* Payment of the government taxes due on the

---

[1] Closing is the name that is given to the meeting at which the actual sale and transfer of title occur.

sale. This is the responsibility of the lawyer working on the file, who is required to withhold taxes from any money due to a client and to pay the required amount to the government. In this way, the lawyer becomes a tax collector **on behalf of** the government.

- *Succession law* Succession law is the law governing the transfer of property at death. The deceased can either die **testate**, i.e. having made a **will,** or **intestate**, i.e. without having **drawn up** a will. It is normally a solicitor who will draft the client's will and then **take out probate** upon the client's death, i.e. apply to the appropriate government authority on behalf of the **executor/executrix** for the right to administer the deceased's **estate**. The property is then distributed to the **beneficiaries** named in the will. However, it is not necessary to have **recourse** to a lawyer to draft a will and, once the will is written, the executor **nominated** in the will can take out probate without using a solicitor.

- *Advocacy* Although in the United States any lawyer can represent his client before the courts, in the United Kingdom and many other common law countries, this work is mainly carried out by barristers who specialize in **pleading**. Barristers traditionally enjoy a monopoly in pleading before the higher courts, but solicitors have always played an important subsidiary role in the litigation process. For example, nearly all the preparatory work for a trial is carried out by a solicitor who **compiles** a **file** referred to as a **brief**. The solicitor then "**briefs**" the barrister who drafts the **pleadings** and pleads the case on behalf of the solicitor's client. The specialist nature of the profession of barrister is reinforced by the fact that a member of the public cannot contact a barrister directly but must do so through his/her solicitor. However, instead of having recourse to a barrister, solicitors may themselves plead before the lower courts. Solicitors may also apply to become a solicitor-advocate, whereby (s)he will enjoy the same **rights of audience** before the courts enjoyed by barristers. Thus, the monopoly enjoyed by barristers, as regards pleading before the courts, is in reality rather limited. Moreover, it should be recalled that individuals have the right to represent themselves before the courts without a lawyer, if they so choose.

- *Drafting of contracts* This is one of the principal jobs of the commercial solicitor. The drafting of contracts is an extremely important activity, as the effect of a contract is to create a type of private law between the parties that **binds** them and limits their future commercial freedom. Obviously, the **scope** or extent of any such restriction must be clearly defined and represent the true intention of the parties. This is effectively the task of the solicitor when drafting the contract, i.e., to give legal effect to the wishes of the parties.

- *Issuing of legal opinions* When not pleading before the courts, the other activity of barristers involves **issuing** legal opinions; junior counsel frequently carry out this work. A legal opinion is a document drafted by a barrister defining the legal rights a party enjoys, and **seeks** to estimate the chance of success of this party were they to bring a case before the courts. A solicitor, after his first meeting with a client, will often request a legal opinion from a barrister before advising a client as to whether they should bring a case before the courts.

- ***Regulatory work*** Modern society has adopted a seemingly endless number of laws regulating human activity. This is especially true as regards commercial activities, and businesses are required to respect these laws. Areas such as competition law, **environmental law**, **labor law**, **intellectual property etc., all come** under this heading and this work is primarily carried out by solicitors. In-house counsel, referred to as compliance lawyers also carry out this work**.** A bank will often employ lawyers to ensure that they **comply with** the countless banking regulations governing consumer protection and the bank's general economic stability. For example, banks have to issue information **notices** to investors and **shareholders**. It will be the compliance lawyer's job to ensure that these notices are issued on time and comply with all the information requirements established by law.

VOCABULARY

Practitioner of law – *juriste*
Lawyer – *avocat*
Attorney/attorney at law – *avocat (US)*
Counsel – *avocat*
Solicitor – *un "avocat" : il remplit des fonctions qui, en France, seraient à la fois celles d'un avocat, d'un conseiller juridique et d'un notaire. En principe un « solicitor » ne peut pas plaider devant les juridictions supérieures*
Barrister – *avocat dont l'activité essentielle est de plaider devant des juridictions, souvent les juridictions supérieures*
In-house lawyer/corporate in-house counsel – *juriste d'entreprise*
Licensed to practice law – *être habilité à exercer une profession juridique*
To denote – *indiquer/marquer*
I.e. (*id est*; that is) – *c'est-à-dire*
Merely – *simplement/seulement*
Patent – *brevet*
Attorney-General – *conseiller juridique du gouvernement*
Law firm – *cabinet d'avocats*
Profession – *profession libérale*
Partnership – *association*
Partnership (to go into) – *s'associer*
Specialized (to be) in pleading – *être spécialisé en plaidoirie*
Plead (to) – *plaider*
Junior Counsel – *avocat « barrister » qui n'a pas le titre de QC*
Senior Counsel – *avocat spécialisé devant les juridictions supérieures*
Queen's Counsel (= QC) – *nom donné au Senior Counsel au Royaume-Uni*
Gown – *robe*
Wig – *perruque*

Solicitor advocate – *solicitor habilité à plaider devant les juridictions supérieures au même titre qu'un barrister*
Trial lawyer/attorney – *avocat spécialisé en plaidoirie aux Etats Unis*
In-house counsel – *juriste d'entreprise*
Notary Public – *notaire*
Commissioner for Oaths – *officier assermenté habilité à recevoir des déclarations sous serment*
Sworn statement – *déclaration sous serment*
Oath – *serment*
Affidavit – *affidavit/déclaration sous serment faite par écrit*
Notarize (to) a document – *certifier/certifier officiellement*
Work (to) in private practice – *exercer dans un cabinet d'avocats*
Work (to) in-house – *travailler en tant que juriste d'entreprise*
Criminal prosecutor – *procureur*
Government agency – *organisme gouvernemental*
Competition law – *droit de la concurrence*
Judge – *juge*
Appointed to the bench – *accède à la magistrature*
Executive branch – *pouvoir exécutif*
Conveyancing – *transfert de propriété*
Legal transfer of ownership – *transfert du titre de propriété*
Ownership – *propriété*
Title to property – *titre de propriété*
Convey (to) – *transmettre (ici : transférer un titre de propriété)*
Conveyance – *acte de cession d'un titre de propriété*
Licensed conveyancer – *rédacteur agrée d'actes de transfert de propriété*
Taking instruction (from a client) – *recevoir/prendre des instructions (d'un client)*
To act for/on behalf of a client – *agir au nom/pour le compte d'un client*
Vendor – *vendeur*
Purchaser – *acheteur/acquéreur*
Stamp duty – *droit de timbre (fiscal)*
Legal fees – *honoraires d'avocat*
Search – *recherche*
Encumbered – *bien grevé*
Closing – *réunion – conclusion d'une vente*
Chain of ownership – *chaîne, liste des propriétaires successifs*
Title – *titre*
Draft (to) – *rédiger*
Deeds to a house – *actes établissant le titre de propriété d'une maison*
Deed (contract) – *acte authentique*
Lend (to) – *prêter*
Loan – *prêt*
Mortgage – *hypothèque*
Mortgagor – *(débiteur hypothécaire) acheteur à qui on a accordé un prêt hypothécaire*
Mortgagee – *créancier hypothécaire (banque ou organisme de crédit qui a octroyé le prêt hypothécaire)*

Purchase cheque – *chèque d'achat*
On behalf of – *au nom de/pour le compte de*
Law of succession – *droit des successions*
Legal beneficiaries – *ayants droits*
Die (to) testate – *le défunt a exprimé ses volontés dans un testament*
Will – *testament*
Intestate – *succession « ab intestat », le défunt n'a pas manifesté sa volonté par testament*
Draw-up (to) – *rédiger*
Take (to) out probate – *effectuer une demande auprès des autorités pour avoir le droit d'administrer le patrimoine du défunt*
Probate – *homologation/validation d'un testament*
Executor/executrix – *exécuteur testamentaire*
Estate – *patrimoine*
Beneficiary – *bénéficiaire*
Have (to) recourse to – *avoir recours à*
Nominated/appointed – *nommé/désigné*
Advocacy – *plaidoirie*
Plead (to) – *plaider*
Brief – *dossier avec toutes les pièces concernant le procès établi par le solicitor et transmis au barrister*
Brief (to) – *donner instruction/transmettre/confier un dossier en vue de préparer la plaidoirie*
Pleading – *dossier de plaidoirie*
Right of audience – *droit de plaider devant une cour, un tribunal*
Bind (to) – *lier (ici, juridiquement)*
Bound (to be) – *être lié/être contraint (juridiquement)*
Scope – *portée/étendue/champ d'application*
Legal opinion – *avis juridique rédigé par un « barrister »*
Issue (to) (a legal opinion) – *émettre (un avis juridique)*
Seek (to) – *chercher/rechercher*
Regulatory work – *travail réglementaire*
Environmental law – *droit de l'environnement*
Labor law – *droit du travail*
Intellectual property law – *droit de la propriété intellectuelle*
Compliance lawyer – *juriste chargé de s'assurer de la conformité d'une activité, d'un comportement avec les lois et règles en vigueur*
Comply (to) (with a law, a rule) – *être en conformité avec/respecter les lois et règlements en vigueur*
Notice – *avis*
Shareholders – *actionnaires*

PART 1 – TEXT 2 – EXERCISES

1. Definitions

Write a sentence defining each of the following terms – one sentence per term

   a)   Partnership

b) In-house lawyer
c) Pleadings
d) Closing
e) Solicitor-advocate
f) Executor
g) Compliance lawyer

2. Sentences

Write sentences with the following pairs of words. Your sentence should, if possible demonstrate your knowledge of the relationship between the words

a) Solicitor/pleading
b) Brief/solicitor
c) Mortgage/building society
d) Intestate/testate
e) Probate/executor
f) Advocacy/labor law
g) Conveyance/stamp duty
h) Draft/contract
i) Jurisdiction/solicitor
j) Deed/property

3. Fill in the missing words

Fill in the missing words using the vocabulary in Text 2

a) The role of the _____ is to prepare a brief for the barrister, who then _____ the case before the court that has _____ to hear the matter.
b) Normally only solicitors specialized in conveyancing will _____ ownership of property from one party to another. However, this work can also be carried out by a _____. The purchaser will normally take out a loan referred to as a _____ in order to be able to buy the house.
c) A solicitor who wishes to have a full right of audience before the courts must become a _____. Otherwise, (s)he may only plead before the courts of lower _____ and must instruct a _____ to represent his/her client before the higher courts.
d) Upon the death of a client, a solicitor will apply to take out _____ and then will distribute the deceased's property to the _____ named in the _____.
e) The _____ solicitor carried out a _____ on the property to ensure it was unencumbered before allowing his/her client to sign the _____ transferring the house.

4. Knowledge test

The following questions may be answered in writing or by way of discussion

a) Compare the profession of lawyer in Anglo-Saxon countries to lawyers in your country.
b) What are the differences between barristers and solicitors?

c)   Would you like to work as a lawyer? Explain your answer.
d)   Why do you think there is no distinction between solicitors and barristers in the United States?
e)   What area of law would you like to specialize in?

PART 2 – QUICK LOOK GRAMMAR REVISION

The Present Tense – The Simple Present and the Present Progressive

1. The Simple Present

The simple present is used to express things that are neither specific nor particular; it is used to express habitual or frequent actions and talk about permanent characteristics or situations. For example:

- daily events – **John *meets* his clients every day**;
- usual activities – **John usually *meets* clients on a Tuesday**;
- general non-specific statements of fact – **John *meets* with clients as part of his work**.

It can be also used to talk about the future, for example:

- **The next train *leaves* in an hour**.

Forms of the **simple present**

a)   When making an affirmative statement, the verb stem is used, with the addition of an "s" for the third person singular:
  - I, you, we, they: WORK/WATCH/PAY/STUDY
  - He, she, it, John: WORK**S**/WATCH**ES**/PAY**S**/STU**DIES**

  Note:

  If the subject of the sentence is in the third person singular it is necessary to add "s" to the verb; however:
  - if the verb ends in "**ch**" (*watches*), "**x**" (*fixes*)", "**ss**" (*passes*), "**sh**" (*flashes*), "**zz**" (*buzzes*), it is necessary to add "**es**";
  - if the subject of the sentence is in the third person singular and ends with a consonant and "**y**", remove the "**y**" and add "**ies**" (*study* becomes *studies*);
  - if the subject is in the third person singular and ends with vowel and "**y**", one only add "**s**" (*pay* becomes *pays*).

b)   When making a negative statement:
  - I, you, we, they: do not (don't) WORK/WATCH/PAY/STUDY
  - He, she, it, John: does not (doesn't) WORK/WATCH/PAY/STUDY

  Note:

  When speaking in the negative:

- "do not" (don't), becomes "does not" (doesn't) in the third person singular;
- the verb is always in its stem form, and so in the third person singular does not change, i.e., it does not take "s", "**es**", "**ies**".

c) When asking a question the auxiliary do/does is used with the verb stem:
- Do I, you, we, they WORK/WATCH/PLAY/STUDY?
- Does he, she, it, John WORK (hard)/WATCH (much television)/ PLAY (a lot)/STUDY (every evening)?

Note:

When asking a question:
- "do" becomes "does" in the third person singular;
- the verb in the third person singular remains in its stem form and does not change, i.e. does not take an "s", "**es**", "**ies**".

2. The present progressive

The present progressive is used to talk about something that has a link with the situation that is being experienced. Often this is an action that is occurring now:

John cannot come to the phone because he *is meeting* with a client.

The present continuous allows for the description and commentary of a situation. It is used to describe:
- things that one witnesses: "I don't believe it! He's doing it again!"
- activities that are in progress: "He's talking to the manager."

It is used to comment on
- the behavior of someone: "He's always stirring up trouble".
- a remark someone has made: "Are you suggesting that I'm lying?"

Forms of the **present progressive**

The auxiliary "be" is conjugated to correspond to the subject, and then followed with the verb stem + ing

a) When making a statement:
- I **am** WORKING;
- He, she, it, John **is** WORKING;
- You, we, they **are** WORKING.

b) When negating, i.e. making a negative statement:
- I **am not** WORKING;
- He, she, it, John **is not** (isn't) WORKING;

  –   You, we, they **are not** (aren't) WORKING.

c)   When asking a question:
  –   **Am** I WORKING?
  –   **Is** he, she, it, John WORKING?
  –   **Are** you, we, they WORKING?

  Note:

  When using the present progressive, one frequently uses contractions, for example:
  –   I am working: **I'm** working.
  –   He/she is working: **he's/she's** working.
  –   It is working: **it's** working.
  –   You are working: **you're** working.
  –   We are working: **we're** working.
  –   They are working: **they're** working.

NB Only use contractions in oral English, NEVER in formal written English

  Note:

  Some verbs are less frequently used in the progressive form. These are the stative verbs, which are often associated with feelings or opinions:
  –   to be;
  –   to believe;
  –   to want;
  –   to hear;
  –   to know;
  –   to like;
  –   to love;
  –   to prefer;
  –   to understand; and
  –   to guess, doubt, imagine, mean, remember, dislike, see, taste, smell, feel……..

  Example
  John will not represent Bob, he:
  –   **prefers** to work for James = CORRECT;
  –   **is preferring** to work for James = INCORRECT.

  John does not believe his client, he:
  –   **thinks** he is lying = CORRECT;
  –   **is thinking** he is lying = INCORRECT.

  John quit his job with his law firm, he:
  –   **wants** to move in-house = CORRECT;
  –   **is wanting** to move in-house = INCORRECT.

PART 2 – GRAMMAR EXERCISES

1. Simple present or present progressive

Fill in the spaces using the simple present or the present progressive

a) At the moment, John cannot speak to you, (he/plead) _____ an important case before the High Court.

b) (John/understand) _____ what his client wants to do, but he thinks it may be against the law.

c) (John/work) _____ in the area of conveyancing?

d) (John/plead/usually) _____ before the court every Tuesday morning.

e) What is John doing with that file? (he/take) _____ out probate of the deceased's will.

f) At present (John/work) _____ as in-house counsel for a large company but before that he was working with a law firm.

g) (John/hate) _____ pleading before the courts, he is too nervous.

2. More of the same ......

At the moment, (John/read) _____ the brief that a solicitor gave him but (he/understand/not) _____ it at all; it is a mess. (He/need) _____ to set up a meeting with the solicitor but (he/know/not) _____ his new phone number. Normally, (he/work) _____ for another firm of solicitors. He is unable to contact his secretary as (he/work) _____ in the law library and is not allowed to use his phone. He is due in Court N°. 1 in two hours, and (he/think/not) _____ he will be able to represent the client. He will have to ask for an adjournment. (He/hope) _____ Judge Michaels agrees; fortunately, (he/know) _____ him well and so it should not be a problem.

3. Fill in the blanks

Fill in the spaces in the following questions and answers. For guidance, look at the example immediately below

(John, have) <u>Does John</u> have the file?
Yes, <u>he does</u>. He <u>has it</u> in his office.

a) (Frank/act) for your client?
Yes, (he/represent/always) _____ him before the courts. (he/hope) _____ to win again.

b) I want to go down to the court; (rain) _____ at the moment?
No, (the sun/shine) _____

c) (John, want) _____ to question the witness?
No, (he/want) _____ to continue with the trial. He (prefer) _____ to call the next witness instead.

PART 3 – AUDIO – LISTENING AND SPEAKING

Comprehension

Listen to the following conversation, make notes of all the relevant facts and then answer the questions below. If you have trouble understanding, follow the conversation while also reading the text.

Conversation between Bob, a solicitor and Charles Fry, a barrister

Charles: "Hello Bob, thanks for getting back to me."

Bob: "Not at all; what can I do for you?"

Charles: "It's about that brief you sent over, you know Ellström v Harte"[2]?

Bob: "Yes, interesting matter, we were hoping to get an injunction against Harte Ltd. preventing them from moving their money out of the UK, at least for as long as they owe my client Ellström money."

Charles: "Unfortunately, I cannot take the file, you see there is a bit of a problem, a conflict of interest in fact."

Bob: "Really?"

Charles: "Yes, unfortunately, I did a bit of work a couple of months back for a subsidiary of Ellström's, a company named Hotwire Corporation. In fact, they were also working for Harte Ltd."

Bob: "Did you indeed? Sorry I didn't know."

Charles: "You couldn't have known; however given that I worked for the other side, it probably isn't appropriate that I now represent Harte[3]."

Bob: "No, you are right and I'm not sure the client would like it either. Well thanks for telling me. I will just have to find someone else to do the application. Do you have anyone you might recommend off the top of your head? The client wants us to try to get this before the court in the next twenty-four hours."

Charles: "Why not try my old chambers[4] Smith & Dunn, old Jim Bradley over there would be delighted to get his hands on a brief like this. Ring him up and mention my name."

Bob: "Will do, thanks Charles and if we have any other work, I'll be in touch."

Charles: "Yes please; the way Anne is spending money these days, I'll have to be working around the clock just to keep my head above water. She's just back from the Maldives with some of her crowd and already is talking about doing St. Moritz again this year."

Bob: "Well you always had expensive tastes Charles. Look after yourself and talk to you soon."

Charles: "Yes, goodbye old chap."

---

[2] Note "v", short for versus; in spoken English "v" (versus) is changed to "and", i.e. Ellström **and** Harte.

[3] Ethical practice rules do not normally allow lawyers to work for and against the same client, as there might well be a conflict of interest for the lawyer.

[4] "Chambers" is the name given to the offices in which barristers work.

PART 3 – AUDIO COMPREHENSION – EXERCISES

1. Comprehension

From the notes you have taken answer the following questions

    a)   For what Company had Charles previously worked?
    b)   What kind of ruling does Bob want from the Court against Harte Ltd.?
    c)   What will be the effect of this remedy?
    d)   Why is Charles unable to represent Bob's client?
    e)   What does Charles suggest as an alternative?
    f)   Why is Charles looking for more work?

2. Speaking practice

In the following series of conversation couplets, develop suitable responses to the questions asked

    a)   Bob: "Hello Charles, how are you?
             Charles: "_____."
    b)   Bob: "How are Anne and the kids?"
             Charles: "_____."
    c)   Bob: "I may have a brief dealing with a court application for an injunction; would you be interested?
             Charles: "_____"
    d)   Bob: "I tried to ring you this morning but you were in court."
             Charles: "_____."
    e)   Bob: "We need a legal opinion on the legality of a conveyance, where it seems the seller did not really own the land. Would you be interested?"
             Charles: "_____."
    f)   Bob: "Would you like to take in a round of golf this weekend; maybe on Saturday afternoon in my club?"
             Charles: "_____."
    g)   Bob: "We have a case where a client thinks he has been unfairly dismissed. Do you know anything about employment law?"
             Charles: "_____."
    h)   Bob: "Did you get a new receptionist? She seems to be very efficient."
             Charles: "_____."
    i)   Bob: "It is a very complicated matter involving US law. Could you give our American attorney a call?"
             Charles: "_____."

3. Speaking practice continued ......

Create five other conversation couplets using in each couplet at least one word from the vocabulary found in Part 1, Text 1 or Text 2

4. Speaking practice continued ......

Listen to the suggested replies and repeat

a) Bob: "Hello Charles, how are you?
    Charles: "Fine thanks Bob. How is business?"

b) Bob: "How are Anne and the kids?"
    Charles: "They are doing very well, thanks. Anne is bringing the kids for a holiday in the south of France next week but unfortunately I cannot go."

c) Bob: "I may have a brief dealing with a court application for an injunction; would you be interested?"
    Charles: "Yes, thanks I would. For when do you need it to be done?"

d) Bob: "I tried to ring you this morning but you were in court."
    Charles: "Yes, I got stuck in Court 5; there was a divorce case before the Court."

e) Bob: "We need a legal opinion on the legality of a conveyance, where it seems the seller did not really own the land he was selling. Would you be interested?"
    Charles: "Yes, as you probably know I am specialized in conveyancing law."

f) Bob: "Would you be able to do an emergency application for us this evening in the High Court?"
    Charles: "No unfortunately I have a case scheduled before the Court of Appeal that is due to begin this afternoon."

g) Bob: "Would you like to take in a round of golf this weekend; maybe on Saturday afternoon in my club?"
    Charles: "Yes Bob I would, that is very nice of you. I need some fresh air."

h) Bob: "We have a case where a client thinks he has been unfairly dismissed. Do you know anything about labor law?"
    Charles: "Well, I have to admit that I do not have much experience in labor law; however, we do have a bright young chap here in Chambers specialized in the area."

i) Bob: "Did you get a new receptionist? She seems to be very efficient."
    Charles: "Yes, she is called Sandra. She is much better than Betty, who is out on maternity leave, thank God!"

j) Bob: "It is a very complicated matter involving US law. Could you give our American attorney a call?"
    Charles: "Of course I will. Send me an e-mail with his contact details and I will give him a ring this afternoon."

5. Associated questions

Discuss the following questions

a) In your country, do lawyers have to be specialized in pleading in order to plead before the courts?
b) Do you think the legal profession in the United Kingdom is well organized?
c) Do you think the separation between the profession of barrister and solicitor is necessary?
d) Which do you consider more interesting, the work of a barrister or a solicitor? Would you prefer to be a barrister or a solicitor?

PART 4 – TRANSLATION EXERCISES

When carrying out the translations it is not necessary to translate directly word for word; rather the emphasis should be on translating the sense of the text. Language is not directly interchangeable and so direct translations do not always convey the meaning in the text.

Translate the following texts from English to French

A. Class actions

Not everyone is happy to see the introduction into Europe of American-style class actions. European businessmen probably come at the top of that list. They are of course afraid of the imposition of astronomic damages similar to the type of awards made in the United States. For example, $145 billion was recently awarded by a Florida jury against five tobacco companies, on behalf of all American smokers. There was also an award of a $1.1 billion settlement against Ahold, a Dutch retailer, in a shareholders' class action in 2005; and a $65 million settlement last year against IBM in an overtime claim by technical and support staff in 2006. Many in Europe argue that the mechanism of class actions is not needed, given the high levels of regulation that already exist. They fear a double imposition of costs, firstly regulatory compliance costs and thereafter excessive court costs, as Anglo-Saxon style class actions provoke an increase in the number of consumer actions before the courts.

B. Regulated conveyancing model is by far the most expensive

The European Commission has published a study by independent consultants on the EU market for legal services associated with house and land sales (conveyancing services). The study finds that consumers have greater choice and are on average paying less for conveyancing services under more deregulated systems, with no loss in quality. The market for conveyancing services is worth about €17 billion per annum; efficiency savings of even a few percent following deregulation would therefore save consumers millions of Euros each year. The Commission is calling on member states to look at the findings and to review and update national laws, which limit competition and the free circulation of services throughout the Single Market. The traditional, highly regulated Latin notary system, which exists in most continental European countries, appears to be the most expensive, without necessarily offering clients a better service. This model is characterized by:

- mandatory involvement of specialist conveyancing lawyers for all land transfers;
- quantitative restrictions on the number of lawyers that can become specialist conveyancers; and
- the imposition of fixed fees set by government.

C. What is it exactly that barristers do?

Barristers are lawyers who do most of their work in court. Normally specialized in a particular branch of law, they above all have detailed knowledge of the latest case law applicable to a specific area. This specialist legal knowledge combined with their experience of court procedure ensures that they can make a substantial difference to the outcome of a case. However, they don't just apply their skills in court. A high proportion of civil cases are settled out of court and the fact of having engaged a leading barrister will normally greatly strengthen the client's hand at negotiation. If the matter goes to trial, a well-argued case will impress a judge and maximize the positive aspects of a client's case and minimize the negatives. In the same way, good cross-examination technique will impress a jury. Given the importance of case law in the common law legal system, hiring a top barrister can make a significant difference to the outcome of a case.

Translate the following texts from French to English

A. Les Rosbifs débarquent!

Les avocats britanniques et américains envahissent le marché français du Droit des affaires et du Droit commercial. Quelques cabinets français inventent des nouvelles stratégies pour résister. En effet, il y a une guerre sourde et feutrée, ignorée du grand public mais dont les enjeux sont colossaux, car ils affectent la façon de travailler dans le monde des affaires: les avocats français affrontent actuellement un débarquement britannique et américain. Sur les vingt premiers cabinets spécialisés en Droit des affaires en France, plus de la moitié sont désormais anglo-saxons. Plus grave encore, de nombreux avocats français réputés rejoignent, avec toute leur équipe, de grands cabinets anglo-saxons. «En débauchant chez nous, les Anglais font coup double », commente le patron d'un grand cabinet parisien. « Ils déstabilisent leurs concurrents français tout en achetant des compétences, des clientèles et des parts de marché.»

B. Vers une baisse du chômage?

La nouvelle génération de l'avion européen Airbus A320 sera assemblée à Hambourg, dans le nord de l'Allemagne, selon des informations du gouvernement allemand rendues publiques lundi. La mise au point des A320 à l'heure actuelle est encore partagée entre Toulouse, en France, et Hambourg. D'autres appareils seront également montés en Chine, a précisé le gouvernement allemand. La décision d'assembler les appareils à Hambourg fait partie des négociations menées entre Airbus et les gouvernements respectifs de l'Allemagne, de la France, de la Grande Bretagne et de l'Espagne dans la perspective d'un emprunt de 3,3 milliards d'euros, afin de permettre à la compagnie de livrer son futur appareil de longue distance, l'A350 d'ici 2013.

C. Donc un solicitor c'est quelqu'un qui ...

Le terme *solicitor* (avocat conseil) désigne une catégorie d'avocats que l'on trouve, dans les pays de *common law* comme le Royaume-Uni, Hong Kong, la République d'Irlande, l'Australie et la Nouvelle-Zélande mais pas aux États-Unis (le mot y a une signification tout à fait différente, car aux Etats Unis, un *solicitor* est plutôt la principale autorité juridique d'une ville). Dans beaucoup de pays de *common law* la profession d'avocat est divisée entre les *solicitor*s qui représentent et conseillent leurs clients, et les *barristers* (avocats spécialisés en plaidoirie), mandatés par un *solicitor* pour plaider dans une audience judiciaire, ou pour donner une opinion juridique. Cependant dans plusieurs pays comme le Canada ou les Etats-Unis, la profession a opéré la fusion de ces deux activités. Là où ce n'est pas le cas, lorsqu'un procès se révèle nécessaire, le client aura d'abord recours à un *solicitor*, qui le conseillera et fournira ensuite un dossier à un avocat chargé de plaider selon le mandat donné par le *solicitor*.

PART 5 – ADVANCED READING

The future of hourly billing

Time recording is probably one of the most tedious tasks that lawyers have to do. Most firms bill the time their lawyers spend on a file at a certain fixed hourly rate: associates charging $200 – $300 an hour, with much more charged for the work of senior associates, junior partners and senior partners. Each hour of a lawyer's day is in fact sub-divided into increments of five to ten minutes and each five-minute period spent on a file is logged into a time recording program, by way of the file number. In this way, it is hoped that clients will pay for every minute a lawyer spends on their case. This structure has been in place for decades in the United States and since the nineties in continental Europe. Normally, lawyers in a firm are set a billable hours target and failure to meet or alternatively to surpass this target is the single most determining factor in the outcome of a lawyer's career. Typical entry level associates would be expected to bill a minimum of 1,300 hours a year but those looking to be considered as partnership prospects should probably be billing closer to 1,600 a year or more. Moreover, those with exceptional billing records receive substantially larger annual bonuses; bonuses that can be larger than the lawyer's annual salary. It has been alleged by some that, given the manner of its application and the emphasis it places on the number of hours billed, hourly billing can make it tempting for younger lawyers to overbill, a practice referred to as padding. Padding involves dishonestly exaggerating the time that is spent on a file. There is another practice that is called weighting and which is not, in principle, dishonest. Weighting involves charging more than the hours actually worked on the file, but here the charge is not based on invented extra hours but is justified by reference to the particularly complicated character of the file and the work done. Thus, the extra charge is justified by reference to the nature of the file itself and should be identified as such in the invoice sent to the client. Given the temptations hourly billing creates for time wasting and padding, some companies are asking their law firms to introduce more reliable and cheaper fee establishment mechanisms. Indeed, it could be argued that the present economic downturn provides smaller firms, which have lower operating costs, with an opportunity to steal a march on their larger competitors. As a result of their lower costs, they are in a position to offer clients lower fees, which larger firms cannot match, because of their higher fixed costs. The present downturn also provides a major opportunity for a new phenomenon known as virtual firms. Such "firms" operate through the creation of a virtual law firm on the "net". Lawyers, many second and third year associates that have been laid off by larger firms, sign on to these virtual firms as available for work in the specific areas in which they have expertise. As they have absolutely no overheads, the virtual law firm, which is in reality just an agency for self-employed lawyers working from home, is in a position to bill clients a lot less than do established bricks and mortar firms. Moreover, the person doing the actual work is probably the same person, as regards experience and qualifications, who would be doing it, had the client contacted a big full-service law firm. Indeed the economic downturn, coupled with the expensive billing practices of some firms, has the potential to revolutionize the billing structure and thus the overall business model relied on by law firms.

Chapter three

WHAT IS THE COMMON LAW?

PART 1 – TEXT 1 – INFORMATION

The common law – sources of law

The common law is the legal system relied on in countries as **diverse** as the United States of America, England and Wales, Ireland, Canada, Australia, New Zealand, South Africa, India, Malaysia, Pakistan, Singapore, Hong Kong and many other **Commonwealth** countries. The common law is a system **founded** on extensive judicial power and consequently particular importance is given to the role of case law. The common law was developed in England following the invasion of the Normans in 1066. Prior to this invasion, England was divided into a number of small **kingdoms**, each applying their own system of local laws. The Normans eventually centralized the system of law in England and developed the common law as a system of law *common* to everyone.

The common law has a number of different sources such as case law, written law and custom.

- *Case law* Unlike the civil law, which is set out in a system of codes, the common law was initially derived from case law. There are two types of case law: common law case law and equity case law. Common law case law was developed from the decisions of the King's courts established by the Normans in the twelfth century. They developed three basic courts: the **Court of King's Bench**, the **Court of Common Pleas**, the **Court of the Exchequer** and the decisions of these courts **made up** the content of the common law. The Court of Common Pleas was the court of **first instance** for **actions** between **commoners**; the King's Bench had both **original and appellate jurisdiction**, hearing appeals from the Court of Common Pleas; and the Court of Exchequer **dealt with** fiscal questions. However, the system of law developed by these courts was technical and **tainted with corruption**. Moreover, the common law courts only offered **complainants** one remedy, **namely damages**. As a result, the Chancellor, the King's principal advisor, who was normally a member of the clergy, developed an alternative system of case law. This system of law was called equity and was developed to **complement** the common law system and to **overcome** its **inadequacies**. Consequently, equity offered remedies other than damages, referred to as equitable remedies. An example of an equitable remedy is an **injunction**. As equity was a separate system of law, it had its own court named the Court of Chancery. However, the common law and equity court systems were **merged** together by the Judicature Acts of the 1880s and as a result courts today can either give a remedy in common law, i.e. damages or alternatively a remedy developed under equity.

- *Statute law* The dominant source of law in common law countries today is statute law, as sovereignty is no longer vested in the King and his courts but in the legislature. Laws **adopted/enacted** by Parliament in the United Kingdom are called **Acts of Parliament** and **once** they are made public and published in the statute books, i.e. **promulgated**, they become known as **statute law**. Statute law is written law but it is different from civil law codes. This is because common law statutes tend to be **broadly** written, lacking the detail of the codified civil law system. This results in the common law courts having **large powers of interpretation** when applying statute law.

- *European Union law* The United Kingdom joined the European Union in 1973. European Union (EU) law is considered to take precedence over the national law of the United Kingdom. The supremacy of EU law over member state law was confirmed by the European Court of Justice in the celebrated case of Costa v ENEL.

- *Custom* A custom becomes a source of law when an established pattern of behavior becomes a right that can be relied on before the courts. For a **custom**, for example a **right of way**, to be considered to be a right in law, the exercise of the custom must be shown to have occurred since **time immemorial**, i.e. **since 1189**. If this cannot be established, alternatively it must be shown to have existed as far back as living memory. Moreover, the custom must be reasonable and not **offend** fundamental notions of justice, i.e. notions of right and wrong. Also, the right **claimed** must have been in constant and continual use and have been exercised **as of right** and not by **stealth**.

VOCABULARY

Diverse – *divers*
Commonwealth countries – *pays du Commonwealth, autrefois membres de l'empire britannique*
Founded on – *fondé sur*
Kingdom – *royaume*
Court of King's Bench – *Cour du Banc du Roi : cour de première instance et également cour d'appel du système de common law. Aujourd'hui la même cour se trouve au sein de la High Court et elle s'intitule* Queen's Bench
Court of Common Pleas – *Cour des Plaids Communs : cour de première instance du système de common law pour les particuliers*
Court of the Exchequer – *Cour de l'Echiquier (responsable pour les questions financières, surtout les litiges concernant les questions fiscales)*
Make (to) up – *constituer/composer*
First instance – *première instance*
Actions – *actions en justice/actions contentieuses*
Commoners – *particuliers/gens du peuple*

Original and appellate jurisdiction – *cour de première instance et cour d'appel*
Deal (to) with – *traiter de/s'occuper de/avoir affaire à*
Tainted with – *entaché de*
Corruption – *corruption*
Complainant – *plaignant/demandeur*
Namely – *à savoir*
Damages – *dommages et intérêts*
Complement (to) – *être le complément de/compléter*
Overcome (to) – *surmonter/dépasser*
Inadequacies – *insuffisances*
Injunction – *injonction/ordonnance de ne pas faire*
Merge (to) – *fusionner*
Adopted – *adopté*
Act of Parliament – *loi adoptée par le parlement mais pas encore promulguée*
Once – *une fois/une fois que/dès que*
Promulgate (to) – *promulguer*
Statute law – *législation (votée par le Parlement et promulguée)*
Broadly – *dans les grandes lignes*
Large power of interpretation – *large/important pouvoir d'interprétation*
Custom – *coutume*
Right of way – *droit de passage/servitude*
Time immemorial – *de temps immémorial, cad 1189 (cette date a été établie par le* Statute of Westminster *[Loi de Westminster] adopté en 1275)*
Since 1189 – *depuis 1189*
Offend (to) – *ne pas respecter/porter atteinte à*
Claim (to) – *revendiquer*
Exercised as of right – *exercé de droit*
By stealth – *furtivement*

PART 1 – TEXT 1 – EXERCISES

1. Vocabulary test

Fill in the missing words using the vocabulary in Text 1

a) The _____ law is based on the notion of extensive _____ power, with _____ developed by the courts having great importance.

b) The Normans established the Court of _____ and the Court of _____, the latter court dealt with fiscal issues.

c) Problems with the common law case law system led the _____ to establish a new system of case law based on _____ principles.

d) Equity was established because the common law was tainted with _____ and the only remedy available to complainants was _____.

e) The common law was established as a system of law _____ to everyone and replaced the system of _____ laws existing at that time.

f) The most important domestic source of law in the UK system is _____ law adopted by _____.

g) Another _____ of law in the common law is custom, however, to be established it is necessary to demonstrate the existence of the custom since time _____.

h)   _____ law adopted by Parliament is broadly written and gives the courts wide powers of _____.

i)   Equity was created to overcome the _____ of the ____ law and was dispensed in the Court of _____.

2. Vocabulary test

Write sentences with the following pairs of words. Your sentence should demonstrate your knowledge of the relationship between the words

a)   Right of way/time immemorial
b)   Adopted/Act of Parliament
c)   Statute law/interpretation
d)   Equity/common law
e)   Court of King's Bench/jurisdiction
f)   Judicial power/case law

3. Knowledge test

Each of the following statements is false; do you know why? Write a sentence stating why

a)   The system established by equity was too rigid and legalistic.
b)   To establish a custom as law, it is necessary to demonstrate that the custom in question has existed for twenty-five years.
c)   An Act of Parliament is the name given to statute law, once it has been promulgated into law.
d)   The Court of Common Pleas was the appellate court in the system of courts established by Henry II.
e)   The Commonwealth is the name given to the different states making up the United States.
f)   Case law is the most important source of law in common law countries.

PART 1 – TEXT 2 – MORE INFORMATION

The common law – sources of law

There are **close to** two hundred nations existing in the world today. Each has its own identity, different political **beliefs** and ambitions; and each has its own legal system representing these differences. **Thus**, certain **behavior** may be illegal in one country and be perfectly legal in another. However, even though the legal system of each of these countries has its own specific character, for reasons of simplicity the world's legal systems can be **classified** under three basic **headings**:

- the Romano-Germanic system of law (Civil Law);
- the Anglo-American system of law (Common Law);
- *Fiqh* – Islamic jurisprudence based on Sharia law.

The importance of the common law is that it has a worldwide presence and is the legal system of choice for some of the world's largest and richest countries. For example, the common law is the legal system in countries as diverse as the

United States of America (with the exception of the State of Louisiana), England and Wales, Ireland, Canada (with the exception of Quebec), Australia, New Zealand, South Africa, Malaysia, Pakistan, Singapore, Hong Kong and many other **Commonwealth** countries. **Indeed**, most countries that have at some time been **colonized** by the United Kingdom use the common law. Other countries, such as India, have taken the common law and mixed it with their own local laws. Thus, although many countries apply a system **based on** the common law, referred to as common law countries, the specific character of the laws developed by each of these countries may vary greatly. However, despite this difference, all these countries share the fundamental approach of the common law, namely: a system founded on extensive judicial power and consequently the important role of case law.

Origins of the common law

The common law was developed in England following the invasion of the Normans in 1066. Prior to the invasion of the Normans, England was divided into a number of small **kingdoms**, each applying their own system of local laws. The Normans sought to centralize the system of justice in England and over time developed the common law, as a system of law *common* to everyone.

When speaking of the common law, it is important to be aware that the term can be used in a number of different ways.

- It can be used as a general term to describe the system of law that was developed in England and that is now used in many different countries around the world. For example, the *common law* is the system of law applied in the United States and civil law is the system relied on in France.
- It can be used as a general term for case law to distinguish case law from statute law, i.e. law adopted by the legislative **branch of government**. Thus, case law is sometimes referred to generally as common law.
- Finally, as we will see, there are two types of case law, one of which is referred to as common law case law developed by the King's common law courts and the other which is called equity case law, developed by the King's chancellors[1]. The term common law is sometimes used as a term to distinguish the law coming from the King's common law courts from that developed by the Chancellor under the heading of equity.

To appreciate the various uses of the term *common law*, it is necessary to understand that the common law has a number of different sources:

- case law;
- legislation, also referred to as statute law;
- other sources.

---

[1] Effectively the King's prime minister, who in medieval times was often a representative of the Catholic Church.

Case law Unlike civil law, which is set out in a structured system of codes, the common law is initially derived from case law. Under the case law **methodology**, certain decisions adopted by higher courts may set a **precedent**, which must then be followed by all courts of equal or lower standing. This is called the **doctrine of stare decisis**. In this way, the content of the law is developed by way of a series of court decisions, referred to as case law. However, a court decision can run to hundreds of pages and, obviously, not the whole decision will be considered binding on subsequent courts. Instead, it is only the rule of law or the principle established by the decision, referred to as the **ratio decidendi** that binds subsequent courts. Sometimes in a decision, a judge will also issue an opinion on a related matter, but one not coming within the actual facts of the case. Such opinions are called **obiter dicta** and are not thought to create a binding precedent. This is because a court is only empowered to **rule in law** on the actual facts of the case before it. However, although such opinions are not binding, they can be influential in subsequent cases, especially if issued by a leading judge. Effectively, with obiter dicta a judge is giving his/her opinion on how (s)he would have decided the case, had the facts been different.

The area of case law is further divided into two types of case law:
- *Common law case law developed by the King's courts* Common law case law was developed from the decisions of the King's common law courts, established from the twelfth century onwards. These courts were the **Court of King's Bench**, the **Court of Common Pleas** and the **Court of the Exchequer**. The Court of Common Pleas was a **first instance jurisdiction**, which **handled** cases between **commoners**. The King's Bench **heard** appeals from the Court of Common Pleas and was also a first instance jurisdiction for cases involving the Crown, i.e. the King. Finally, the Court of Exchequer had **jurisdiction** over cases involving **fiscal disputes**. However, the system of common law developed by these courts was procedurally very technical and over time it **lost touch** with more fundamental notions of justice, such as right and wrong. Moreover, it became **tainted with corruption**, whereby people with money could influence the outcome of their trial. Lastly, the common law courts only offered **complainants/plaintiffs**[2] one remedy, **namely damages**[3]. As a result, the Chancellor, the King's principal advisor, who was normally a member of the clergy, created an alternative system of case law referred to as equity. Equity was developed not so much to compete with the King's common law but as a discretionary remedy designed to **complement** the common law when it failed to provide a complainant with an appropriate solution. Equity was **dispensed** in its own separate court referred to as the Court of Chancery.
- *Equity case law – the Court of Chancery* To **deal with** the inadequacies of the common law case law system created by the King's courts, the

---

[2]   The term *claimant* has now replaced the term *plaintiff* in the United Kingdom.
[3]   This is still the case today. Thus, someone bringing an action based on common law case law may only receive damages.

Chancellor developed equity, a new source of law based on principles of right and wrong. As it was put in place to respond to problems with common law case law, equity from the beginning was only applied when the remedy provided by common law case law was inappropriate and this is still the case today. Thus, it is said to be a discretionary remedy. Unlike the common law, which is a technical legalistic system based on notions of legal and illegal, equity is based on Christian principles of fairness and natural law. Substantive areas of law created by equity include **trusts** and **succession law**. Moreover, in place of the common law remedy of damages, equity developed **remedies** such as **injunctions** and **specific performance**, to better answer the needs of complainants. For example, sometimes, instead of receiving damages from someone because they did not respect their contractual duties, it might be better to apply for an order of specific performance in equity, forcing them to perform their contractual duty. To the contrary, an injunction is an equitable remedy preventing someone from doing something. For example, if X entered into a contract with Y to sell him his car, Y could apply for an injunction to stop X from selling the same car to Z, in breach of his earlier contract with Y. **Needless** to say, equity became quite popular and the two systems grew up together, each developing specific areas of expertise – the common law in the King's common law courts and equity in the Chancellor's Court of Chancery. However, over time conflicts developed between the two systems and in the 1880s the common law and equity case law systems were merged into one unified system of courts. **Nowadays** an applicant before a court can seek either a remedy in common law or a remedy in equity. Nonetheless, two important points should be made:

- equity remains a discretionary remedy, and thus a remedy in equity will only ever be given where the solution offered by the common law is inappropriate or non-existent;
- if there is a **conflict** between rights created by the two systems of law, i.e. if their respective rules contradict one another, rights in equity take **precedence** over common law rights.

However, the most important source of law in common law countries is **statute law**, which takes precedence over both common law case law and equity.

Statute law The second source of law in the common law is statute law. The first Parliaments in modern England date from the 13th and 14th centuries and since then the **influence** of Parliament has **grown**, as the country slowly became a democracy. Statute law is now the **major** or dominant source of law in the UK. Laws **adopted** by Parliament in the United Kingdom are called **Acts of Parliament** and **once** they are published in the statute books, become known as statute law. Statute law is written law but should not be confused with civil law codes, which are normally more detailed. Traditionally, common law statutes tend to be **broadly** written, allowing the courts to retain **large powers of interpretation**.

Other sources of law Under this heading we can find **custom** and **canon law**. Custom becomes a source of law when an established pattern of behavior becomes a right that can be relied on before the courts. For a custom such as a **right of way** to be considered law, it must have existed since **time immemorial**, i.e. since 1189. If this cannot be established, the custom must be shown to have existed as far back as living memory. If it is shown that reliance on the custom was interrupted at some time between 1189 and the present, then the custom will not be accepted as a source of law. The custom that one wishes to have recognized as a right must be reasonable and also must not **offend** fundamental notions of right and wrong. Moreover, the **scope** of the custom must be definite and specific. For example, a vague **claim** to have right of use over a certain area of land, which is not specific as to the exact location of the land and the nature of the use of the land, will not be **entertained** by the courts. Finally, the right claimed under the heading of custom must be in constant and continual use and exercised **as of right**, i.e. not exercised by way of **stealth**.

Canon law or the law of the Roman Catholic Church has been an important element in **shaping** the common law, especially as regards equity, which was first developed by **ecclesiastics**. More generally, canon law concepts of right and wrong, the **sanctity of marriage** and the special position of the family **underlie** many of the areas of law making up the common law today.

Sources of common law specific to the United Kingdom

After World War II, European countries decided that, in place of the nationalism that had **led** to two world wars, it was necessary to try and **promote** cooperation between them. As part of this process, the Council of Europe was established in 1949. Thereafter, the **European Economic Community** (EEC) was created in 1957. This organization is now called the European Union.
* *The Council of Europe and the European Convention on Human Rights* The European Convention on Human Rights was drawn up by the Council of Europe in 1950 and entered into force in 1953. However, it did not become an integral part of UK law until the adoption of the 1998 Human Rights Act. **Pursuant to** this Act, the UK courts and administrative bodies must respect the **provisions** of the Convention when adopting decisions. The Convention has its own court, the European Court of Human Rights, and its own administrative body. Under the Convention, if a UK citizen considers that the authorities have **breached** his human rights, he/she will first bring an action before the UK courts. If he/she is unhappy with their decision, an action may then be brought before the Court of Human Rights located in Strasbourg.
* *The law of the European Union* The United Kingdom **joined** the European Economic Community in 1973. In 1992, the organization expanded the scope of its activities and is now called the European Union (EU). The two most important types of EU law are **regulations** and directives. After adoption by the European Union, regulations apply directly in the Union's twenty-eight member states. Directives

once adopted at European level have to be **implemented** into the law of the United Kingdom by way of an Act of Parliament. Since the decision of the European Court of Justice in Luxembourg in Costa v ENEL, European Union law is considered to take precedence over the national law of the United Kingdom.

VOCABULARY

Close to – *près de*
Belief – *croyance/conviction*
Thus – *ainsi/donc*
Behavior – *comportement/conduite*
Classify (to) – *classer*
Headings – *rubriques/titres*
Commonwealth countries – *pays du Commonwealth, autrefois membres de l'empire britannique*
Indeed – *en effet/effectivement*
Colonized – *colonisé*
Based on – *fondé sur*
Kingdom – *royaume*
Branch of government – *branche/corps du gouvernement (au sens de pouvoir: législatif, exécutif...)*
Methodology – *méthodologie*
Precedent – *précédent (judiciaire)/élément de jurisprudence*
Doctrine of Stare Decisis – *règle selon laquelle les cours sont obligées de suivre les décisions prises précédemment par les juridictions de même niveau et les juridictions plus hautes (s'en tenir à la chose jugée)*
Ratio decidendi – *règle de droit contenue dans une décision que d'autres cours devront suivre en se fondant sur la doctrine du précédent*
Obiter dicta – *opinion émise par les cours supérieures sur un point de droit non déterminant pour le point de droit jugé en l'espèce et permettant d'indiquer une direction à suivre à l'avenir (la règle du Stare Decisis ne s'applique pas)*
Rule (to) in law – *statuer en droit*
Court of King's Bench – *Cour du Banc du Roi : cour de première instance et également cour d'appel du système de common law*
Court of Common Pleas – *Cour des Plaids Communs : cour de première instance du système de common law crée par Henry II pour les particuliers*
Court of the Exchequer – *Cour de l'Echiquier, responsable pour les questions financières, surtout les litiges concernant les questions fiscales*
First instance jurisdiction – *juridiction de première instance*
Handle (to) – *s'occuper de/traiter de*
Commoners – *particuliers/gens du peuple*
Hear (to) a case – *juger une affaire/statuer sur une affaire*
Jurisdiction – *compétence juridictionnelle*
Fiscal dispute – *litige fiscal*
Lose (to) touch with – *perdre contact avec*
Tainted with – *entaché de*

Corruption – *corruption*
Complainant/plaintiff – *plaignant/demandeur*
Namely – *à savoir*
Damages – *dommages et intérêts*
Complement (to) – *être le complément de/compléter*
Dispense (to) – *administrer/accorder*
Deal (to) with – *s'occuper de/traiter*
Trust (A) – *fiducie*
Succession law – *droit des successions*
Remedy – *recours*
Injunction (not to do something) – *injonction (de ne pas faire quelque chose)*
Specific performance – *ordonnance d'exécution forcée (en cas de non-exécution d'un contrat notamment)*
Needless to say – *inutile de dire/cela va sans dire*
Nowadays – *de nos jours*
Conflict – *conflit*
Take (to) precedence over – *prévaloir sur/primer sur*
Statute law – *législation (votée par le Parlement)*
Influence – *influence*
Grow (to) (grew, grown) – *croître/grandir*
Major source – *source très importante/principale*
Adopted (to be) – *adopté*
Act of Parliament – *loi adoptée par le Parlement mais pas encore promulguée*
Once – *une fois/une fois que/dès que*
Broadly – *dans les grandes lignes*
Large powers of interpretation – *large, important pouvoir d'interprétation*
Custom – *coutume*
Canon law – *droit canon*
Right of way – *droit de passage/servitude*
Time immemorial – *de temps immémorial, c'est-à-dire 1189, date établie par le* Statute of Westminster *(Loi de Westminster) adopté en 1275 au début du règne de Richard I*
Offend (to) – *ne pas respecter/porter atteinte à*
Scope – *champ d'application/portée/étendue*
Claim (to) – *revendiquer/demander*
Entertain (to) – *prendre en considération*
Exercised as of right – *exercé de droit*
By stealth – *furtivement/à la dérobée*
Shape (to) – *modeler/influencer*
Sanctity of marriage – *caractère sacré du mariage*
Underlie (to) – *sous-tendre*
Lead (to) – *mener*
Promote (to) – *promouvoir*
European Economic Community – *Communauté Economique Européenne*
The latter – *ce dernier/cette dernière*
Pursuant to – *selon/en vertu de*
Provisions – *dispositions*
Breach (to) (a right) – *violer (un droit)*

Join (to) – *devenir membre de/adhérer à*
Regulation – *règlement*
To the contrary – *au contraire*
Implement (to) – *mettre en œuvre/transposer*

PART 1 – TEXT 2 – EXERCISES

1. Definitions

Write a sentence defining each of the following terms – one sentence per term

- a) Equity
- b) Injunction
- c) Stare decisis
- d) Right of way
- e) Statute law
- f) Canon law
- g) Implement a directive
- h) Specific performance

2. Sentences

Write sentences with the following pairs of words. Your sentence should if possible demonstrate your knowledge of the relationship between the words

- a) Precedence/equity
- b) Court of King's Bench/Chancellor
- c) Damages/injunction
- d) Act of Parliament/promulgate
- e) Commonwealth/colonize
- f) Precedent/common law
- g) Complement/equity
- h) Specific performance/contract
- i) Custom/time immemorial
- j) Council of Europe/European Convention on Human Rights

3. Fill in the missing words

Fill in the missing words using the vocabulary in Text 2

- a) The _____ law system established by the King's courts was too technical and as a result the _____ established a second system of law referred to as equity.
- b) To establish the existence of a _____ establishing a right of way, it is necessary to demonstrate that it has been relied on since _____. Moreover, it is necessary to show that it was exercised _____ and not by stealth.
- c) Once a law is passed by Parliament it becomes an _____. Thereafter, once it is _____ in the statute books, it is referred to as _____ law.
- d) There are two types of legal provision relied on by the European Union

_____ and _____. The first applies directly in the law of a _____ and the second must be _____ into national law.

e)   Equity developed remedies such as _____ and _____. The former requires someone to carry out a duty, while the second prevents a party from acting.

4. Knowledge test

The following questions may be answered in writing or by way of discussion

a)   Compare the common law system with the system of law in your country.

b)   Does the French civil law system have the same system of precedents as used in the common law?

c)   In your opinion, are judges too powerful in the common law system?

d)   It is said that the common law system is a flexible system of law. Why?

e)   If you could reform the common law system, what changes would you make?

PART 2 – QUICK LOOK GRAMMAR REVISION

The Past Tense – The Simple Past and the Past Progressive

1. The Simple Past

The simple past is used for events or situations that began and ended in the past. It is the tense used to narrate a sequence of events. For example:

- **John *walked* to his clients' office yesterday**;
- **John *arrived* back at his office on Tuesday last week**.

Forms that the **simple past** take:

a)   When making a statement, "ed" is added to the verb stem if the verb is a regular verb:
- I, you, he, she, it, we, they: WORKED/WATCHED/STUDIED yesterday.

b)   When negating, i.e. making a negative statement, the auxiliary DID is used with NOT:
- I, you, he, she, it, we, they: did not (didn't) WORK/WATCH/ STUDY.

c)   When asking a question, the auxiliary DID is used with the verb stem:
- Did I, you, he, she, it, we, they WORK/WATCH/ STUDY yesterday?

d)   When answering the question, it is common to use only the auxiliary:
- **YES**, I, you, he, she, it, we, they **did** (work yesterday);
- **NO**, I, you, he, she, it, we, they **did not (didn't)** (work yesterday).

Note:

The simple past of regular verbs is formed by adding "ed" to the verb. However, note:
- Verbs ending in "**e**" (*smile/hope*) – just add "**d**" to the stem
  = **smiled/hoped**;
- One syllable verbs ending in a single vowel and a consonant (*stop/plan*) – double the last consonant and add "**ed**"
  = **stopped/planned**;
- Two syllable verbs that also end in a single vowel followed by a consonant in which the second syllable is stressed (carries the tonic stress) (*prefer/admit*) – double the last consonant and add "**ed**"
  = **admitted/preferred**;
  If the verb ends in a consonant + "y" (*study/worry*) – change the "y" into an "i" and add "ed" = **studied/worried**.

NB If the verb ends in a vowel and "y", keep the "y" and do not change it to "i", for example, play = played.

NB If the first syllable of a two syllable verb is stressed, do not double the consonant, for example, visit = visited NOT visit/ted

Note:

Irregular verbs in the simple past:
be (**was, were**), become (**became**), begin (**began**), bend (**bent**), bite (**bit**), blow (**blew**), break (**broke**), bring (**brought**), broadcast (**broadcast**), build (**built**), buy (**bought**), catch (**caught**), choose (**chose**), come (**came**), cost (**cost**), cut (**cut**), dig (**dug**), do (**did**), draw (**drew**), drink (**drank**), drive (**drove**), eat (**ate**), fall (**fell**), feed (**fed**), feel (**felt**), fight (**fought**), find (**found**), fly (**flew**), forget (**forgot**), forgive (**forgave**), freeze (**froze**), get (**got**), give (**gave**), go (**went**), grow (**grew**), hang (**hung; hanged for a person**), have (**had**), hear (**heard**), hide (**hid**), hit (**hit**), hold (**held**), hurt (**hurt**), keep (**kept**), know (**knew**), lay (**laid**), lead (**led**), leave (**left**), lend (**lent**), let (**let**), light (**lit**), lose (**lost**), make (**made**), mean (**meant**), meet (**met**), pay (**paid**), put (**put**), quit (**quit**), read (**read**), ride (**rode**), ring (**rang**), rise (**rose**), run (**ran**), say (**said**), see (**saw**), sell (**sold**), send (**sent**), set (**set**), shake (**shook**), shoot (**shot**), shut (**shut**), sing (**sang**), sit (**sat**), sleep (**slept**), slide (**slid**), speak (**spoke**), spend (**spent**), spread (**spread**), stand (**stood**), steal (**stole**), stick (**stuck**), strike (**struck**), swear (**swore**), sweep (**swept**), swim (**swam**), take (**took**), teach (**taught**), tear (**tore**), tell (**told**), think (**thought**), throw (**threw**), understand

(**understood**), upset (**upset**), wake (**woke**), wear (**wore**), win (**won**), withdraw (**withdrew**), write (**wrote**).

2. The past progressive/past continuous/continuous past

As we have seen, the simple past is used to refer to activities that began and ended in the past; the past progressive refers to a past that is placed in contrast with another event occurring in a shorter time-span:

I **was eating** my dinner when my friend called at 12:30pm.

Forms of the **past progressive**

a)   When making a statement, the verb "be" is used in its past simple form (WAS or WERE) plus the verb stem + ING
   –   I, he, she, it, John **was** WORKING;
   –   You, we, they **were** WORKING.

b)   When making a negative statement, WAS/WERE are used with NOT, plus the verb stem + ING:
   –   I, he, she, it, John **was not** (wasn't) WORKING;
   –   You, we, they **were not** (weren't) WORKING.

c)   When asking a question, there is an inversion of the subject and the auxiliary WAS/WERE and the subject + the verb stem +ING:
   –   **Was** I, he, she, it, John WORKING?
   –   **Were** you, we, they WORKING?

   NB Only use contractions in oral English, NEVER in formal written English.

   Note:

   Time clauses such as WHEN, WHILE can take the progressive or simple past:
   –   *when/while* I **was working** at my desk, the phone rang;
   –   *when/while* the phone **rang**, I was working at my desk.

   Note:

   Most verbs in the past progressive are formed by just adding "**ing**". However, exceptions do exist:
   –   For verbs that end in "e" (*smile/hope*) – drop the "e" and add "ing"
        = **smil*ing*/hop*ing***.
   –   For one syllable verbs ending in a single vowel and a consonant (stop/plan) – double the consonant and add "ing"
        = **stop*ping*/plan*ning***.

– For two syllable verbs where the second syllable is stressed (*prefer/admit*) – double the last consonant and add "**ing**"
= admit***ting***/prefer***ring***.
– If the verb ends in "ie" (*die/tie*) – drop the "ie" and replace it with "y" = **d*ying*/t*ying***.

NB If the first syllable of a two syllable verb is stressed, DO NOT double the consonant, for example visit = visiting NOT visitting.

See grammar section in Chapter 10

PART 2 – GRAMMAR EXERCISES

1. Present tense to past tense

Put the verbs in the following text in the past tense

I **get up** at 8:00am. I **put** my clothes on. I **eat** my breakfast and **read** the newspaper. I **feed** my cat and **exercise** for one hour. I **grab** on my coat and **run** to the bus stop. I **look** out the window and **see** it **is raining**. When I **arrive** at my law firm, I **say** hello to the receptionist and I **take** the elevator to my third floor office. I **turn on** my computer and **fix** a cup of coffee. I **check** my e-mails and **open** the file I **am working on**. I **work** until 1:00pm and then I **go** for lunch. After lunch I **attend** meetings with clients and I **take** notes of everything they **say**. After the meetings, I **return** to my office and at 8:00pm I **go** home. I **prepare** my dinner and **watch** TV. At 11:00pm, I **go** to bed and **dream** of winning the lottery.

2. Present tense to past tense

Write a sentence using the simple past form of each of the irregular verbs listed below

begin
build
come
drink
know
make
quit
sell
shoot
sleep
strike
teach
understand
wear
write

3. Fill in the blanks

Fill in the spaces in the following questions and answers. For guidance, look at the example immediately below

(John, have) <u>*Did John*</u> have the file?
Yes, *he had* it in his office.

  a)   (Frank/act) _____ for that client?
        Yes, before he retired, he always (to represent) _____ him in court.
  b)   (John/want) to go down to the court?
        Yes, but he was unable to go because (it/rain) _____.
  c)   (John/hope) _____ to question the witness?
        Yes, but (his boss/prefer) _____ to call the next witness instead.
  d)   (Frank/take) _____the Bar exam last year?
        Yes, but unfortunately (he/fail) it again.
  e)   (John, study) _____ in the library last year?
        Yes, (he/study) all the time; that was why (he/pass) the Bar Exam at his first attempt.

4. Fill in the blanks

Fill in the spaces in the following questions and answers

  a)   At 9:00am Bob (sit) down at his desk and began to work. That morning he (write) _____ a memo to his client.
  b)   John (want) _____ to go down to the court, but he was unable to because it (rain) _____.
  c)   John (hope) _____ to go on holiday last Thursday, but his client (ask) _____ him to work on his case instead.
  d)   Frank (take) _____the Bar exam last year, but unfortunately he (fail) it again.
  e)   John (work) _____in his office late every night and that is why he was promoted and (receive)_____ a pay rise.
  f)   Sally (eat) _____her lunch when her client (call) _____ her on the telephone.

PART 3 – AUDIO – LISTENING AND SPEAKING

Comprehension

Listen to the following conversation, make notes of all the relevant facts and then answer the questions below. If you have trouble understanding, follow the conversation while also reading the text.

Conversation between Professor Bob and his student James

James: "Sorry Professor, could I speak with you for a moment?"
Bob: "Ah, James, how are you?"
James: "Fine thanks Professor, although I am having difficulty following your course."

Bob: "Really, what's the problem?"

James: "It has got to do with the common law and the fact that the term common law can mean a number of different things."

Bob: "Yes, well that is actually pretty difficult to understand; students often have difficulty with this area."

James: "Could you explain it to me again, briefly?"

Bob: "Yes, I suppose I could, but I don't have lots of time, let's see. Do you understand what we mean by the term common law, when we are speaking generally?"

James: "Yes, it refers to the Common Law as a system of law that is relied on in Anglo-Saxon countries and their former colonies; just like when we speak of the Civil Law, we are speaking of the system of law used in countries like France and Italy."

Bob: "OK, well that is the first meaning of the common law; it is in fact the general name for the system of law applied in the UK and the US and many other countries in the world. The second meaning of the term common law refers to the fact that within the common law system, there is both written law, called statute law adopted by the Parliament and there is also case law created by the courts. Now sometimes to describe the area of case law, which is one of the sources of law in the common law system, we use the word common law."

James: "Oh OK, so the second meaning describes one of the sources of law within the common law system, namely case law?"

Bob: "Yes, not unlike the fact that within the Civil Law system there is an area of law called civil law or what the French call *droit civil*."

James: "OK, I understand; thanks for explaining it to me."

Bob: "Hold on a minute James, I'm not finished yet."

James: "You mean there is another meaning as well?"

Bob: "Yes, this is where students sometimes have difficulty understanding, so listen carefully."

James: "OK."

Bob: "Well, you remember the area of equity?"

James: "Yes, it is the area of law created by the Chancellor back in medieval times to make up for the inadequacies of the common law case law developed by the King's Courts."

Bob: "Yes, exactly and what kind of law is equity, written law or case law?"

James: "Written law, no I mean case law, sorry, it is case law developed by the Court of Chancery."

Bob: "So there are two types of case law: common law case law developed by the common law courts and equity case law developed by the Chancellor. The term common law is also used to describe the case law developed by the King's courts."

James: "Wow! This is complicated."

Bob: "I know. So do you think you can tell me the three different meanings for the term common law?"

James: "Yes, I think I can. It is a general term to describe the system of law relied on in Anglo-Saxon countries; it is a general term used to describe case law, so as to distinguish case law from written law or statute law and finally, it is also used to distinguish common law case law developed by the King's courts from equity case law developed by the Chancellor."

Bob: "Very good. I will be expecting top marks from you in the exam!"

James: "Well I don't know about that, but thanks for explaining it to me so clearly."

PART 3 – AUDIO COMPREHENSION – EXERCISES

1. Comprehension

From the notes you have taken, answer the following questions

 a)   What exactly did James ask Professor Bob to explain to him?
 b)   What is the first meaning of the term common law, according to Professor Bob?
 c)   What kind of marks does Professor Bob expect from James in the future?
 d)   According to Professor Bob how many meanings can be given the term common law?
 e)   What is the area that students sometimes have particular difficulty with according to Professor Bob?

2. Speaking practice

In the following series of conversation couplets, develop suitable responses to the questions asked

 a)   James: "Hi Professor Bob, would you like to attend a dinner that some of the students in our class are organizing?"
      Prof. Bob: "_____."
 b)   James: "Could you tell me what equity is exactly?"
      Prof. Bob: "_____."
 c)   James: "Is case law the primary source of law in the common law system?"
      Prof. Bob: "_____"
 d)   James: "Could I have an extension on the deadline for handing in my essays?"
      Prof. Bob: "_____."
 e)   James: "So how many meanings are there for the term common law?"
      Prof Bob: "_____."
 f)   James: "What is the difference between the common law courts and the Court of Chancery?"
      Prof. Bob: "_____."
 g)   James: "Where is the common law applied today?"
      Prof. Bob: "_____."
 h)   James: "What are the main sources of law in the common law?"
      Prof. Bob: "_____."
 i)   James: "What exactly is an order of specific performance Professor Bob?"
      Prof. Bob: "_____."

j)   James: "Does the term common law describe case law in the common law system?"
Prof. Bob: "_____."

3. Speaking practice continued ......

Create five other conversation couplets using in each couplet at least one word from the vocabulary found in Part 1, Text 1 or Text 2

4. Speaking practice continued ......

Listen to the suggested replies and repeat

a)   James: "Hi Professor Bob, would you like to attend a dinner that some of the students in our class are organizing?
Prof. Bob: "That depends James, when do you intend to have the dinner? Unfortunately, I have a very busy schedule at the moment."

b)   James: "Could you tell me what equity is exactly?"
Prof. Bob: "Equity is a form of case law that was developed in England from medieval times onwards."

c)   James: "Is case law the primary source of law in the common law system?"
Prof. Bob: "No, statute law is now the primary source of law in the common law system but case law was the first source of law and remains very important."

d)   James: "Could I have an extension on the deadline for handing in my essays?"
Prof. Bob: "I am afraid not James, if I gave an extension to you, then everyone would want one."

e)   James: "So how many meanings are there for the term common law?"
Prof Bob: "Well, in my lecture I spoke of three main meanings for the term common law."

f)   James: "What is the difference between the common law courts and the Court of Chancery?"
Prof. Bob: "Well James, the common law courts were developed by the King. The Court of Chancery was created by the Chancellor."

g)   James: "So where is the common law applied today?"
Prof. Bob: "In many different countries all over the world; mainly in those countries that previously formed part of the British Empire."

h)   James: "What are the main sources of law in the common law?"
Prof. Bob: "Well in the common law the main sources of law are statute law, case law, custom and canon law."

i)   James: "What exactly is an order of specific performance Professor Bob?"
Prof. Bob: "Specific performance is a remedy developed in equity as an alternative to damages."

j)   James: "Is the term common law used to describe case law in the common law system?"
Prof. Bob: "Yes, as we have seen, the term common law has a number of different meanings, one of which describes the system of case law, which is one of the sources of law in the common law."

5. Associated questions

Discuss the following questions

a)   Does the term civil law have different meanings, as is the case with the common law?
b)   Do you think your system of law is superior to the common law? If so why?
c)   What are the benefits of a system based on case law?
d)   In reality is the common law really that different from other systems of law?

PART 4 – TRANSLATION EXERCISES

When carrying out the translations it is not necessary to translate directly word for word; rather the emphasis should be on translating the sense of the text. Language is not directly interchangeable and so direct translations do not always convey the meaning in the text.

Translate the following texts from English to French

A. Equity

Case law remedies come from two separate sources:
- common law remedies; and
- equitable remedies.

The only remedy available under the common law is monetary compensation, referred to as damages. Equity provides alternative remedies such as specific performance and injunctions. Thus, a single wrong may give rise to a right to several potential different remedies. For example, a breach of contract might entitle the injured party to damages under the common law and/or an equitable order requiring the party in breach of their contract to perform their contractual obligations, i.e. an order of specific performance. However, it should be recalled that equity is a discretionary remedy. Thus, normally only damages are available to a party before the courts and if they wish to receive equitable relief, he/she will have to demonstrate that damages are not a suitable solution and that a solution in equity is necessary.

B. What is a trust?

Equity also created areas of law such as trusts. A trust is a legal vehicle whereby two owners are recognized: a legal owner and an equitable owner. A trust establishes a relationship in which a person, called a trustor/settlor, transfers property to another person, called a trustee, who becomes the legal owner. The trustee then manages and controls this asset for the benefit of a third person, called a beneficiary, who is the equitable owner. Trusts have many uses. For example, if a person wishes to invest the money for their retirement, in common law countries they will often do so by way of a Unit Trust. Pursuant to the Unit Trust agreement signed with the bank, the investor is both the trustor and beneficiary, and the bank is the trustee. Thus, the investor (trustor) gives the money to the bank (trustee), which becomes the legal owner of the funds. However, pursuant to the trust document signed with the bank, it has to exercise ownership for the benefit of the investor (beneficial owner). In other words, the bank has a fiduciary duty towards the beneficiary.

C. The Battle of Hastings

When Edward the Confessor, King of England, died in 1065, William, Duke of Normandy, known as William the Bastard, laid claim to the English throne, disputing the claim of Harold, husband of one of the dead King's daughters. William justified his claim through his blood relationship with Edward; they were distant cousins. Moreover, he claimed that, some years earlier, Edward had officially appointed him as his successor. However, when Edward died, Harold claimed the throne for himself. William immediately invaded England in 1066, Harold died in the Battle of Hastings and William took the throne for himself, changing the course of English history forever.

Translate the following texts from French to English

A. La common law

Par le terme de *common law*, qui n'a pas vraiment de traduction en Français, on désigne surtout le système juridique mis en place en Angleterre par les rois normands et qui repose sur la création du droit par les cours. A l'origine, la jurisprudence a été développée par les cours royales, créations du roi Henri II. Le terme *common law* fait aussi référence à l'ensemble du système juridique de l'Angleterre et des autres pays de *common law*. Cependant, ces systèmes sont nombreux et variés. Connaître le fonctionnement de la *common law*, c'est comprendre le fonctionnement des systèmes juridiques de beaucoup de pays à travers le monde, un système dont l'importance ne fait aujourd'hui que s'accroître dans un monde dominé par le capitalisme.

B. L'Equity

L'*Equity* a été crée pour remédier aux lacunes du droit de *common law* et s'est développée par le biais de pétitions envoyées au Chancelier du roi. Finalement, l'*Equity* devint droit positif grâce à la jurisprudence de la cour créé à la fin du XVe siècle, la Cour de la Chancellerie. Cette cour a conçu des remèdes autres que ceux dont on disposait dans les cours de *common law*, en l'occurrence les dommages et intérêts. En effet, l'*Equity* a instauré des principes auxquels le juge a recours, s'il s'avère que l'application à la lettre de la loi (*common law*) était facteur d'injustice à l'égard du justiciable. Donc l'*Equity* a donné naissance à des remèdes comme l'injonction, en vertu de laquelle il fallait s'abstenir de faire, ou renoncer à un certain type de conduite.

C. L'Equity et la common law

La *common law*, lors de son essor au cours du XIe siècle, a progressivement supplanté les coûtumes locales en matière de justice, grâce à l'action des cours royales (*Curia regis*). Droit créé par les juges et non par la loi, la *common law* donne la primauté aux précédents jurisprudentiels. Cependant, petit à petit, la *common law* s'est figée dans des règles difficiles à modifier, les juges étant trop liés par la jurisprudence déjà adoptée. C'est pourquoi, le Chancelier a développé l'*Equity*, pour mettre en place une nouvelle juridiction parallèle. Ces règles, fondées sur les principes d'équité, permettent de pallier les insuffisances de la *common law* et ses rigidités. Ainsi, la *common law* permettait d'octroyer des dommages-intérêts à la partie lésée par l'inexécution d'un contrat. Cependant, si le plaignant ne souhaite pas une réparation financière, mais préfère que l'autre partie contractante soit contrainte d'exécuter ce contrat, il doit intenter une action en *Equity* et il obtiendra l'accord du juge, s'il parvient à établir que les dommages et intérêts ne sont pas, dans ces circonstances-ci, le remède adéquat.

PART 5 – ADVANCED READING

The birth of the common law and equity

The birth of the common law dates from the creation of a centralized legal system by the newly arrived Norman kings after 1066. It really began under Henry II, grandson of William the Conqueror, who sent curiales (judges) from the *curia regis* (the King's administrative office) on occasional eyres (journeys) around the country, to hold pleas (hear court cases) and to supervise the work of the older local courts. Over time this practice was formalized, with the judges coming to be known as judge *errantes*. As it was organized by and for the Norman aristocracy, for many years its language of procedure was French. At the same time, an increase in litigation before the papal curia in Rome from all over Christendom Europe led to the decentralization of these actions through the creation of national papal delegates. These papal delegates represented the pope and their decisions led to the introduction of Christian principles into the judicial process in each of the Christian kingdoms. Slowly this led to the development of church courts in each Christian kingdom, staffed by professional judges trained in canon law, i.e. church law. In the face of these two new centralized systems of justice, especially the King's common law system, the old local courts dating from Saxon times slowly faded into insignificance. It is important to note that the Normans did not directly interfere with the system of local courts that predated their arrival. For a number of centuries after their invasion, Saxons continued to use these courts, whilst Normans went before the King's courts. However, the proliferation of the common law court system through the use of errant judiciary, backed by the King's military authority, slowly led to the decline in the local system, signaling the final conquest of Saxon England. Thus, the King's system of law dispensed in his common law courts slowly developed a monopoly over justice and, like many monopolies, began to underperform. For example, the system restricted the types of claims applicants could bring before the courts, thereby limiting people's ability to receive a solution for their problems. Moreover, the procedure that governed the hearing of those claims became painfully technical and expensive, and at times the honesty of the system was called into question. As a result, litigants began to sideline the courts and appeal directly to the King for justice, on the basis that all judicial power emanated from, and thus ultimately resided in, the Crown. The King passed these petitions to the Chancellor, the equivalent of the King's prime minister and usually a clergyman. As a man of the church he looked to canon law principles of right and wrong developed by the church courts, rather than to common law notions of legal and illegal, to resolve these disputes. In so doing he slowly created a new source of case law, which was called equity. Procedure before the Chancellor was simplified and was conducted in English. Over time the Chancery office, headed by the Chancellor, began to resemble a judicial authority and became known as the Court of Chancery. Equity grew out of problems with the common law and thus was developed as an alternative response that was only applied if and when the common law failed to function properly. This complementary or discretionary character of equity law continues to this day and, consequently, it is only possible to receive a remedy in equity if the common law remedy is not suitable or appropriate.

Chapter four

THE POLITICAL SYSTEM IN THE UNITED STATES

The organization of political power in the United States of America

Political power in the United States is expressed at different levels, namely at:
*   federal level;
*   state level; and
*   local level.

Thus, there is one federal government and fifty individual state governments. All are organized around Montesquieu's theory of the separation of powers, i.e. each having a separate **executive**, **legislative** and **judicial branch** of government. The fifty states are separate **legal entities** and not just administrative **units** created by the federal government to **facilitate** governing the country. Both federal and state elections generally take place within the context of a two-party system represented by the **conservative leaning** Republican Party and the more **liberal** Democratic Party.

How does the federal government co-exist with the state governments?

The federal and state systems co-exist on the basis of two principles, the:
*   *supremacy of federal law* Pursuant to article 6 of the US federal Constitution, federal law, where applicable, takes **supremacy** over the laws of the individual states. Thus, if illegal under federal law, such **behavior** cannot be considered legal under state law;
*   *federal government is a government of **limited powers*** Although federal law is the supreme law of the land, the power that the federal government **possesses** is, in theory at least, strictly limited to the express powers conferred on it by the US Constitution. These powers are sometimes referred to as the **enumerated powers** of the federal government.

Federal branches of government

As we have seen, the federal government has three branches of power: the legislative, executive, and judicial branches.
*   *Legislative power – the United States Congress* Pursuant to article 1 of the US Constitution, legislative power is conferred on Congress, which is **comprised of** two houses or assemblies: the House of Representatives and the Senate. Each of the congressional chambers,

i.e. the House of Representatives and the Senate, enjoy different powers. For example, the Senate's agreement is required for many important Presidential nominations, such as the **appointment** of judges to the Supreme Court; while the House of Representatives has exclusive power over the introduction of **fiscal measures** aimed at raising tax revenue.

- *Executive power – the President* Pursuant to article 2 of the US Constitution, federal executive power is **vested in** the President of the United States. The President is the head of state, as well as the military **commander-in-chief** and chief diplomat. Many of the President's powers have to do with the area of foreign affairs; for example (s) he may, with the consent of two-thirds of the Senate, make treaties with foreign nations. (S)he also has a limited right of veto as regards legislation coming from Congress.

- *Judicial power – the Supreme Court* In accordance with article 3 of the US federal Constitution, federal judicial power is vested in the Supreme Court, which has **jurisdiction over** cases concerning the federal government and disputes between states. It has both **original** and **appellate jurisdiction** and its most important power is its power of **interpretation**, as regards the **provisions** of the federal Constitution. Other courts at federal level are the US Courts of Appeal and the US Federal District Courts which, pursuant to article 3, were established by Congress. There are also specialized federal courts, such as the United States Tax Court.

State branches of government

As the states have jurisdiction over all the areas not coming within the power of the federal government, they have in fact **wide regulatory powers** over many **fields**, including education, company law, contract law and fiscal policy, to mention just a few. As we have seen, each of the individual states, like the federal power, is also organized **pursuant to** Montesquieu's system of the separation of powers and each state has its own individual governmental system and constitution. Thus, executive power is held by state governors, who normally hold office for a four-year term (two years in a minority of states). Legislative power is held by the state parliaments, all of which are split into two houses/ assemblies (bicameral system), with the exception of the State of Nebraska, which has only one assembly (unicameral system). Finally, each state has its own separate judicial system, empowered to apply state law.

Local government

The United States also has a **widespread** system of **local government** governing different geographical zones such as **counties**, **municipalities**, **townships** and **school districts**. Local government bodies are responsible for **providing** everything, from police protection to the development of **sanitary codes**, **health regulations** to education and public transportation to **housing**.

VOCABULARY

Executive – *exécutif (pouvoir)*
Legislative – *législatif (pouvoir)*
Judicial – *judiciaire (pouvoir)*
Legal entities – *entités juridiques/personnes morales*
Units (administrative) – *unités (administratives)*
Facilitate (to) – *faciliter*
Conservative – *conservateur*
Conservative leaning – *de tendance conservatrice (*lean (to) = *pencher pour)*
Liberal – *libéral (au sens anglo-saxon = progressiste)*
Supremacy – *prééminence/prépondérance (ici, prime sur)*
Behavior – *comportement*
Limited powers – *pouvoirs limités*
Possess (to) – *posséder, détenir*
Enumerated powers – *pouvoirs recensés/dénombrés (principe de compétences d'attribution)*
Comprised (to be) of – *se composer de*
Appointment – *nomination/désignation*
Fiscal measures – *mesures fiscales*
Vest (to) – *investir (quelqu'un de quelque chose) /assigner (quelque chose à quelqu'un)/être dévolu à/être attribué à/conférer à*
Commander-in-chief – *commandant en chef*
Jurisdiction (to have) over – *avoir compétence pour*
Original jurisdiction – *compétence en première instance*
Appellate jurisdiction – *juridiction d'appel/pouvoir de recevoir ou examiner les appels*
Interpret (to) – *interpréter*
Provisions – *dispositions*
Regulatory powers – *pouvoirs réglementaires*
Wide powers – *vastes pouvoirs/pouvoirs étendus*
Fields – *domaines*
Pursuant to – *selon/en vertu de*
Widespread – *étendu*
Local government – *collectivités locales*
County – *comté (division administrative géographique)*
Municipality – *municipalité*
Township – *commune*
School district – *district scolaire*
Provide (to) – *fournir/dispenser*
Sanitary code – *code/règlement sanitaire*
Housing and health regulations – *logement/règles sanitaires*

PART 1 – TEXT 1 – EXERCISES

1. Vocabulary test

Fill in the missing words using the vocabulary in Text 1

a) In the United States, there are _____ individual states, each one being a separate _____ entity largely independent from the federal government.

b) The federal government is said to be a government of _____ powers, insofar as all its powers are specifically _____ in the US Constitution.

c) The President is the _____ of state and commander _____ of the military.

d) Article 1 of the US Constitution vests legislative power in the _____ and article 2 places _____ power in the hands of the President.

e) The United States has a _____ system, with the Republican Party on the conservative right and the _____ Democratic Party representing the centre.

f) Power is held on three main levels in the United States: at _____ level representing the entire country, at _____ level and finally at local level.

g) The states have significant regulatory powers extending to areas such as _____ law governing agreements entered into between businesses and _____ law dealing with the creation and governance of separate legal business entities.

h) The legislative powers of the Houses of _____ are established _____ article 1 of the US Constitution.

i) Pursuant to article 3 of the Constitution, the US _____ has both original and appellate _____.

j) Congress is _____ two assemblies, the House of Representatives and the _____.

2. Vocabulary test

Write sentences with the following pairs of words. Your sentence should demonstrate your knowledge of the relationship between the words

a) Federal law/state law
b) Article 1/ US Constitution
c) Fiscal measures/Congress
d) Federal government/enumerated
e) Article 2/pursuant to
f) Sanitary codes/government

3. Knowledge test

Each of the following statements is false; do you know why? Write a sentence stating why

a)   State law can sometimes take precedence over the provisions of US federal law.
b)   The Democratic Party promotes conservative values in American politics.
c)   There is practically no local government in the United States.
d)   Article 3 of the Constitution establishes the three levels of federal courts: the federal courts of first instance, the federal appeal courts and the Supreme Court.
e)   The US President, along with being head of the executive, is also the head of the legislative branch of government.
f)   Both the state and federal governments are governments of enumerated powers.

PART 1 – TEXT 2 – MORE INFORMATION

The organization of political power in the United States of America

The political system in the United States is organized around a federal system of government that **sits astride** the fifty different separate state systems. It is important to note from the **outset** that the fifty states are separate **legal entities** and not just **administrative units** created by the federal government to **facilitate** governing the country. Indeed, it was the state governments that created the federal government, **ceding** some of their powers to the new federal entity. **Thus**, the states **guard** the powers that they did not transfer to the federal government **jealously**, not unlike the member states of the European Union. However, unlike the European Union there is a collective national identity in America that **reinforces** the role of federal power. Both federal and state governments are organized around Montesquieu's theory of the separation of powers, each having an **executive**, **legislative** and **judicial branch** of government. Federal and state elections generally take place within a two-party system, represented by the **conservative-leaning** Republican Party and the more **liberal** Democratic Party.

How does the federal government co-exist with the state governments?

As we have seen, the American legal system is **built around** two **distinct** legal systems, the:
• federal system established by the US federal Constitution, which **came into effect** in 1789; and
• legal systems of the fifty individual states, which existed prior to the creation of the federal state.

The federal and state systems co-exist together on the basis of two principles, the:
• *supremacy of federal law* Pursuant to article 6 of the US federal Constitution, federal law takes **supremacy** over the laws of the

individual states. Thus, if **behavior** infringes federal law, it will be considered illegal even if state law provides to the contrary;

- *federal government is a government of **limited powers*** Although federal law is supreme, the federal government only **possesses** those powers that were expressly given to it by the original thirteen states, i.e. the powers listed in the US Constitution. These are sometimes referred to as the **enumerated powers** of the federal government.

Thus, the federal government and its laws are supreme but the scope of its power is strictly limited to those areas expressly set out or enumerated in the US Constitution. In the areas not coming within the scope of federal law, the individual US states are free to adopt the laws they wish. Consequently, each state adopts the laws it considers appropriate and as a result **each** of the fifty US states has its own **specific character.** This is particularly true as state law governs most of the areas that **impact** people's lives on a daily basis. For example, areas such as family law, contract law, company law and education all **come within** the **remit** of the individual states.

Indeed, although the United States is a **single economic unit**, each state remains responsible for many of the rules regulating businesses established in its jurisdiction. However, although each state has jurisdiction or responsibility over the businesses established on its territory, each state is nonetheless required to **mutually recognize** the laws adopted in other states and consequently the businesses established thereunder. As a result, **goods** and services originating in one state automatically have the right to be marketed and sold in the remaining forty-nine states. For example, a company **incorporated** in the State of Delaware must respect Delaware State company law, but once it does this it is then recognized as a legally incorporated company throughout the US. The State of Delaware for its part has to also **recognize** companies incorporated under the laws of other states and allow them to offer their goods and services on its territory. However, every company, no matter its state of origin, must respect all applicable US federal law provisions.

Federal branches of government

The **federal government of the United States** was established pursuant to the provisions of the United States Constitution. Federal power is divided into three branches: the legislative, executive and judicial branches of government. Thus there are three individual powers but the system of the separation of powers is not applied rigidly, insofar as it operates alongside the system of **checks and balances**. Under this system, each branch of power exercises partial control over the exercise of power by the other federal branches. Thus, the **undue concentration** of power in any one branch of government is prevented. Each of the three branches can be said to have two types of power:

- one giving it the **authority** to act on its own (*the separation of power*);
- another that it **shares** with the other branches of government *(the balance)*, which power can also be considered as an ability to check

or control the exercise of power by another branch of government *(the check)*.

- *Legislative power – United States Congress* Congress is **comprised of** the House of Representatives and the Senate. The House of Representatives has over 400 elected members, each of whom represents a **congressional district** in the United States and **serves** for a two-year **period** or **term**. Seats in the House of Representatives are **apportioned by reference** to population numbers. Thus, more heavily populated areas, such as New York State, will have more House *representatives* than less populous areas, such as the State of Montana. In contrast, in the Senate each state is represented by two Senators, no matter the size of its population. Consequently, the tiny State of Rhode Island has two Senators, as does California, which has a much larger population and is a global **economic powerhouse in its own right**[1]. As there are fifty states, consequently there are 100 senators, each of whom serves a six-year term. However, one third of the Senate stands for election every two years and thus, every two years, significant Senatorial and House of Representative elections take place in the United States. As we have seen, under the system of checks and balances each of the congressional chambers enjoy both exclusive powers and complementary powers. For example, the approval of the Senate is required for many important Presidential **appointments**, whilst the House of Representatives has the exclusive power to introduce or propose **fiscal measures** or **bills**. However, the support of the Senate is required if such **revenue bills** are to pass into law. Indeed, the consent of both chambers is required for the adoption of legislation, which then may only be **promulgated** into law after signature by the President. If the President decides to **veto** legislative proposals coming from Congress, both houses of Congress must then readopt the legislation by a two-thirds majority in each chamber, if they are to by-pass the Presidential veto and ensure the measure **passes** into law. The actual powers of Congress are limited to those areas specifically enumerated in article 1 section 8 of the Constitution and include, *inter alia*, the power to **levy** and collect taxes, provide for common defense, establish **post offices** and roads, issue **patents**, create federal courts inferior to the Supreme Court, declare war, raise armies, provide and **maintain** a navy, etc.
- *Executive power – the President* Executive power in the US federal government is **vested** in the President of the United States. The President is the head of state and government, the military **commander in chief** and chief diplomat. The main powers of the President are *to take care that the laws of the United States be **faithfully executed** and to also preserve, protect and defend the Constitution*. Moreover, as we have seen, the President has the power to either approve legislation

---

[1] If California was a separate country, it would have the eighth largest economy in the world.

passed by Congress into law or alternatively the power to veto it. The President may also, with the consent of two-thirds of the Senate, make treaties with foreign nations. He/she also has the power to **pardon** or **release** criminals **convicted of** offenses against the federal government and to **enact** executive orders. Executive orders are a secondary form of **legislative instrument**, like a **decree**, and the President's power to adopt such orders has been criticized by some as a **usurpation** of Congress's legislative role. Indeed, nowhere does the Constitution specifically give the President the right to adopt such orders; rather it is **inferred** from the duty to ensure that the laws of the US are faithfully executed. Finally, with the **consent** of the Senate, the President has the power to **appoint** Supreme Court justices and federal judges.

- *Judicial power – the Supreme Court* The Supreme Court is the highest court in the federal court system and **deals with** cases concerning the federal government and disputes between states. It has both **original** and **appellate jurisdiction** and its most important power allows it to **interpret** the **provisions** of the United States Constitution. Pursuant to this latter power of interpretation, the Supreme Court can **declare** legislation adopted by Congress or an executive action of the President to be unconstitutional and consequently **null and void**. This is referred to as the power of **judicial review**, i.e. the power to review judicially the legality of the acts of the other branches of federal government. The Supreme Court can also declare unconstitutional acts of the 50 state executive, legislative or judicial powers, as federal law is the supreme law of the land. Members of the federal judiciary may be **impeached** by Congress, as may the President.

State branches of government

As in the federal system, power in each individual US state is organized **pursuant to** Montesquieu's system of the separation of powers. Every state has a legislative power, an executive power, and a state judiciary. Moreover, each state has its own constitution. State governors representing the executive power normally hold office for a four-year term (although in a few states the term is only two years). All the states, with the exception of Nebraska, have a **bicameral** legislative system in place; Nebraska has a **unicameral** legislative system. As the states have **regulatory powers** over all the areas not specifically granted to the federal government, they have **wide powers** over education, company law, contract law and fiscal policy, to mention just a few areas. It is the function of the state courts to apply state law governing these areas.

Local government

There is a **widespread** system of **local government** in the United States governing geographical areas referred to as **counties**, **municipalities**, **townships** and **school districts**. Each of these areas has a locally elected **ruling body**, referred to collectively as local government. Local government bodies are responsible for **providing** services such as police protection, the development of **sanitary codes**, **health regulations**, education, public transportation and

housing. Cities are generally run by a **Mayor** who then appoints officials to head each of the city's administrative departments, normally acting with the **approval** of the city council, a type of city legislature. The city council is usually responsible for city ordinances, the setting of rates, i.e. taxes on property, managing the city budget and **apportioning** money among the various city departments.

Political pressure groups

Special interest groups play a very important role in the legislative adoption process in the United States. These groups **support** the political and economic **agendas** of their members and **lobby** politicians to this end. Thus, employer organizations will **canvas** politicians to promote legislation providing for the adoption of low **corporate taxes** and restrictions on imports; **whereas labor unions** will support minimum wage legislation. There is a feeling in **some quarters** that these groups have to some extent **hijacked** the democratic process in the United States and that it is the **interests** of these groups, **rather than** the interests of the general **populace**, that Congress **promotes**. One important type of private interest group that has grown in influence is the *political action committee* (PAC). Numerous PACs have been established and are often organized around a single issue or **cause**, for example a group might be pro or indeed anti abortion and contribute money to political candidates that support their **policy position**. Although PACs may be limited in the amounts they can contribute directly to candidates, there are no **restrictions** on the amounts PACs can spend independently to promote their candidate. Thus, they often pay for advertisements in favor of the candidates they support. It is suspected that election candidates often use friendly PACs to **make known** and focus general opinion on negative details concerning their opponents; details that they themselves might be unwilling to directly speak about, given the sometimes odious nature of the accusations. A candidate for the Senate might for example use a friendly PAC to publicize information revealing that an opponent once used drugs. In this way, the information is made public but the candidate is not directly associated with its revelation.

The result of the interaction between federal, state and local powers level is a dynamic form of democracy reinforced by the fact that there are significant elections taking place annually. This has been criticized **on the grounds** that it results in the election of political leaders overly influenced by **short-term** public concerns. Although possibly true, it is also a significant ingredient in a system where change is welcome and where people truly feel that *yes, they can.*

VOCABULARY

Sit (to) astride – *dominer/chevaucher*
Outset – *début/commencement*
From the outset – *d'entrée de jeu/d'emblée*
Legal entities – *personnes morales*

Administrative units – *unités administratives*
Facilitate (to) – *faciliter*
Cede (to) – *céder/concéder*
Thus – *donc/ainsi*
Guard (to) – *conserver*
Jealously – *jalousement*
Reinforce (to) – *renforcer*
Executive – *exécutif (pouvoir)*
Legislative – *législatif (pouvoir)*
Judicial branch – *pouvoir judiciaire*
Conservative – *conservateur*
Conservative leaning – *de tendance conservatrice*
Liberal – *libéral (sens anglo-saxon = progressiste)*
Built around – *construit autour de*
Distinct – *distinct*
Come (to) into effect – *entrer en vigueur*
Supremacy – *prééminence/primauté*
Behavior – *comportement*
Limited powers – *pouvoirs limités*
Possess (to) – *posséder/détenir*
Enumerated powers – *pouvoirs énumérés (principe des compétences d'attribution)*
Each – *chacun*
Specific character – *nature spécifique/caractéristique propre*
Impact (to) – *avoir une incidence*
Remit – *responsabilité/attribution*
Come (to) within the remit of – *relever de la compétence de*
Single economic unit – *seule/unique unité économique*
Mutual recognition – *reconnaissance mutuelle*
Goods – *marchandises/biens*
Incorporate (to) – *incorporer*
Recognize (to) – *reconnaître*
Federal government of the United States – *gouvernement fédéral des Etats Unis*
Checks and balances – *système d'équilibre et de contrôle entre les différentes branches du pouvoir (exécutif, législatif, judiciaire)*
Undue concentration – *concentration excessive/abusive*
Authority – *autorité*
Share (to) – *partager*
Comprised (to be) of – *se composer de/consister en*
Congressional district – *circonscription électorale*
Serve (to) – *exercer (un mandat)*
Period/term – *mandat (électif)*
Apportion (to) – *répartir*
By reference to – *par rapport à/en fonction de*
Economic power house – *puissance économique*
In its own right – *en lui-même/à part entière*
Appointment – *nomination/désignation*
Fiscal measures – *mesures fiscales*

Bill – *projet de loi*
Revenue bill – *projet de loi fiscale*
Promulgate (to) – *promulguer*
Veto – *veto*
Right of veto – *droit de veto*
Pass (to) a law – *adopter une loi*
Inter alia – *parmi d'autres/entre autre*
Levy (to) – *prélever/percevoir/imposer*
Post office – *bureau de poste*
Patent – *brevet*
Maintain (to) – *entretenir*
Vest (to) – *investir (quelqu'un de quelque chose) /assigner (quelque chose à quelqu'un)/être dévolu à (quelque chose à quelqu'un) /conférer à (quelque chose à quelqu'un)*
Commander-in-chief – *commandant en chef*
Faithfully (to) execute – *appliquer/exécuter fidèlement*
Pardon (to) – *gracier*
Release (to) – *libérer/relâcher*
Convicted (to be) of – *être reconnu coupable/être condamné*
Enact (to) – *décréter*
Legislative instrument – *instrument législatif*
Decree – *décret*
Infer (to) – *déduire*
Consent – *consentement*
Appoint (to) – *nommer/désigner*
Deal with (to) – *s'occuper de/traiter de*
Original jurisdiction – *compétence en première instance*
Appellate jurisdiction – *juridiction d'appel/pouvoir de recevoir ou examiner les appels*
Interpret (to) the provisions – *interpréter les dispositions*
Declare (to) something null and void – *déclarer quelque chose nulle et non avenue*
Judicial review – *contrôle juridictionnel de légalité d'une norme*
Impeachment – *mise en accusation pouvant déboucher sur une destitution*
Pursuant to – *selon/en vertu de*
Bicameral – *bicaméral*
Unicameral legislature – *corps législatif monocaméral*
Regulatory powers – *pouvoirs réglementaires*
Wide powers – *vastes pouvoirs/pouvoirs étendus*
Widespread – *étendu*
Local government – *collectivité locale*
County – *comté (division administrative)*
Municipality – *municipalité*
Township – *commune*
School district – *district scolaire*
Ruling body – *corps dirigeant/décisionnel*
Provide (to) – *fournir/dispenser*
Sanitary code – *code/règlement sanitaire*

Housing/health regulations – *logement/règles sanitaires*
Mayor – *maire*
Approval – *approbation*
Apportion (to) – *répartir/distribuer*
Support (to) – *soutenir*
Economic agenda – *programme (agenda) économique*
Lobby (to) – *faire pression sur*
Canvas (to) – *démarcher (chercher à obtenir le soutien de qq'un)*
Corporate taxes – *impôts sur les sociétés*
Whereas – *tandis que*
Labor union – *syndicat*
There is a feeling in some quarters – *il y en a qui ont le sentiment/l'impression que/il est parfois estimé que*
Hijack (to) – *détourner/pervertir*
Interests – *intérêts*
Rather than – *plutôt que*
Populace – *population*
Promote (to) – *promouvoir*
Cause – *cause*
Policy position – *position politique sur une question spécifique*
Restriction – *limitation*
Make (to) known – *diffuser/répandre (dans le domaine public)*
On the grounds that – *au motif que*
Short-term – *à court terme*

PART 1 – TEXT 2 – EXERCISES

1. Definitions

Write a sentence defining each of the following terms – one sentence per term

- a) Sovereignty
- b) Enumerated
- c) Congress
- d) Levy
- e) Impeach
- f) Bicameral
- g) Enact legislation

2. Sentences

Write sentences with the following pairs of words. Your sentence should if possible demonstrate your knowledge of the relationship between the word

- a) Pursuant/US Constitution
- b) Local government/counties
- c) Impeach/US President
- d) Fiscal measures/Congress
- e) PACs/public policy
- f) Pardon/President

g)   Appoint/judiciary
h)   Checks and balances/Montesquieu
i)   Congressional District/election
j)   Patents/Congress

3. Fill in the missing words

Fill in the missing words using the vocabulary in Text 2

a)   In the United States, the federal government is said to be a government of _____ powers and thus can only use those powers given to it under the _____.
b)   The political organization in the US is based on Montesquieu's theory of the separation of powers and also uses the system of _____ to prevent the _____ concentration of power in any one branch of government.
c)   In 1789 the US Constitution came into_____ and created the _____ government.
d)   Political Action Committees are an example of a political _____ group that seek to influence legislation adopted by _____.
e)   One of the most important powers of the federal Supreme Court is its power of_____ _____, whereby it can rule on the constitutionality of the acts adopted by the other _____ of government.

4. Knowledge test

The following questions may be answered in writing or by way of discussion

a)   Do you think the division of powers between the US federal government and the US states is an appropriate model for federal multistate unions? Can you think of another model that could be used; how does the US differ from the European Union?
b)   Why do you think Americans have such a strong central identity given the obvious differences between the fifty different US States?
c)   What are the main principles governing the relationship between the US federal government and the individual US state governments?
d)   Is it appropriate that interest groups such as PACs should play such a significant role in the election of politicians and the adoption of legislation? Are there any dangers attached to such a system?

PART 2 – QUICK LOOK GRAMMAR REVISION

The Future Tense – *be going to/will/shall*

"Be going to + verb stem" and **"will + verb stem"** are used to express the future.

Note:

The problem of using "shall" to create an obligation in legal documents such as contracts is that it does not necessarily always create an obligation to do something.

Take the following sentence as an example:
"I am dying and no one shall save me."

Shall in this case can mean either:
- "I am dying and *I realize that no one will make an effort to save me*"; or
- "I am dying and *I am instructing people that they should not save me*."

In fact the only time that "shall" creates a clear obligation is when it is imposing a duty on the subject of the sentence, for example:

"The Agent shall supply the clients of the Manager every week."

A good test to note if "shall" has been used correctly in order to create an obligation is to see whether it can be replaced by the words "has a duty to."

For example:
"The Manager shall receive supplies from the Agent every week."

"The Agent has a duty to supply the clients of the Manager every week."

It is only in the second sentence that an actual duty is created for the agent as regards the supply of goods. Thus, in contracts and other documents seeking to create an obligation, it is advisable to replace 'shall" with another term such as "must" or "has a duty to".

Note:

When used in everyday speech, Americans are inclined to pronounce **"going to"** as **"gonna"**. For example, *he is **going to** be at the football match* can become *he is **gonna** be at the football match.*

When used in everyday speech "will" is usually reduced to "ll", for example *he **will** be at the football match* becomes ***he'll** be at the football match.*

1. Difference between "going to + verb" and "will + verb"

Going to + verb expresses certainty for the future; when there is a clear intention in the present to do something in the future, when something has been planned or organized, or when there are clear signs in the present that something will occur in the future, for example:

"I *am going* to take the plane tomorrow at 9am."
"Look at those clouds! It's going to rain."

When will + verb is used to talk about a future event, it expresses a decision taken at the moment of speaking, and may indicate that the speaker has not thought about the matter beforehand. It can also be used to predict a future event that may or may not occur:

"I *will* take the plane tomorrow at 9 am."
"The phone's ringing".... "OK, I'll get it."
"I reckon the budget deficit will be below 3 % by the end of the year."

2. Forms using *"will"*

a) When making a statement:
- I, you, he, she, it, we, they WILL WORK/PLAY/STUDY tomorrow;
or in spoken form
- I'll, you'll, he'll, she'll, it'll, we'll, they'll WORK/PLAY/STUDY tomorrow.

b) When making a negative statement:
- I, you, he, she, it, we, they WILL NOT WORK/PLAY/STUDY tomorrow;
or in spoken form
- I, you, he, she, it, we, they WON'T WORK/PLAY/STUDY tomorrow.

c) When asking a question:
Will I, you, he, she, it, we, they WORK/PLAY/STUDY tomorrow?

d) When answering a question:
Yes, I, you, he, she, it, we, they WILL WORK/PLAY/STUDY tomorrow.

No, I, you, he, she, it, we, they WILL NOT (WON'T) WORK/PLAY/STUDY tomorrow.

3. Forms using *"going to"*

a) When making a statement:
I **AM**
You **ARE**
He, she, it **IS**
We, they **ARE**
.... GOING TO WORK/PLAY/STUDY tomorrow;
or in spoken form
I'**M**,
You'**RE**,
He'**S**, she'**S**, it'**S**,
We'**RE**, they'**RE**
.... GOING TO WORK/PLAY/STUDY tomorrow.

b)   When speaking in the negative:
I AM NOT
You ARE NOT
He, she, it IS NOT
We, they ARE NOT
………………………. GOING TO WORK/PLAY/STUDY tomorrow;
                    or in spoken form
You AREN'T
He, she, it ISN'T
We, they AREN'T
………………………. GOING TO WORK/PLAY/STUDY tomorrow.

c)   When asking a question:
AM I
ARE you
IS he, she, it
ARE we, they
……………………... GOING TO WORK/PLAY/STUDY tomorrow?

d)   When answering a question:
Yes, I **AM (I'M)**
Yes, you **ARE (you're)**
Yes, he, she, it **IS (he'S, she'S, it'S)**
Yes, we, they **ARE (we'RE, they'RE)**
………………………. GOING TO WORK/PLAY/STUDY tomorrow.

No, I **AM NOT (I'M NOT)**
No, you **ARE NOT (you're NOT)**
No, he, she, it **IS NOT (he'S, she'S, it'S NOT)**
No, we, they **ARE NOT (we'RE, they'RE NOT)**
………………………. GOING TO WORK/PLAY/STUDY tomorrow.

PART 2 – GRAMMAR EXERCISES

1. Contractions

Write the appropriate contraction for the words in brackets

(He will)   *He'll* be home tonight.

a)   (I will)   ____ see you in court on Wednesday.
b)   (We will)   ____ probably get an acquittal on Thursday.
c)   (It will)   ____ certainly be too late to have the meeting.
d)   (She will)   ____ take her Bar exams after finishing her law degree.
e)   (they will)   Their plane has just landed so ____ probably make
     the meeting at 5:00pm.

2. More contractions

*In spoken English the noun and will are often joined together in speech. Read the sentences below out loud and practice contracting **will** with the **noun** attached*

(Jane will)   *Jane'll* be in court tomorrow.

    a)   *Dinner will* be after the meeting at 9:00pm.
    b)   The *meeting will* start this afternoon.
    c)   *Frank will* help us move into our new office on Saturday.
    d)   My *clients will* be here soon.
    e)   The *witness will* be here tomorrow.

3. Probably + *will* and *won't*

*Using **probably** with a **pronoun** and **will not/won't** complete the sentences below*

I stayed at the office last night, and *I will probably stay* tonight as well.

    a)   Jane did not come to the office today because she was sick, and
          _____ tomorrow either.
    b)   I attended the court case yesterday evening but _____ the court
          case tomorrow too.
    c)   We were not at work last night and _____ at work tomorrow
          night.
    d)   My clients did not attend the meeting last night and _____ the
          meeting tonight either.
    e)   She went to bed early last night but _____ to bed early tonight
          as well.

4. Activities in the future

*Write sentences about future activities using the words provided, and using **will** and **going to**. Write one sentence for each*

Tomorrow, to work – *I am going* to work tomorrow/*I will go* to work tomorrow.

    a)   Tomorrow afternoon, to meet Jane.
    b)   Late tonight, to eat.
    c)   Later today, to appear in court.
    d)   Next year, to change office.
    e)   Very soon, to be promoted.

PART 3 – AUDIO – LISTENING AND SPEAKING

Comprehension

Listen to the following conversation, make notes of all the relevant facts and then answer the questions below. If you have trouble understanding, follow the conversation while also reading the text.

Phone conversation between Xavier and Frank Collins. Xavier is ringing Frank Collins

Frank: "Hello Mr. Enriquez, this is Frank Collins; what can I do for you?"

Xavier: "Hello, Mr. Collins, my name is Xavier Enriquez as you know and I work with a French law firm called Bide, Florette & Partners. I am ringing you on the recommendation of Bob Marshall, a US lawyer who works with our Firm, here in France."

Frank: "Ah Bob, how is he doing over there in France? We were in University together."

Xavier: "He is doing very well thanks and asked me to give you his regards. In fact the reason I am calling you is because we have a client here in France, Arnaud Dupont, who agreed to act as an Agent for a US Company and signed an agency agreement to that effect. However, despite having secured numerous sales, the US Company has refused to pay him the commissions he is owed."

Frank: "What is the name of the US Company?"

Xavier: "Just give me a second to look at the file……. They are called Teeny Bopper Inc., it is a company incorporated in the State of Delaware and they sell fashion accessories for the teenage girl market. "

Frank: "And your client was appointed as Agent for their products in France?"

Xavier: "Yes, that is right. He was in fact appointed as an exclusive Agent for the French territory."

Frank: "And briefly, what were the terms of remuneration?"

Xavier: "Well, under the agreement, Mr. Dupont was to receive 5% of net income resulting from all Teeny Bopper sales on the French market."

Frank: "And from your understanding of the agreement, would you say Mr. Dupont was acting as an independent agent or not?"

Xavier: "I don't fully understand, could you repeat the question?"

Frank: "Sorry, looking at the terms of the agreement between Mr. Dupont and Teeny Bopper, do you think Mr. Dupont was working as a separate legal entity independent of Teeny Bopper or was he actually working for them as an employee or representative?"

Xavier: "Well I would have to look at the agreement more closely to answer that."

Frank: "OK, I presume you are ringing me because the applicable law in the contract is US law?"

Xavier: "Yes, the applicable law is the Californian State law. In fact, I am not very clear on this; does the fact that the law of California applies to the agreement mean that US federal law does not apply to the agreement?"

Frank: "Each individual state has jurisdiction over the area of contract law and so this agreement will be primarily governed by the agency rules of the State of California, unless of course there is applicable federal law on the matter."

Xavier: "Well I guess we need your help then."

Frank: "OK, why don't you send me a copy of the agreement and any correspondence you have between Teeny Bopper and Mr. Dupont as soon as you can? I am in court all this week and so my cousin James will be dealing with it. From our side, we will do a company search on Teeny Bopper and try and find out exactly who they are."

Xavier: "I will try to have the contract sent to you by this evening. Would you be able to get back to me with your first impression in two days time? That way I can have something to tell the client."

Frank: "That shouldn't be a problem. Once we have had a look, James will give you a call and he can also talk about fees at that time as well."

Xavier: "OK, thanks Mr. Collins."

Frank: "Please call me Frank."

Xavier: "Thanks Frank and please call me Xavier."

Frank: "OK Xavier, James will ring you at this time in two days to give you our first impression of Mr. Dupont's legal position."

Xavier: "Wonderful."

Frank: "Goodbye Xavier."

Xavier: "Goodbye Frank."

PART 3 – AUDIO COMPREHENSION – EXERCISES

1. Comprehension

From the notes you have taken of the conversation, answer the following questions

    a)   Why did Xavier choose to ring Frank Collins?

    b)   What exactly is the problem that Arnaud Dupont has?

    c)   When will Frank next contact Xavier?

    d)   Does Arnaud work for Teeny Bopper Inc. as an independent agent?

    e)   What is the law governing the Agency Agreement?

    f)   What papers does Xavier have to fax to Frank?

2. Speaking practice

In the following series of conversation couplets, develop suitable responses to the questions asked

    a)   Xavier: "Would you be able to assist us on a contract law matter involving the law of the State of California?"
            Frank: "_____."

    b)   Xavier: "Could you explain to me the relationship between state law and federal law in the United States?"
            Frank: "_____."

    c)   Xavier: "Could you tell me if it is state law or federal law that applies to the agreement that Mr. Dupont has with Teeny Bopper Inc.?"
            Frank: "_____"

    d)   Xavier: "OK I will call you tomorrow, what is the time difference between California and France?"

Frank: "_____"

e) Xavier: "Could you send me the documentation by fax?"
Frank: "_____."

f) Xavier: "Is the area of contract law governed by federal law or state law?"
Frank: "_____."

g) Xavier: "What was the agreement as to remuneration, I mean how much was Mr. Dupont meant to receive?"
Frank: "_____."

h) Xavier: "What documentation would you like me to fax to you?"
Frank: "_____."

i) Xavier: "In what country is Teeny Bopper Inc. incorporated?"
Frank: "_____."

j) Xavier: "What does Teeny Bopper Inc. do exactly?"
Frank: "_____."

3. Speaking practice continued ......

Create five other conversation couplets using in each couplet at least one word from the vocabulary found in Part 1, Text 1 and Text 2.

4. Speaking practice continued ......

Listen to the suggested replies and repeat

a) Xavier: "Would you be able to assist us on a contract law matter involving the law of the State of California?"
Frank: "Yes of course, we would be delighted to help you in any way we could."

b) Xavier: "Could you explain to me the relationship between state law and federal law in the United States?"
Frank: "Well fundamentally there are two different systems: state law and federal law. Federal law takes supremacy over state law but has limited application."

c) Xavier: "Could you tell me if it is state law or federal law that applies to the agreement that Mr. Dupont has with Teeny Bopper Inc.?"
Frank: "The area of contract law comes within the jurisdiction of the individual states and consequently the law applicable to the agreement will be Californian state law."

d) Xavier: "OK I will call you tomorrow, what is the time difference between California and France?"
Frank: "There is roughly a nine hour time difference between Paris and L.A., so when it is 6:00pm in France it's 9:00am in California."

e) Xavier: "Could you send me the documentation by fax?"
Frank: "Yes of course. What is your fax number?"

f) Xavier: "Is the area of contract law governed by state law or federal law?"

Frank: "Contract law is primarily governed by the provisions of state law."

g) Xavier: "What was the agreement as to remuneration; I mean how much was Mr. Dupont meant to receive?"
    Frank: "He was to receive a 5% cut of all sales."

h) Xavier: "What documentation would you like me to fax to you?"
    Frank: "Could you send me a copy of the Agency Agreement and any correspondence that you may have between the client and Teeny Bopper Inc?"

i) Xavier: "In what state is Teeny Bopper Inc. incorporated?"
    Frank: "Teeny Bopper is incorporated under the law of Delaware."

j) Xavier: "What does Teeny Bopper Inc. do exactly?"
    Frank: "They make teenage fashion accessories."

5. Associated questions

Discuss the following questions

Would you like to work as a lawyer in the area of international commerce?

a) Do you think it is essential to speak English today to work in the area of business?
b) Briefly summarize the law in your country governing agency agreements.
c) Discuss the type of research you would do if you were Frank and had to prepare to call Xavier in two days.

PART 4 – TRANSLATION EXERCISES

When carrying out the translations it is not necessary to translate directly word for word; rather the emphasis should be on translating the sense of the text. Language is not directly interchangeable and so direct translations do not always convey the meaning in the text.

Translate the following texts from English to French

A. Judicial review

The power of judicial review can involve a review by the courts of the constitutionality of acts adopted by the other branches of government. However, another facet of judicial review allows the courts to rule on the legality of administrative acts, i.e. the decisions adopted by either public or private administrative authorities; for example, a decision of the New York Bar preventing a lawyer from practicing. Thus, in common law countries, administrative control is carried out by way of judicial review by the ordinary civil courts. Civil law countries such as France and Germany have established a system of administrative courts with exclusive jurisdiction over administrative questions.

B. State rights

Since its creation the United States has been the subject of an ongoing political tug of war between state and federal powers. The federal government was created by the states, but once they had created the federal state, it is clear that they already doubted its wisdom. Thus, they immediately adopted the tenth amendment to underline that all powers that were not expressly given to the federal government by the Constitution were reserved to them. In this way they hoped to strictly limit the power of the federal state. However, the following two hundred years were characterized by growing federal power, especially during the Roosevelt presidency. With the election of Ronald Reagan in 1980, the pendulum was supposed to swing back toward state power; however it seems easier to criticize federal power, than to actually get rid of it.

C. Roosevelt and the Supreme Court

The President appoints members of the Supreme Court for life. They may be removed only by death, resignation or impeachment. One of the most important powers of the Supreme Court is its power of judicial review, pursuant to which it may declare acts of Congress or the President to be unconstitutional and therefore invalid. When democrat Franklin D. Roosevelt came to power, the Court was dominated by republican nominees and these justices used their power of judicial review to declare unconstitutional legislation being adopted by Roosevelt. On 2nd February 1937, Roosevelt made a speech attacking the Supreme Court, pointing out that seven out of the nine judges had been appointed by Republican presidents. Roosevelt had just won re-election by a large majority and resented the fact that the unelected justices could veto legislation that clearly had the support of the vast majority of the public. He threatened to increase the number of sitting judges, so as to introduce a democratic majority. However, the republican judges backed down and stopped blocking the adoption of Roosevelt's legislation.

Translate the following texts from French to English

A. Fédération ou confédération ?

Le terme confédération s'oppose à celui de fédération et les deux termes ne sont pas interchangeables. Dans une confédération, la souveraineté relève exclusivement des entités qui composent l'ensemble. Dans une fédération, la souveraineté est partagée entre l'État fédéral et les États fédérés; toutefois, le pouvoir est principalement détenu par le gouvernement fédéral. Il y a des confédérations comme la Suisse, même si celle-ci est en réalité maintenant une fédération et une confédération seulement par le nom, et il y a des fédérations comme les Etats-Unis, et des organisations qui se situent quelque part entre ces deux modèles-là. L'Union européenne, par exemple est une organisation politique dont les États demeurent majoritairement souverains, bien qu'il y ait une préséance du droit communautaire sur les droits nationaux. Dans la majorité des cas, la confédération n'est qu'une étape vers la fédération.

B. Le contrôle de constitutionnalité

Le contrôle de la constitutionnalité d'une loi aux États-Unis s'effectue *a posteriori*, ce qui signifie qu'il a lieu après que la loi a été promulguée. Donc, la constitutionnalité d'une loi n'est examinée que dans le cadre d'une affaire particulière liée à l'application de cette loi. Il est alors possible que la loi soit jugée totalement ou en partie inconstitutionnelle, pour des raisons de légalité externe (par exemple, elle a été adoptée par une autorité qui n'en avait pas le pouvoir) ou interne (son contenu est en contradiction avec les dispositions de la Constitution, par exemple avec les droits fondamentaux). Ce modèle de contrôle de constitutionnalité est parfois appelé « modèle américain », en opposition à un modèle qu'on dit européen. Le modèle européen se caractérise avant tout par un contrôle centralisé, c'est-à-dire relevant de la compétence d'une seule cour constitutionnelle.

C. Judicial review aux Etats-Unis

On peut définir le contrôle de constitutionnalité aux Etats-Unis comme un système dans lequel les juges peuvent décider si ce qui leur est soumis est conforme à la constitution. C'est le pouvoir de *judicial review*; ce n'est pas un pouvoir de révision ni d'annulation car le juge ne révise ni n'annule l'acte qui est présumé inconstitutionnel. En revanche, la cour le prive de toute force légale en ne l'appliquant pas. En outre, ce pouvoir ne se limite pas aux lois : il concerne aussi bien les actes du pouvoir législatif que du pouvoir exécutif. L'article fondateur est l'article 6 de la Constitution de 1787 établissant la primauté de la Constitution et des lois fédérales. Les juges se voient donc investis d'un très grand pouvoir, à tel point qu'on entend parler de « gouvernement des juges ».

PART 5 – ADVANCED READING

Regulatory control: harmonization v mutual recognition and the phenomenon of the *race to the bottom*

The United States is made up of fifty separate states, each with its own separate political and legal system. These states along with the US federal power together form the entity known as the United States of America. Regulatory control in the USA is thus expressed on two levels:

- *Federal level* In some areas, the regulation of economic activity occurs at federal level. For example, many of the rules that businesses must respect when seeking a listing on the stock market or dealing with shareholders have been adopted at federal level. Federal control implies that the rules are the same throughout the fifty US states and thus some of the law in the area of financial services is said to have been *harmonized* at federal level.
- *State level* In those areas where the federal government does not enjoy competence, each of the states enjoys individual jurisdiction. One of many such areas is the field of company law and company creation. Consequently, in the United States, each of the fifty states has responsibility for granting company franchises and each is responsible

for establishing a regulatory framework applicable to companies. In other words, there are no companies established under US federal law but rather companies created under the laws of one of the fifty US states. However, although each of the states has individual jurisdiction in this area, their competence is subject to the principle of *mutual recognition*. Pursuant to this principle, each state is bound, on the basis of reciprocity, to recognize companies created or incorporated in the other 49 states. As a result, a company incorporated in the State of California has the right to establish and offer its services in the State of New Jersey without having to receive authorization from the New Jersey authorities. Thus, although each state establishes its own regulatory framework, it does not enjoy a complete monopoly over the regulatory process, insofar as its regulatory model is open to competition from company entities formed in other states.

The creation of a system based on mutual recognition can result in regulatory competition. As states need to attract companies to their territory to create employment and tax revenue, they can choose to do so through the adoption of regulatory models attractive to businesses. Thus, the purpose of regulation can be diverted from one of controlling business to one of attracting business. Indeed, it is this facet of regulatory competition intrinsic to the notion of mutual recognition that has led to a fierce debate in academic circles. Those in favor of the application of a system based on mutual recognition argue that its effect on regulation is positive. For such commentators, the application of mutual recognition requires regulatory powers in each state to be aware of the negative effects of overly burdensome regulation; clearly, in such a system an inappropriate, uncompetitive regulatory model will be punished, as businesses will simply re-establish in other states providing more efficient control. However, other commentators have argued that mutual recognition forces states to compete as regards the content of their regulatory models, distorting the regulatory process and undermining the primary role of regulation. In their opinion, the role of regulation thereby necessarily becomes one of attracting rather than controlling business. Given that businesses will be attracted by pro-business and possibly even lax regulation, this will in turn, it is argued, inevitably lead to a *race to the bottom* in regulatory standards. This phenomenon is also referred to as the *Delaware effect*, after the State of Delaware, which is a *popular* state in the United States for company incorporation.

Chapter five

THE COURT SYSTEM IN THE UNITED STATES OF AMERICA

PART 1 – TEXT 1 – INFORMATION

The court structure of the United States

As we have seen, the United States is more than a country; it is a **federation** made up of fifty separate states. The individual fifty states and the federal state together make up the political entity known as the United States of America. Consequently, there are fifty-one different legal systems in the United States and every US citizen is **subject to** two governments:

- the federal government established in 1787 and organized pursuant to the US federal Constitution, adopted in 1789; and
- their individual state government. Each state has its own individual constitution, as well as its own legislative, executive and judicial power responsible for adopting and applying its laws.

The federal court system

The US federal judiciary was established **pursuant to** Article 3 of the Constitution, providing for the establishment of a Supreme Court and any other inferior courts **deemed** necessary by Congress. Jurisdiction for applying the Constitution and the laws adopted **thereunder** is specifically given to the federal courts by the Constitution. The federal courts operate on three different levels and their jurisdiction is restricted to **cases and controversies** arising under federal law. Thus, they have no competence in state law matters except where a state law violates federal law, in which case the federal court may **strike it down**.

The federal courts are organized in the following way:

- *US District Courts* The United States is **divided** into ninety-four federal judicial **districts**, with **each** district having its own federal district court. The district courts are the **first instance** federal trial courts and have general **jurisdiction** over cases and controversies coming under the **heading** of federal law.
- *US Courts of Appeal* The ninety-four federal districts are grouped into twelve regional **circuits**. Each circuit is represented by an appellate court, which **hears** appeals from the different federal district courts coming within its jurisdiction.
- *US Supreme Court* Finally, the most important court in the federal system is the US Supreme Court. Pursuant to Article 3 of the Constitution, the Supreme Court has both **appellate jurisdiction** and

original jurisdiction i.e. first instance jurisdiction. It has appellate jurisdiction as regards matters coming from the US federal Courts of Appeal and from the different state supreme courts where a question of federal law is involved. The Supreme Court's original jurisdiction extends to cases affecting ambassadors, other public ministers and consuls, and to cases to which a state is a party.

The state court system

Each state has its own constitution and legal system that is applied by its own independent judiciary. Although federal law is superior to state law, the scope and area of application of federal law is limited to those areas set out in the US Constitution. Consequently, state law governs many of the day-to-day activities of its citizens, for example family law matters (including divorce, **child custody cases** and adoption), personal injury cases, contracts, **probate** and traffic violations. However, state courts do not have jurisdiction to hear cases involving issues such as **bankruptcy**, immigration, patents and **copyright**, as the federal courts **handle** these matters exclusively.

Although each state has its own separate court system, generally state courts are organized on three basic levels:
- *State trial courts* The **state trial courts** (state courts of first instance) exist at two different levels, those hearing minor matters, often referred to as **municipal courts**, and those with the power to hear more important matters, often referred to as **superior** or **general jurisdiction courts**.
- *State Courts of Appeal* If one of the participants to an action in a state trial court is unsatisfied with the result **handed down** by the trial court judge, the decision may be appealed to the state Court of Appeal.
- *State Supreme Court* Finally, each state has its own Supreme Court **empowered** to **hear** appeals coming from lower state courts. Decisions of the state Supreme Courts are final and may only be appealed to the federal courts where a question of federal law is involved.

VOCABULARY

Federation – *fédération*
Subject to – *soumis à*
Pursuant to – *conformément à*
Deem (to) – *estimer/considérer/juger*
Thereunder – *à ce titre/en vertu de*
Case – *affaire/cas*
Controversy – *controverse (ici, au sens de différend)*
Cases and controversies – *termes employés dans la Constitution des Etats-Unis, article III, section 2. Peut être traduit par « les affaires »*
Strike (to) down a law – *prononcer la nullité d'une loi*
Divide (to) (into) – *diviser (en)*

District – *district*
Each – *chacun*
First instance – *première instance*
Jurisdiction – *juridiction/compétence*
Jurisdiction (to have) over – *avoir compétence pour, sur*
Heading (under the heading) – *titre (au titre de)*
Circuit – *circuit/réseau*
Hear (to) (a case) – *avoir à connaître de/statuer sur*
Appellate jurisdiction – *compétence d'appel*
Original jurisdiction – *compétence de première instance*
Child custody – *exercice de l'autorité parentale*
Probate – *homologation/validation d'un testament*
Bankruptcy – *faillite*
Copyright – *droit d'auteur*
Handle (to) – *s'occuper de/traiter*
State trial court – *cour d'état de première instance*
Municipal court – *cour d'état statuant sur des affaires mineures*
Superior/general jurisdiction court – *cour d'état statuant sur les affaires plus importantes*
Hand down (to) – *rendre (une décision/un arrêt)*
Empowered to – *habilité à*
Power to hear (a matter) – *compétence pour connaître, statuer sur (une affaire)*

PART 1 – TEXT 1 -EXERCISES

1. Vocabulary test

Fill in the missing words using the vocabulary in Text 1

a)   Every American citizen is the _____ of two governments, the federal government and his own state government.

b)   The federal Supreme Court has jurisdiction over all cases and _____ arising under the US Constitution.

c)   The US district courts are the federal trial courts, i.e. they are the courts of first _____ in the federal court system.

d)   The federal courts of appeal have jurisdiction to _____ appeals from the federal district courts.

e)   _____ to article 3 of the US Constitution, the federal Supreme Court has both original and appellate jurisdiction over cases and controversies arising under federal law.

f)   The state trial courts are divided into the _____ courts and the superior/general courts; the former deal with small claims and misdemeanors.

g)   If a litigant is not happy with a decision _____ down by the state municipal court, (s)he can appeal it to the state court of appeal.

h)   Decisions of the State Supreme Court are normally final but may be appealed to the _____ where a question of federal law is involved.

i)   The federal courts of appeal are organized around twelve _____ and hear appeals from the federal district courts.

2. Vocabulary test

Write sentences with the following pairs of words. Your sentence should demonstrate your knowledge of the relationship between the words

- a) State Supreme Court/federal Supreme Court
- b) To hear/state Court of Appeal
- c) Bill of Rights/US Constitution
- d) Federation/states
- e) Article 3/pursuant to
- f) Cases and controversies/jurisdiction

3. Knowledge test

Each of the following statements is false; do you know why? Write a sentence stating why it is false

- a) The US federal Supreme Court has no jurisdiction over the decisions of the state courts.
- b) A litigant can choose to bring an action either before the state courts or the federal courts.
- c) Decisions from the Municipal Courts can be appealed to the State Supreme Court.
- d) The United States is divided into twelve federal judicial districts.
- e) The state courts of general jurisdiction are the lowest ranking federal trial courts.

PART 1 – TEXT 2 – MORE INFORMATION

The court structure of the United States

The United States is more than a country; it is a **federation** of fifty separate states that **covers** a **vast** territory made up of over 300 million people, **stretching** from the Atlantic to the Pacific. Each American citizen is the **subject** of two governments, **namely** the state government and the **federal** government. The laws of the fifty states can differ greatly. For example, in Massachusetts and California it is possible to have **same-sex weddings** and use marijuana[1]; however, **the same is not true** for southern states such as Alabama, which tend toward religious conservatism. **Moreover**, some states such as California and Texas are economic and financial **powerhouses** and would **rank amongst** the world's **wealthiest countries**, if they were independent countries. **On the contrary**, states like Mississippi and Louisiana are much **poorer.** However, **despite** social and financial inequalities and vastly different notions as to what it is to be American, there **nonetheless** remains a common American ideal or dream that most US citizens appear to share or aspire to.

State v Federal Courts

The state courts are found in each of the fifty states. The federal courts

---

[1] For medical reasons.

were established pursuant to the U.S. Constitution. State courts have broad jurisdiction, for example they enjoy jurisdiction over family law, criminal law, **tort law** and indeed most areas of law concerning the day-to-day life of their residents. Over 90% of all trials in the United States occur at state level. By contrast, jurisdiction of the federal courts is limited to **cases and controversies** arising under the Constitution.

Most criminal cases involve **violations** of state law and are tried in state courts, but criminal cases involving federal laws will be **tried** in a federal court. For example **robbery** is a crime, but under state law or federal law? By and large, it is state law and not federal law that criminalizes robbery. There are in fact only a few federal laws **dealing with** the crime of robbery, such as a federal law making it a federal crime to rob banks, where the **deposits** of the bank are insured by a federal agency. Other federal criminal offences include **smuggling** drugs into the country and using the U.S. mail to **swindle** consumers or for other illegal purposes. Crimes committed on federal property (such as national parks or military reservations) are also prosecuted before the federal courts.

Some kinds of conduct are illegal under both federal and state laws. For example, federal laws prohibit discrimination in the area of employment and most states have laws **mirroring** this **prohibition**. A person who is a victim of such discrimination can bring an action before either the federal court or his/her own state court, but normally people choose their own state court. Indeed, as we have seen, the state courts **handle** by far the majority of court cases and consequently have more contact with the US public than do the federal courts.

Federal courts may hear cases concerning state laws if the issue is whether the state law **violates** the federal Constitution. For example, let us imagine that a state law **forbids** the **slaughtering** of animals in urban areas. Under this law, a **neighborhood association** brings a case in the state court against Mr. X who has **sacrificed goats** in his **backyard**, as part of a **religious rite** or ceremony. When the state court applying state law **issues** an **order** requiring him/her to refrain from further animal sacrifices, the defendant may choose to **challenge** the state law before the federal courts, as **amounting to** an **infringement** of his/her constitutional right to exercise his/her religion.

How are the US courts organized?

There are fifty-one different legal systems in the United States and consequently there are also fifty-one different court systems:
* one federal court system; and
* fifty different state court systems.

  Federal Court System
  The federal courts operate on three different levels:
  * *US District Courts* The United States is **divided** into ninety-four federal judicial **districts, each** one having a federal district court. The district courts are the **first instance** federal trial courts and

have **jurisdiction** over cases and controversies for most matters coming under the **heading** of federal law. Areas coming within first instance jurisdiction of the federal district courts include:
- civil and criminal actions involving federal law;
- legal actions between citizens of different states where the amount exceeds $75,000;
- admiralty, maritime and bankruptcy cases.

- *US Courts of Appeal* **On top of** the ninety-four districts, there are twelve regional **circuits,** each one having a Court of Appeal. The twelve different Courts of Appeal have jurisdiction to **hear** appeals from the federal district courts coming within their jurisdiction.

- *US Supreme Court* Finally, the most important court in the federal system is the US Supreme Court. **Pursuant to** Article 3 of the Constitution, the US Supreme Court has the power to hear:
    - cases in law and **equity arising** under the Constitution, the laws of the United States, and **Treaties entered into under their authority**;
    - cases concerning ambassadors and other public ministers;
    - controversies to which the United States is a **party**;
    - controversies between two or more states; between a state and citizens of another state.

  In all cases affecting ambassadors, other public ministers and consuls, and those in which a state is a party, the Supreme Court has original jurisdiction. In all the other cases, the Supreme Court has **appellate jurisdiction**. The Supreme Court is made up of a Chief Justice and eight associate judges. However, the US Constitution does not actually state how many judges should serve on the Court. This power resides with the President, who may nominate judges acting with the consent of the Senate, i.e. with the approval of the majority of the Senate.

- Specialized federal courts also exist: such as the Bankruptcy courts with jurisdiction to enforce federal **bankruptcy** laws; the Court of Federal Claims responsible for hearing **lawsuits** brought against the United States government; the Court of International Trade to rule on disputes involving the imposition of **customs duties**; and the Tax Court ruling on questions related to the imposition of federal taxes.

The federal courts also have an important power referred to as **judicial review**. Under this power, established in the **celebrated case** of *Marbury v Madison*, the federal courts have the power to review the constitutionality of the acts of the other federal branches of government. The power of judicial review also applies to the acts of the state governments. Thus, the federal courts and ultimately the federal Supreme Court control all the other branches of power in the US political system, whether at federal or state level. This role gives the federal courts a considerable political character, as it is these courts that decide on issues such as the legality of the death penalty, abortion, euthanasia and same-sex marriage.

State Court System
As we have seen, the fifty states making up the union have jurisdiction over all areas not expressly given to the federal government by the federal constitution. Each state has its own specific system of courts but they all follow the same basic structure. As with the federal system, state courts are organized on three basic levels:

- *State trial courts* The **state trial courts**, i.e. the state courts of first instance, normally exist at two different levels, those hearing minor matters, often referred to as **municipal courts**, and those with the power to hear more important matters, often referred to as **superior** or **general jurisdiction courts**. Normally, for civil matters, the jurisdiction of the municipal courts will be fixed at a certain amount, for example $25,000, and claims above this amount must be brought in the superior jurisdiction trial courts. Similarly, as regards criminal matters, minor crimes, referred to as **misdemeanors**, will be heard in the lower jurisdiction courts and more serious crimes, called **felonies**, are heard before the courts of superior jurisdiction.
- *State Court of Appeal* If one of the participants to an action in a state trial court is unsatisfied with the result **handed down** by the trial court judge, the decision may be appealed to the state Court of Appeal. However, an acquittal in a criminal matter may not be the subject of an appeal by the **prosecution**, pursuant to the **double jeopardy guarantee set out** in the fifth amendment of the US Constitution. As federal law, this rule binds both state and federal courts.
- *State Supreme Courts* Finally, each state has its own Supreme Court **empowered to hear** appeals coming from the State's Court of Appeal. Decisions of the state Supreme Courts are final and may only be appealed to the federal Supreme Court where they concern a question of federal law. For example, if a party claims that his/her first amendment right to free speech under the US Constitution has been **violated** under state law, if unsuccessful before the state courts, (s)he may seek to appeal this matter to the US federal Supreme Court, as free speech is guaranteed under federal law.
- *Juvenile Courts, Probate Courts, Family Courts* Most states have specialized courts dealing with questions of family law, succession and youth crime.

VOCABULARY

Federation – *fédération*
Vast – *étendu/démesuré/vaste*

Stretch (to) – *s'étendre/s'étirer*
Subject to (to be) – (être) *soumis à/dépendant de*
Namely – *à savoir*
Federal – *fédéral*
Gay wedding – *mariage entre personnes de même sexe*
The same is not true – *il n'en est pas de même*
Moreover – *de plus/en outre*
Powerhouse – *"locomotive"/puissance (économique et financière)*
Rank (to) amongst – *se classer parmi*
Wealthy – *riche*
Wealthiest countries – *pays les plus riches*
To the contrary – *au contraire*
Poorer – *plus pauvre*
Despite – *en dépit de/malgré*
Nonetheless – *néanmoins*
Tort law – *responsabilité civile extracontractuelle*
Cases and controversies – *expression employée dans la Constitution des Etats-Unis, article III, section 2. Peut être traduit par « les affaires »*
Violation – *violation/atteinte*
Try (to) an offence – *juger une infraction*
Robbery – *vol*
Deal (to) with – *traiter*
Deposits of a bank – *réserves d'une banque*
Smuggle (to) – *faire de la contrebande/du trafic*
Swindle (to) – *escroquer*
Mirror (to) – *refléter*
Prohibition – *interdiction*
Handle (to) – *s'occuper de/traiter de*
Violate (to) – *violer*
Forbid (to) – *interdire*
Slaughter (to) – *abattre*
Neighborhood association – *association de voisinage*
Sacrifice (to) – *offrir en sacrifice/immoler*
Goat – *chèvre*
Backyard – *arrière-cour*
Religious rite – *rite religieux*
Issue (to) an order (a court) – *rendre/délivrer une ordonnance (de la cour)*
Challenge (to) – *contester*
Amount (to) to – *(ici) équivaloir à*
Infringement – *atteinte/violation*
Divided into – *divisé en*
District – *district*
Each – *chacun*
First instance – *première instance*
Jurisdiction – *juridiction/compétence*
Have (to) jurisdiction over – *avoir compétence pour/sur*
Heading (under the heading) – *titre (au titre de)*
On top of – *au-dessus de*

Circuit – *circuit/réseau*
Hear (to) (a case) – *auditionner/statuer sur*
Pursuant to – *conformément à*
Equity – *equity (ensemble de règles et principes juridiques destinés à compléter les règles de Common Law)*
Arise (to) – *provenir/survenir/apparaître (ici, découler de)*
Treaties entered into under their authority – *traités conclus conformément à la constitution ou aux lois adoptées conformément à celle-ci*
Party – *partie (ici : partie prenante/partie en cause)*
Appellate jurisdiction – *compétence d'appel*
Bankruptcy – *faillite*
Lawsuit – *action en justice (droit civil)*
Customs duties – *droits de douane*
Judicial review – *contrôle juridictionnel de légalité*
Celebrated case – *arrêt célèbre*
State trial court – *cour d'état de première instance*
Municipal court – *cour d'état statuant sur des affaires mineures*
Superior/general jurisdiction court – *cour d'état statuant sur les affaires plus importantes*
Misdemeanor – *infraction*
Felony – *crime*
Hand (to) down – *rendre (une décision/un arrêt)*
Prosecution – *accusation/Ministère Public*
Prosecutor – *procureur*
Double jeopardy guarantee – *règle non bis in idem*
Set (to) out – *établir*
Empowered to – *habilité à*
Power to hear – *pouvoir/compétence pour connaître d'une affaire*
Violate (to) – *violer/enfreindre*
Juvenile Court – *tribunal pour enfants et adolescents*
Probate Law – *droit des successions*
Probate Court – *tribunal spécialisé dans les affaires de succession*
Family Court – *tribunal dans les affaires familiales*

PART 1 – TEXT 2 – EXERCISES

1. Definitions

Write a sentence defining each of the following terms

   a)   Federation
   b)   Supremacy clause
   c)   Government of limited powers
   d)   Checks and balances
   e)   Double jeopardy
   f)   Bill of Rights
   g)   Regulatory competition

2. Sentences

Write sentences with the following pairs of words demonstrating the relationship between the words

- a)   State courts/federal courts
- b)   Appellate jurisdiction/federal Supreme Court
- c)   Checks and balances/concentration of power
- d)   Double jeopardy/appeal
- e)   Municipal courts/federal district court
- f)   Original jurisdiction/ambassador
- g)   Enumerated powers/federal government
- h)   Pursuant/legislative power
- i)   Municipal courts/state law
- j)   Cases and controversies/Supreme Court

3. Fill in the missing words

Fill in the missing words using the vocabulary in Text 2

- a)   In the United States, the federal government is said to be a government of _____ powers and thus can only use those powers given to it under the _____.
- b)   The political organization in the US is based on Montesquie's theory of the separation of powers and uses the system of _____ to prevent the _____ concentration of power in any one branch of government.
- c)   In 1789 the US Constitution came into _____ and created the _____ government.
- d)   Pursuant to the _____ rule, no one can be tried twice for the same _____.
- e)   At federal level there are also _____, such as the Court of Federal Claims, hearing lawsuits brought against the United States and the Court of International Trade, ruling on matters relating to _____.

4. Knowledge test

The following questions may be answered in writing or by way of discussion

- a)   Do you think the division of powers between the US federal government and the US states is an appropriate model for the European Union?
- b)   Why do you think Americans have such a strong identity, given the differences between the fifty US States?
- c)   What are the main principles governing the relationship between the US federal government and the US state governments?
- d)   In the United States, it is the US federal Supreme Court that has decided fundamental questions for American society, such as the legality of the death penalty, abortion and euthanasia. In your opinion, should such decisions be taken by the judicial branch or by the legislative branch of government?

PART 2 – QUICK LOOK GRAMMAR REVISION

Expressing the future tense in *time* clauses and *if* clauses

*1. Time **clauses***

A time clause occurs after words such as **before, after, when, as soon as**.

A future time clause arises where the speaker is talking about two events in the future, for example going to work and eating his dinner:

> *Before I go to work, I am going to/will eat my dinner*

> **Note:**
>
> As we can see, the simple present: *before **I go** to work* is used in future time clauses in place of *be going to* and *will*, which are however found later in the sentence *I am **going to** eat my dinner*.
>
> **The rule is that in time clauses introduced by before, after, when, as soon as, the simple present and not the future is used.**
>
> For example:
> – **As soon as** the rain **stops** pouring, I will go to the office – ***stop** is in the present tense, even though the event will occur in the future*.
> – I will give the message to my lawyer **when** I **see** him tomorrow- ***see** is in the present tense, even though the event will occur in the future*.
> – **After** I **eat** my lunch, I am going back to my office – ***eat** is in the present tense, even though the event will occur in the future*.

*2. If **clauses***

As is the case with time clauses, the present simple is used after **"if"**, even though the meaning of the sentence is in the future. **Going to** or **will** are not used.

For example:
> **If** it **snows** tomorrow I will go skiing – *the verb **to snow** is in the present tense, even though the event will occur in the future*.

PART 2 – GRAMMAR EXERCISES

1. Combining sentences

Combine the two sentences into one sentence, using the words in brackets

> (After)   *First*: I am going to finish my work.
> *Then*: I am going to go to bed.
> *After I finish my homework, I am going to go to bed;*
> or
> *I am going to go to bed after I finish my homework.*

a) (before)   *First*: I am going to write a letter to my client.
              Then: I am going to go for lunch.
b) (when)   *First*: I am going to Brussels next week.
              Then: I am going to eat some chips.
c) (before)   *First*: Jane will finish writing her letter.
              Then: She will have to meet her clients.
d) (after)   *First*: John will go home this evening.
              Then: He is going to surf the Internet.
e) (as soon as) *First*: The snow will stop.
              Then: John is going to go to the courthouse.
f) (when)   *First*: I will call Frank tomorrow.
              Then: I will ask him to attend the meeting.

2. Finish the sentences using the correct tense

Complete the following sentences......

a) I am going to eat lunch before I ......
b) As soon as the meeting finishes this evening, I ......
c) I am going to call my client after ......
d) When I am in London next month, I ......
e) I will call you as soon as I ......

3. Combining sentences

Combine the two sentences using an "if" clause

Condition: Maybe it will rain tomorrow.
Result: I am going to stay in the office.

If it rains tomorrow, I am going to stay in the office;

or

I am going to stay in the office if it rains tomorrow.

a) *Condition*: Maybe I will not receive a letter tomorrow.
   Result: I will call my client.
b) *Condition*: Maybe Frank will have enough time.
   Result: To finish his work tonight.
c) *Condition*: Maybe it will be sunny tomorrow.
   Result: I am going to take a day off.
d) *Condition*: Maybe I will study for my Bar exams.
   Result: I will probably pass.
e) *Condition*: Maybe I will not study tonight.
   Result: I probably will not pass my Bar exams.

4. Complete the sentences

Complete the sentences by using the words in brackets

>	Before Frank **(go)** *goes* to work, he **(brush)** *will brush* his hair.

a)	Before Tom (leave) _____ the office this evening, he (write) _____ a letter to his client.
b)	Before Rodger (go) _____ to the office, he (take) _____ a shower.
c)	As soon as Tom (wake up) _____ tomorrow morning, he (ring) _____ his client.
d)	After Tom (arrive) _____ home from work, he (drink) _____ a cup of tea.
e)	John (meet) _____ me at the airport when my plane (arrive) _____ tomorrow.
f)	When I (be) _____ in London next week, I (stay) at the Connaught.

PART 3 – AUDIO – LISTENING AND SPEAKING

Comprehension

Listen to the following conversation, make notes of all the relevant facts and then answer the questions below. If you have trouble understanding, follow the conversation while also reading the text.

Phone conversation between James and Xavier; James is ringing Xavier

Xavier: "Hello James, thank you for getting back to me so quickly."
James: "Not at all Xavier, it is my pleasure. I wanted to give you an update on where we are with Teeny Bopper Inc. and your client Arnaud Dupont. So we tried to get in contact with Teeny Bopper Inc. and see if it was possible to come to an amicable solution and have them pay Mr. Dupont the commission money he is owed."
Xavier: "Yes, indeed James, how did you get on?"
James: "Not that well unfortunately. They no longer seem to have an address in California at all; that is where they were established at the time your client entered into the Agency contract with them. So I looked to see whether they have an office in Delaware, given that they reincorporated in that state. They are listed as having a phone number in Delaware but you just get an answering machine and their Delaware address is just a PO Box. It seems it could be a shady[2] operation."
Xavier: "Were you actually able to get in touch with them at all?"
James: "I'm afraid not. I rang and left a number of messages on their voice mail but got no answer. I have also sent them a registered letter but I wouldn't hold my breath."
Xavier: "So what do you think we should do? I feel pretty bad just telling the client that we were unable to contact them and not offering anything else. "
James: "Oh I'm not for one second suggesting that we should leave it at that. They might just be playing dead hoping that we will leave them alone. Personally

---
[2]	Shady – semi-illegal.

I think we should start legal proceedings against them; however, the client has to be willing to pay the costs."

Xavier: "I don't know. Would it be a federal action before the federal courts? I mean that sounds very expensive."

James: "No, not at all, as I think Frank already mentioned, this matter comes within state jurisdiction. Thus, we would be bringing the action before the state courts. At present, Teeny Bopper Inc. owe €75,000 to Mr. Dupont as well as 9 months interest … let me see I did the arithmetic earlier, yes that is well over $100,000, interest included. Now according to the contract between Mr. Dupont and Teeny Bopper Inc., disputes between the parties are to be resolved before the Californian courts …, so we would have to bring the action before the Californian Superior Court. Of course there is the problem that Teeny Bopper Inc. no longer seems to have an actual presence in California."

Xavier: "I don't know, it is beginning to sound expensive. I'm not sure how much money the client has to devote to this."

James: "Well, if he does nothing he is going to be out over $100,000 dollars. That's not going to help him sleep at night!"

Xavier: "No, but you can't get blood out of a stone either[3]. Before starting to bring an action, is there any way we can investigate Teeny Bopper Inc. a little more and try to find out just how deep their pockets[4] are?"

James: "Yes, you are right Xavier; perhaps that would be the best thing. Also, while we are looking more closely at Teeny Bopper Inc. we can serve them with papers. I can do that for a set amount and it should not cost too much. That way we can get the ball rolling and who knows, once we serve them with a summons, perhaps they will want to talk."

Xavier: "OK, but before we do anything I will have to check with Mr. Dupont."

James: "Of course."

Xavier: "I'll try to ring him now and go over the matters you have raised. Could you perhaps send me an e-mail, confirming how much your fixed fee would be for starting an action against Teeny Bopper Inc. before the Californian courts? Once the client knows this, he would be in a better position to take a decision. Perhaps you might also send me a detailed record of your costs to date."

James: "That won't be a problem. However, it might take me until tomorrow to get that information to you. Why not hold off calling the client until I have sent you my costs and also inform you as to how much it will cost to start an action against Teeny Bopper Inc. I will also try to give you an estimate as to the costs for further investigating Teeny Bopper's financial position."

Xavier: "OK James. I will wait to hear from you."

---

[3]   You cannot get blood out of a stone – you cannot get money from someone if they have none.
[4]   Deep pockets – to have a lot of money.

PART 3 – AUDIO COMPREHENSION – EXERCISES

1. Comprehension

From the notes you have taken of the conversation, answer the following questions

a)   Why is James ringing Xavier back?
b)   Was James able to get in touch with Teeny Bopper Inc.?
c)   When will James next contact Xavier?
d)   Have they decided to sue Teeny Bopper Inc.?
e)   What is the applicable jurisdiction for the resolution of disputes between Teeny Bopper Inc. and Arnaud Dupont?
f)   What information does James have to supply Xavier with?

2. Speaking practice

In the following series of conversation couplets, develop suitable responses to the questions asked

a)   Xavier: "How much would it cost to bring an action against Teeny Bopper Inc.?"
     James: "_____."
b)   Xavier: "Do you expect to be coming to Paris anytime soon? That way you could meet the client."
     James: "_____."
c)   Xavier: "Under the terms of the contract, are disputes to be solved by arbitration or before the ordinary courts?"
     James: "_____"
d)   Xavier: "How long does an action normally take before the Californian courts?"
     James: "_____."
e)   Xavier: "Could you send me a summary of your costs to date?"
     James: "_____"
f)   Xavier: "Is it a question that is resolved by the state courts or the federal courts?"
     James: "_____."
g)   Xavier: "What is the time difference between Paris and California?"
     James: "_____."
h)   Xavier: "Do you think I should advise Mr. Dupont to bring an action against Teeny Bopper Inc.?"
     James: "_____"
i)   Xavier: "Sorry, I have a very important call on another line, would you mind if I called you back in ten minutes?"
     James: "_____."
j)   Xavier: "So is Teeny Bopper Inc. willing to pay my client the Commission money they owe him?"
     James: "_____."

3. Speaking practice continued ......

Create five other conversation couplets, using in each couplet at least one word from the vocabulary found in Part 1, Text 1 and Text 2

4. Speaking practice continued ......

Listen to the suggested replies and repeat ...

a) Xavier: "How much would it cost to bring an action against Teeny Bopper Inc.?"
   James: "Well as you know that depends on a lot of things; it is difficult to give an exact figure."

b) Xavier: "Do you expect to be coming to Paris anytime soon? That way you could meet the client."
   James: "Yes, I will be in France on another matter in two months time. It would be nice to meet with you and your client if you were free."

c) Xavier: "Under the terms of the contract, are disputes to be solved by arbitration or before the ordinary courts?"
   James: "Yes, any disputes are to be heard by a three-man arbitration panel in Paris, under the ICC[5] rules."

d) Xavier: "How long does an action normally take before the Californian courts?"
   James: "It's difficult to say Xavier, but I would hope to have a result inside six months."

e) Xavier: "Could you send me a summary of your costs to date?"
   James: "Sure, I'll get up on the screen right now[6] and mail[7] it to you immediately."

f) Xavier: "Is it a question that is resolved by the state courts or the federal courts?"
   James: "Contract questions come within the jurisdiction of the states and not the federal power."

g) Xavier: "What is the time difference between Paris and California?"
   James: "I don't know; it is about ten in the morning here, what time is it there?"

h) Xavier: "Do you think I should advise Mr. Dupont to bring an action against Teeny Bopper Inc.?"
   James: "Fundamentally it is Mr. Dupont's decision but I don't think he will get his money any other way."

i) Xavier: "Sorry, I have a very important call on another line, would you mind if I called you back in ten minutes?"
   James: "No problem Xavier, I'll be at this number for the rest of the morning, take your time."

j) Xavier: "So is Teeny Bopper Inc. willing to pay my client the commission money they owe him?"

---

[5] International Chamber of Commerce.
[6] Get it up on my screen – open the file on my computer.
[7] Mail it to you – it is understood that James will e-mail it to Xavier.

James: "To be honest Xavier, it does not look like it. They are on the verge of bankruptcy."

5. Associated questions

Discuss the following questions

a)   What are the advantages of resolving a contractual dispute by way of arbitration, as opposed to using the court system?

b)   How long does it take to bring a civil law action like that between Arnaud Dupont and Teeny Bopper Inc. before your national courts?

c)   What would you advise Arnaud Dupont to do in the present situation? Are there any steps he could have taken to avoid this problem?

d)   Practice a conversation whereby you try to have James reduce the legal fees he is going to charge. What words and expressions would you use?

PART 4 – TRANSLATION EXERCISES

When carrying out the translations it is not necessary to translate directly word for word; rather the emphasis should be on translating the sense of the text. Language is not directly interchangeable and so direct translations do not always convey the meaning in the text.

Translate the following texts from English to French

A. The jurisdiction of the Supreme Court

The court rules in first instance in only a few rare cases: for example, in cases involving one of the States of the Union, a foreign State or a foreign diplomat. In most matters, the Court has appellate jurisdiction and its decisions may not be appealed. It is only interested in cases involving important questions of law and it chooses from amongst the thousands of appeals presented to it every year, only those cases it actually wishes to hear. Its rulings on the Constitution are final and "the Constitution is what the Supreme Court says it is". Thus, it is the Supreme Court that defines the scope of citizens' fundamental rights, sometimes broadly, sometimes narrowly, depending on the standards applicable at the time.

B. The jurisdiction of the state courts

Nearly all cases concerning state civil law or criminal law begin before the state jurisdictions. Indeed, the state courts have jurisdiction over all questions concerning divorce, child custody, real estate and matters concerning minors; and they rule on most criminal trials, actions involving contract law, road and traffic offenses and personal injury claims. Moreover, specialized courts judge certain types of litigation, for example there is a court dealing only with questions relating to succession law.

C. US Circuit Courts of Appeal

There are twelve Courts of Appeal. Every state and district is brought together in one of these twelve circuits. Each Appeal Court is responsible for hearing appeals from the decisions of the District Courts coming within its circuit. Appeal lies from decisions of the Courts of Appeal to the federal Supreme Court[8]. There is also a relatively new court called the US Court of Appeal for the Federal Circuit. This court is responsible for civil law appeals being brought against the US government, as well as appeals concerning patent law matters or international business law questions.

Translate the following texts from French to English

A. Les juridictions fédérales et fédérées

Aux États-Unis, il y a deux niveaux de juridictions indépendantes, au plan fédéral et au niveau des états. On trouve des juridictions de première instance, des juridictions intermédiaires d'appel et des juridictions d'appel de dernier recours, tant au niveau fédéral qu'à celui des états. Aux deux niveaux, il existe aussi des juridictions spécialisées compétentes pour certains sujets particuliers. Tout comme en France pour la Cour de cassation, il n'est pas possible de saisir directement la Cour suprême aux États-Unis : normalement la plus haute instance judiciaire du pays ne peut intervenir qu'en dernier recours, lorsqu'un citoyen estime que ses droits constitutionnels ont été bafoués et que les procédures d'appel ont échoué.

B. La Cour Suprême

La Cour Suprême des Etats-Unis est la plus haute institution du système judiciaire fédéral. Elle est composée de huit juges associés et d'un juge président appelé le *Chief Justice*. Elle ne peut examiner que les questions de droit. La Cour Suprême peut examiner les décisions des Circuit Courts d'appel fédérales (1) soit par une demande, formulée par une des parties, pour obtenir un *writ of certiorari*, par laquelle la Cour Suprême demande à une cour de niveau inférieur de lui transmettre l'affaire, (2) soit par voie d'appel impératif, ce qui signifie que la Cour Suprême est dans l'obligation d'examiner l'appel. Elle peut également examiner les jugements rendus en dernier recours par la plus haute juridiction d'un état, si la validité constitutionnelle/la constitutionnalité d'une loi est contestée.

C. Le Président et le système des "checks and balances"

En réalité, aux Etats Unis on assiste davantage à un savant dosage des pouvoirs qu'à une séparation rigide. Ainsi, chaque organe dispose, vis-à-vis des autres organes, de moyens d'action puissants permettant un équilibre des pouvoirs. C'est le système des « poids et contrepoids » qui assure un équilibre entre les pouvoirs. Le président a en charge les relations diplomatiques et représente son pays sur la scène internationale. Il nomme les ambassadeurs, les consuls, il négocie et signe les traités internationaux, mais avec l'aval du Sénat. Il est le commandant en chef des forces armées. Il détermine la politique militaire des

---

[8] If it is possible to appeal a case from Court X to Court Y, in legal English it is said the appeal *lies from* Court X to Court Y.

États-Unis. Il peut décider d'engager les forces américaines à l'étranger sans avoir recours à une déclaration de guerre.

PART 5 – ADVANCED READING

Federal power versus state power in the USA

As we have seen, there are two separate sources of power in the USA. Originally, there were thirteen independent territories, which came together to fight for their independence from the United Kingdom. After the War of Independence, the thirteen former colonies decided to create a union between them and to collectively refer to themselves as the United States of America. The US Constitution sets out the rules governing the relationship between the states and the federal power. The most important provision of the Constitution in this regard is Article 6, which provides:

> *"This Constitution, and the Laws of the United States which shall be made in Pursuance thereof; and all Treaties made, or which shall be made, under the Authority of the United States, <u>shall be the supreme Law of the Land</u>; and the Judges <u>in every State</u> shall be bound thereby, <u>Laws of any State to the Contrary notwithstanding</u>"*.

This is known as the Supremacy Clause and clearly places federal law above state law. However, as if attempting to redress this imbalance, the Tenth Amendment provides: "The powers not delegated to the United States by the Constitution, nor prohibited by it to the States, *are reserved to the States* (…)". It was hoped by the drafters of the Constitution that these two clauses would keep an even balance between state and federal power. However, this did not occur and instead, since its adoption, the Constitution has been witness to the creation of an ever larger and more powerful federal state. This partly results from the interpretation given by the Supreme Court to the *necessary and proper clause* set out in article 1 of the Constitution. Article 1(8) lists the powers of Congress as including *inter alia*, the power to:
- lay and collect taxes;
- regulate commerce with foreign nations;
- establish uniform laws on the subject of bankruptcies throughout the United States;
- coin money and fix the standard of weights and measures;
- constitute tribunals inferior to the Supreme Court;
- declare war;
- raise and support armies;
- provide and maintain a navy; and finally
- make all laws which shall be *necessary and proper* for the execution of the foregoing powers.

As we have already seen, the federal government was envisaged by the states as being a government of enumerated powers, restricted to those areas listed in the Constitution. However, the last clause of article 1(8) provides for a secondary *indirect* power, namely the power to do anything that is *necessary and proper* for carrying out its other powers. Thus, for example, if Congress has the duty to build roads, should it also have the power to make compulsory purchases of land, so as to be able to fulfill its road-building duty? This begs the question as to what is considered *necessary and proper* and it has fallen to the federal Supreme Court to define the *term*. It has chosen to do so in a broad manner, thereby increasing federal power, perhaps far beyond anything envisaged by the drafters of the Constitution.

Chapter six

CONSTITUTIONAL LAW IN
THE UNITED STATES

PART 1 – TEXT 1 – INFORMATION

Constitutional law in the United States

When talking of constitutional law in the United States, it is necessary to speak of both *state* constitutional law and *federal* constitutional law, as the federal government and each of the fifty states all have constitutions. The federal Constitution is a **relatively** short and simple document. **Pursuant to** its **terms**, power in the US is organized under Montesquieu's theory of the **separation of powers**. **Consequently**, the first three articles of the federal Constitution establish the powers of the **legislative**, **executive** and **judicial** branches of federal power. Legislative power is **vested in** the Houses of Congress, **made up of** the **House of Representatives** and the Senate (Article 1). Executive power is vested in the President (Article 2) and judicial power in the Supreme Court and the other inferior federal courts **established** by Congress (Article 3).

The federal Supreme Court

The Supreme Court is comprised of one Chief Justice and eight Associate Justices. They are appointed for life and may only be removed by way of **impeachment proceedings**. One of the most important powers of the federal Supreme Court is its power to rule on the constitutionality of acts adopted by both the federal and state governments. This is referred to as its power of **judicial review**. When applying the power of judicial review, the justices of the Supreme Court have different approaches, which greatly influence the conclusions they **reach**. For example, some judges apply an **instrumentalist** approach to constitutional interpretation. For instrumentalist judges, the Constitution is a living, changeable document, which should be interpreted to reflect changes in society. This is sometimes referred to as **judicial activism** and describes the process whereby Supreme Court justices effectively create law by way of the broad interpretation that they choose to give to the Constitution. There are also Supreme Court justices who do not share this view and consider the Constitution to be a **fixed document** that should not be modified in any way despite changes in society. These justices are called **originalists**[1] and their originalist approach to interpreting the Constitution is popular amongst more conservative judges.

---

[1] Also referred to as strict constructionists.

Civil liberties in the United States

Civil liberties or human rights in the United States are **set out** in the Bill of Rights, which is the collective name given to the first ten amendments to the Constitution. The Bill of Rights was adopted on December 15, 1791 and **guarantees** the freedoms and rights enjoyed by US citizens. The Bill of Rights is unique if one considers that since 1791, US citizens have benefitted from civil rights still not enjoyed in many countries in the world today. Below is a list of the most important rights.

- *First Amendment* Freedom of **speech**, freedom of **assembly**, freedom of the press, freedom of religious practice and freedom from **state imposed** religion.
- *Second Amendment* The right to **bear arms**.
- *Fourth Amendment* Freedom from **warrantless searches**.
- *Fifth Amendment* Where a defendant is being prosecuted for a serious criminal offence by the federal authorities, (s)he has the right to a hearing allowing for a preliminary review by *grand jury* of the state's evidence. This ensures that the state is justified in bringing the accused to trial and the hearing is referred to as a **grand jury hearing**. The Fifth Amendment also establishes the:
    - **double jeopardy rule,** i.e. no one can be tried twice for the same offence;
    - **self incrimination rule,** i.e. the accused cannot be required to give evidence against him/herself and consequently has the right to remain silent when being interrogated by the police or the court; and
    - right to **just compensation** for property **confiscated** by the state.
- *Sixth Amendment* The right to a **speedy trial**.
- *Eight Amendment* Freedom from **cruel and unusual punishment**.

Initially the Bill of Rights was only applied to the federal government but now most of the rights contained therein are also applied to the individual state governments, in accordance with the Supreme Court's interpretation of the 14th amendment's due process **clause**. The due process clause requires that citizen's **due process rights** be respected by the states and consequently the rights in the Bill of Rights, coming within the notion of due process, apply not only to the federal government but also to the state governments.

VOCABULARY

Relatively – *relativement*
Pursuant to – *conformément à/en vertu de*
Term – *terme/clause*
Separation of powers – *séparation des pouvoirs*
Consequently – *en conséquence*
Legislative – *législatif*
Legislature – *pouvoir/corps législatif*

Executive – *exécutif*

Judicial – *judiciaire*

Judiciary – *pouvoir/organisation judiciaire*

Vested (to be) in – *investir (quelqu'un de quelque chose)/assigner (quelque chose à quelqu'un) /être dévolu à/être attribué à/conférer* à

Made (to be) up of – *être composé de*

House of Representatives – *Chambre des Représentants*

Establish (to) – *établir/créer/instaurer*

Impeachment proceeding – *procédure dite d'"impeachment" (mise en accusation en vue d'une destitution)*

Judicial review – *contrôle juridictionnel de légalité (dans le texte, de constitutionnalité)*

Reach (to) a decision/conclusion – *parvenir à/rendre une décision*

Instrumentalist – *méthode d'interprétation qualifiée de pragmatique ou de dynamique en Europe. On parle de courant réaliste aux Etats-Unis (à la lumière des conditions de vie actuelles), par opposition au courant légicentriste*

Judicial activism – *activisme judiciaire ou « pouvoir des juges » ou « gouvernement des juges » (le juge n'est pas seulement la bouche de la loi, il est aussi de facto créateur de droit)*

Fixed document – *document figé (d'où une interprétation stricte de la lettre)*

Originalist – *méthode d'interprétation stricte et littérale (s'inscrit dans le courant légicentriste)*

Civil liberties – *libertés civiles*

Set (to) out – *exposer/définer*

Guarantee (to) – *garantir/assurer*

Freedom of speech – *liberté d'expression*

Freedom of assembly – *liberté de réunion*

State imposed religion – *liberté de ne pas se voir imposer une religion officielle par un Etat*

Bear (to) an arm – *porter une arme*

Warrant – *mandat*

Warrantless searches – *perquisitions non motivées par un mandat*

Grand jury hearing – *audition devant un Grand Jury (le Grand Jury est réuni pour déterminer s'il y a ou non des charges suffisantes qui justifient l'ouverture d'une procédure judiciaire pénale et une mise en examen)*

Double jeopardy rule – *règle de non bis in idem*

Self-incrimination rule – *droit au silence (principe selon lequel nul ne peut être contraint à témoigner contre lui-même)*

Just compensation – *indemnisation juste et équitable en cas d'expropriation*

Confiscate (to) – *confisquer/exproprier*

Speedy trial – *procès rapide (célérité de la procédure)*

Cruel and unusual punishment – *peine cruelle ou inhabituelle*

Clause – *clause/disposition*

Due process right – *droit à une procédure régulière afin d'assurer une application régulière de la loi (principe selon lequel le gouvernement fédéral mais aussi d'un Etat doit respecter l'intégralité des droits dont une personne bénéficie en vertu de la loi)*

PART 1 – TEXT 1 – EXERCISES

1. Vocabulary test

Fill in the missing words using the vocabulary in Text 1

a) The Fourth Amendment protects US _____ from _____ searches.
b) Under the _____ clause of the Fifth _____, US citizens must be compensated for property that is confiscated by the state.
c) A Supreme Court justice is appointed for life and can only be _____ by way of _____ proceedings.
d) The Bill of Rights sets out citizens' _____ liberties in the first _____ amendments of the US Constitution.
e) Pursuant to the _____ jeopardy _____ of the Fifth Amendment, no citizen can be _____ twice for the same offence.
f) The _____ to _____ arms is established by the Second Amendment.
g) _____ justices can be classified as originalists or as _____, depending on the manner in which they consider the US Constitution ought to be interpreted.
h) A right to a _____ hearing exists in the case of serious _____, to ensure that there is sufficient evidence against the accused, justifying his being sent for trial.
i) _____ to Montesquieu's theory of the separation of power, power is divided between the _____, _____ and _____ branches.

2. Vocabulary test

Write sentences with the following pairs of words. Your sentence should demonstrate your knowledge of the relationship between the words

a) Double jeopardy/accused
b) Freedom of speech/First Amendment
c) Civil liberties/1791
d) Speedy trial/Bill of Rights
e) Confiscate/compensation
f) Instrumentalist/judicial activism

3. Knowledge test

Each of the following statements is false; do you know why? Write a sentence stating why it is false

a) There is only one Constitution in the United States governing both federal and state activities.
b) The Bill of Rights only applies to the federal government.
c) In the United States there is a strict separation of power between the legislative, executive and judicial branches of federal government.
d) The double jeopardy clause of the Fifth Amendment means that an accused has the right to a grand jury hearing before being sent for trial.
e) The originalist justices in the Supreme Court believe that the Constitution is a living document that should change with the times.

f)   The President has the power to nominate and remove Supreme Court justices with the consent of the Senate.

PART 1 – TEXT 2 – MORE INFORMATION

The nature of Constitutional law in the United States

When talking of constitutional law in the United States, it is necessary to speak both of *state* constitutional law, as each of the fifty states has its own constitution, and of *federal* constitutional law **arising out of** the federal constitution adopted in 1787. It is proposed to **dedicate** this chapter to a discussion of US *federal* constitutional law. The US Constitution not only **sets out** the role of the different **branches of power** at federal level, **demarcating** the relationship between federal and state powers, it also defines the civil rights of US citizens. These rights are contained in the Bill of Rights, as set out in the first ten Amendments to the Constitution adopted in 1791.

US Constitutional law and the Supreme Court

Pursuant to article 3 of the Constitution, the Supreme Court is **empowered** to **rule** on all **cases and controversies** arising under the Constitution. It is this power to **interpret** the sometimes **vague** and general provisions of the Constitution that has **allowed** the Supreme Court through its decisions, to **define** the nature and character of the United States today. **In so doing,** it has become one of the **most powerful** courts in the world. Primarily this results from the US Supreme Court's power of **judicial review, whereby** it can review acts of the other branches of the federal and state governments to **ensure** that they respect the provisions of the federal Constitution. If they do not, the Supreme Court can declare their actions to be unconstitutional and thus illegal. Nowhere does the US Constitution expressly provide for the US federal courts to have the power of judicial review; **rather** this power was **implied** to exist by the Supreme Court itself. The Supreme Court came to this conclusion by virtue of its interpretation of the Constitution, namely:

* article 6, the supremacy clause; and
* article 3, the cases and controversies clause.

The Supreme Court considers that if federal law is supreme under article 6 of the Constitution and article 3 gives the Supreme Court the right to apply federal law, then the Court has the right to ensure that acts of both the federal and state branches of power **come within** the provisions of federal law, as established by the Constitution. The power of judicial review is **extremely** important given that the Supreme Court's interpretation of the Constitution is **binding** on the legislative, executive and lower judicial branches of the federal government and the legislative, executive and judicial branches of the state governments. Consequently, in the United States, it is the Supreme Court and not the legislative power that ultimately decides on the legality of issues such as the death penalty, euthanasia or abortion, insofar as it rules on the constitutionality of the laws adopted in these areas. The Supreme Court's power of judicial review as regards controlling the legality of the acts of the federal branches of government was established in the case of *Marbury v Madison*. In the later decision of *Fletcher v Peck*, the Supreme Court ruled that it also had the power to review the constitutionality of the acts of the state branches of governments.

However, the Supreme Court **tends** to use its power **frugally** and will, for example, only rule on the constitutionality of a law, if the case cannot be resolved in any other way. Indeed, the Court has developed a number of rules to allow it to avoid ruling on such issues, unless it is truly necessary.

- *The Ripeness Doctrine* Pursuant to the Ripeness Doctrine, the Supreme Court will not decide on an issue **in advance, i.e.,** it will not rule on a matter in advance of, or prior to, the problem actually materializing. Consequently, even if a law adopted by Congress is clearly unconstitutional, the Supreme Court will not rule on the issue of its constitutionality until it has actually been applied in an unconstitutional way. It is said that the Supreme Court will not **anticipate** a problem.
- *Cases and controversies clause* Article 3 of the Constitution empowers the federal courts to hear cases and controversies arising under the Constitution. Thus, in order to be able to bring a case before the Supreme Court, the case must be based on a specific problem arising under the Constitution and there must be the possibility of **redress**, i.e. the possibility of a solution. The Court will not hear **spurious claims**. The Supreme Court first considered the scope of the cases and controversies clause when President George Washington **forwarded** to the **Supreme Court** a request asking for its **guidance** as to how he might maintain a policy of neutrality during a war between France and the United Kingdom, in a way that would be consistent with the provisions of the Constitution. The Court ruled that it was not **authorized** to help the President, as the Constitution only permitted the Court to interpret the Constitution in the context of a real *case or controversy* and that consequently it had no power to **render** an advisory opinion as to how government policy could be developed to respect the provisions of the Constitution. In the opinion of the Court, it could only judge whether the Constitution had been respected once the President had actually adopted government policy. Another aspect of the cases and controversies clause is known as the standing or *locus standi* requirement. Under this principle, people wishing to bring an **action** before the courts must show that they have personally suffered the *injury* that is the subject of the action being brought before the court. Consequently, one cannot bring an action if it is founded on injuries suffered by others. For example, if the rights of another are being infringed, one cannot bring an action on their behalf, unless that person is their **guardian**. It is necessary that the injured party bring the action in their own name.
- *Mootness Doctrine* An issue is **moot** when the judgment of the case will have no effect on the resolution of the problem, for example, an attempt to **prosecute** someone for a crime, if that person is already dead.

- *Political questions* If the question before the Supreme Court is **fundamentally** a political issue rather than a legal one, the Court will consider that it is **prohibited** from hearing the **affair**. In this regard, the court has shown an **unwillingness** to **get involved** in issues that are primarily political rather than legal. However, even if the matter is primarily political, where the underlying question is fundamentally a legal one, the Court will not hesitate to rule on the affair, even though such a **ruling** may have important political implications. For example, the Supreme Court's decision on the legitimacy of the Florida State vote during the 2000 Presidential election; in this case, the decision of the court **effectively handed** the presidential victory to George Bush Jr.

To a certain extent it could be said that the:
- Ripeness Doctrine requires that the problem actually exist; it is not enough to show that it is going to exist;
- cases and controversies clause and standing requirement necessitate that the matter be a real issue presenting a problem under the Constitution and that the plaintiff has personally suffered the injury that is the subject of the action;
- Mootness Doctrine requires that the problem on which the action is based continue to exist and be relevant at the moment the action is being brought.

The Supreme Court is made up of one Chief Justice and eight Associate Justices. The President, whose choice must then be approved by the Senate, appoints Justices. They are appointed for life and may only be removed by impeachment proceedings before the Senate. Much of the Supreme Court's power **derives** from the willingness of some of its judges to interpret the Constitution in a **dynamic** way. This is called the **instrumentalist** approach to constitutional interpretation. Such judges consider the Constitution to be a living, changeable document that should be interpreted to reflect changes in society. Instrumentalism allows judges to interpret the Constitution broadly, **going beyond** its literal meaning. Supreme Court justices are assisted in this approach by the fact that the US Constitution is drafted in a very general way. For example, the Constitution prohibits cruel and unusual punishment; this notion is clearly very vague. It is then the work of the Supreme Court to decide whether forms of punishment such as the death penalty can be thought to amount to cruel and unusual punishment. Ultimately this is a subjective evaluation. Indeed, it could be said that the Court develops new laws deriving not from what the Constitution actually **states**, but from what the judge believes it to state, in the context of either the judge's values or what the judge supposes to be the values in society. For example, although the application of the death penalty in a case of robbery might not have been cruel and unusual punishment in 1791, it is probable that it would be considered an extreme form of punishment today. Thus, the judges that interpret its terms actually define the scope of the Constitution, and some judges do this more broadly than others. This willingness to effectively create law by interpreting the Constitution broadly or dynamically is sometimes referred to as **judicial activism**. There are however other Supreme Court justices who do not share the view of the instrumentalists and they believe the Constitution to be a **fixed** document that should be interpreted literally, not taking changes in society into account. These justices are called **originalists**, and the *originalist* approach to interpreting the Constitution is popular amongst more conservative judges. Many judges come somewhere between these two extremes.

Civil liberties in the United States

Civil liberties in the United States are set out in the Bill of Rights, which is the collective name given to the first ten amendments to the Constitution. The Bill of Rights was adopted on December 15, 1791 and **guarantees** the freedoms and rights enjoyed by US citizens or people residing on US territory. From the list below we can see that many important rights are contained in the Bill of Rights.

- *First Amendment* Freedom of **speech**, freedom of **assembly**, **freedom of the press, freedom of religion** and **freedom from state-imposed religion**.
- *Second Amendment* The right to **bear arms**.
- *Fourth Amendment* Freedom from **warrantless searches**.
- *Fifth Amendment* The right to a **grand jury hearing**. Pursuant to this right, if the federal authorities are prosecuting the defendant for a serious criminal offence, he/she has the right to a pre-hearing, called a grand jury hearing, allowing for a preliminary review by a jury of the state's evidence against the defendant. This is to ensure that the state is justified in bringing the accused to trial. The Fifth Amendment also establishes the:
  - Right not to be tried twice for the same offence, referred to as the **double jeopardy rule**.
  - **Self-incrimination rule,** i.e. a person cannot be required to give evidence against himself/herself; consequently an accused has the right to remain silent when questioned by the police or the courts.
  - Right to **just compensation**, i.e. the right to receive money from the state if the latter deems it necessary to **confiscate** the property of an individual for the public good. For example, to acquire a person's land in order to build a public road.
- *Sixth Amendment* The right to a **speedy public trial** with an **impartial jury** for criminal offences.
- *Eight Amendment* The right to **bail** and the right not to have imposed cruel and unusual punishment.

The Bill of Rights initially only applied to the federal government and was not binding on the individual states, which were free to treat their citizens in accordance with their own rules. In fact, the adoption of the Bill of Rights in 1791 probably represented an **attempt** by the original thirteen states to protect their citizens from an overreaching federal power. They probably never intended the Bill of Rights to control the relationship between the state governments and their citizens. Indeed, this goes some way to explaining the vast scope of the rights set out in the Bill of Rights. However, in the **aftermath** of the American Civil War, the Fourteenth Amendment introduced a constitutional guarantee specifically requiring the fifty US states to respect the **due process rights** of their citizens. This is referred to as the *due process clause* and is a universal guarantee that requires states to generally respect the rights of their citizens and treat them fairly and equitably. Relying on the due process clause of the Fourteenth Amendment, the Supreme Court subsequently began to apply the Bill of Rights to the states. One of the first cases in which this was done was *Gitlow v New York*. In this case the Supreme Court held that the right of freedom of expression, as set out in the First Amendment, prevented the State of New York from **denying** its citizens this right. In the opinion of the Supreme Court, the due process guarantee of the 14th Amendment required states to respect those rights in the Bill of Rights coming within the more general notion of due process and freedom of expression was considered to be one such right. The process of applying the rights set out in the Bill of Rights to the individual states, under the heading of the due process guarantee, is referred to as the **theory of selective incorporation**. Under this theory, if a right set out in the Bill of Rights comes within the notion of due process, then that right will apply to the states and not just the federal government. In this way, most of the Bill of Rights now also applies to the state governments.

In interpreting the sometimes vague terms of the US Constitution, the Supreme Court has in many ways become the referee of American society. For example, in the famous case of *Roe v Wade*, the Supreme Court recognized the legality of state abortion laws effectively legalizing abortion in the United States. In other countries this is a decision that would be taken by the legislative power. Indeed, the influence of the US Supreme Court cannot be underestimated and in many ways the Court plays a role similar to that of the *Guardians* in Plato's *Ideal Republic*. However, despite its wide powers, important political power is also vested in the legislative and executive branches of US federal government and the state governments, ensuring that the United States continues to enjoy a balanced and equitable separation of powers.

VOCABULARY

Arise (to) out of – *résulter de/être la conséquence de/découler de*
Dedicate (to) – *consacrer*
Set out (to) – *exposer/définir*
Branch (of power) – *branche*
Demarcate (to) – *démarquer/délimiter*
Pursuant to – *conformément à/en vertu de*
Empowered (to be) to rule – *être habilité à décider/statuer*
Cases and controversies – *expression employée dans la Constitution des Etats-Unis, article III, section 2. Peut être traduit par « les affaires »*
Interpret (to) – *interpréter*
Vague – *vague/imprécis*
Allow (to) – *permettre*
Define (to) – *définir*
In so doing – *ainsi*

One of the most powerful – *l'un des plus puissants*
Judicial review – *contrôle juridictionnel de légalité (ici de constitutionnalité)*
Whereby – *par lequel/au moyen duquel*
Ensure (to) – *s'assurer/garantir*
Rather – *mais/plutôt/davantage*
Implied (to be) – *être sous-entendu*
Come (to) within – *entrer dans/s'inscrire dans le cadre de*
Extremely – *extrêmement*
Binding – *contraignant*
Tend (to) to – *avoir tendance à*
Frugally – *avec prudence/parcimonie*
In advance – *à l'avance*
I.e. – *c'est-à-dire*
Anticipate (to) – *anticiper*
Redress – *réparation*
Spurious – *fallacieux/faux*
Forward (to) something (to the Court) – *envoyer/soumettre/transmettre (quelque chose à la Cour)*
Request for guidance – *demande d'avis/de conseil*
Authorize (to) – *autoriser*
Render (to) – *rendre/fournir*
Bring (to) an action – *intenter une action*
Guardian – *tuteur*
Moot (to) – *discutable/sans fondement*
Prosecute (to) – *poursuivre (en justice)*
Fundamentally – *fondamentalement/essentiellement*
Prohibited (to be) from – *être interdit légalement*
Affair – *affaire/cas*
Unwillingness – *réticence*
Involved (to get) – *être impliqué*
Ruling/decision – *décision/arrêt*
Effectively – *effectivement/efficacement*
Hand (to) something to someone – *donner/offrir/livrer/apporter quelque chose à quelqu'un*
Derive (to) from – *résulter de/découler de*
Dynamic – *dynamique (ici, adjectif qualifiant la méthode interprétative)*
Instrumentalist – *méthode d'interprétation qualifiée de pragmatique ou de dynamique en Europe. On parle de courant réaliste aux Etats-Unis (à la lumière des conditions de vie actuelles), par opposition au courant légicentriste*
Going beyond – *aller au-delà de*
State (to) – *affirmer*
Judicial activism – *activisme judiciaire ou « pouvoir des juges » ou « gouvernement des juges » (le juge n'est pas seulement la bouche de la loi, il est aussi de facto créateur de droit)*
Fixed document – *document figé (d'où une interprétation stricte de la lettre)*
Originalist – *juge qui donne de la constitution une interprétation stricte et littérale*
Civil liberties – *libertés civiles*

Guarantee (to) – *garantir/assurer*
Freedom of speech – *liberté d'expression*
Freedom of assembly – *liberté de réunion*
Freedom of the press – *liberté de la presse*
Freedom of religion – *libre exercice de la religion de son choix*
Freedom from state imposed religion (the establishment clause) – *liberté de ne pas se voir imposer une religion officielle imposée par un Etat*
Bear (to) an arm – *porter une arme*
Warrant – *mandat*
Warrantless search – *perquisition non motivée par un mandat*
Grand jury hearing – *audition devant un Grand Jury (le Grand Jury est réuni pour déterminer s'il y a ou non des charges suffisantes qui justifient l'ouverture d'une procédure judiciaire pénale)*
Double jeopardy rule – *règle de* non bis in idem
Self-incrimination rule – *droit au silence (principe selon lequel nul ne peut être contraint à témoigner contre lui-même)*
Just compensation – *indemnisation juste et équitable en cas d'expropriation*
Confiscate (to) – *confisquer/récupérer/exproprier*
Speedy public trial – *procès rapide et public (célérité et publicité du procès)*
Impartial jury – *jury impartial*
Bail – *caution*
Attempt – *tentative*
In the aftermath of – *à la suite de*
Due process right – *droit à une procédure régulière afin d'assurer une application régulière de la loi (principe selon lequel le gouvernement fédéral mais aussi d'un Etat doit respecter l'intégralité des droits dont une personne bénéficie en vertu de la loi)*
Deny (to) – *refuser*
Theory of selective incorporation – *théorie de l'incorporation sélective*

PART 1 – TEXT 2 – EXERCISES

1. Definitions

Write a sentence defining each of the following terms – one sentence per term

a)   Judicial activism
b)   Double jeopardy
c)   Bail
d)   Mootness doctrine
e)   Dynamic interpretation
f)   Judicial review
g)   Warrant

2. Sentences

Write sentences with the following pairs of words. Your sentence should demonstrate your knowledge of the relationship between the words

a)   Standing/plaintiff

b)   Just compensation/property
c)   Freedom of speech/First Amendment
d)   Establishment clause/religion
e)   Political questions/Supreme Court
f)   Grand jury hearing/serious offences
g)   Arms/Second Amendment
h)   Bill of Rights/civil liberties
i)   Speedy trial/accused
j)   Bail/Bill of Rights

3. Fill in the missing words

Using the vocabulary in Text 2, fill in the missing words

a)   The Bill of Rights is set out in the first ten _____ of the Constitution and _____ US citizens against government intrusion.
b)   Under the _____ rule an accused cannot be required to give _____ against him/herself.
c)   In 1791 the Bill of Rights came into_____ granting US citizens' basic civil _____ .
d)   Pursuant to the _____ , US citizens are protected from _____ searches.
e)   Pursuant to the _____ requirement, the _____ must have a personal interest in any action (s)he brings before the courts.

4. Knowledge test

The following questions may be answered in writing or by way of discussion

a)   Do you think the division of powers between the US federal government and the US states is an appropriate model for other regional groupings, such as the European Union or ASEAN countries to follow?
b)   Why do you think Americans have such a strong national identity, given the obvious differences between the 50 US States?
c)   Discuss the main principles governing the relationship between the US federal government and the US state governments.
d)   In the United States, it is the US federal Supreme Court that has decided fundamental questions such as the legality of the death penalty, abortion and euthanasia. In your opinion, should such decisions be taken by the judicial or legislative branch of government?

PART 2 – QUICK LOOK GRAMMAR REVISION

The Present Perfect

The present perfect is formed with the auxiliary **have/has** and the **past participle** of the verb.

Past participle

English verbs can be considered to have four forms. For example the regular verb "to work", is formed as follows:
- the simple form **work**;
- the simple past **worked**;
- the present participle **working**;
- the past participle **worked**.

The past participle of regular verbs takes the same form as the simple past form, i.e., both end in "**ed**"

> **Note:**
>
> With irregular verbs the form of the past participle can vary, for example, the verb "to see":
> - the simple form **see**;
> - the simple past **saw**;
> - the present participle **seeing**;
> - the past participle **seen**.

How do we form the present perfect?

When making a positive statement
When making a *positive* statement, the present perfect is formed by using **have/has** + the past participle:
- I, you, we, they **have worked** hard on the file for the last year.
- He, she, it **has worked** hard on the file for the last year.

Frequently the present participle is contracted in spoken English:
- I**'ve**, you**'ve**, we**'ve**, they**'ve worked** hard on the file for the last year.
- He**'s,** she**'s**, it**'s worked** hard on the file for the last year[2].

When making a negative statement
When making a *negative* statement, the present perfect is formed by combining have/has + not before the past participle:
- I, you, we, they **have not worked** hard on the file this year.
- He, she, it **has not worked** hard on the file this year.

The present perfect in its negative form is sometimes contracted as follows:
- I, you, we, they have**n't worked** hard on the file this year.
- He, she, it has**n't worked** hard on the file this year[3].

When asking a question using the present perfect
When asking a question, the verb **have/has** precedes the subject:
- **Have** I, you, we, they **worked** hard on the file this year?
- **Has** he, she, it **worked** hard on the file this year?

---

[2]   This should not be used in written English.
[3]   This should not be used in written English.

When answering a question

The verb have/has is often used in a short form of an answer using the past perfect:

- **Have** you **worked** hard on the file this year?
- Yes I **have**/No I **have not**/**haven't worked** hard on the file this year.

When do we use the present perfect?

If one is referring to an event in the past, and the exact time that event occurred is specified, then the simple past tense is used, for example:

John **met** the client **yesterday/two years ago/in 2008**

The present perfect will be relied upon in the following situations:

a) Describing an event in the past, where the time is unspecified and when this has a link with the present
The present perfect is relied on to express activities or situations – single or repeated – that occurred at some unspecified time in the past in order to give important information for the present; the present perfect expresses the result in the present, for example:

John *has met* the client **before**
= John knows this person.

b) Describing activities that occurred many times in the past
If the event referred to has occurred many times and not just on one occasion, then the present perfect may be used, for example:

John *has met* the client on **many occasions**.

c) Following *since* and *for*
When used with *since* and *for* to describe an event that began in the past but that continues into the present, for example:

John *has worked* for the client *for* the last ten years.
John *has been* in the office *since* ten o'clock this morning.

PART 2 – GRAMMAR EXERCISES

1. Putting verbs in the past participle

Put the verb in past participle form (attention many of these are irregular verbs)

Example: work – worked; see – saw

a) go – _____
b) meet – _____
c) begin – _____

d)   have – _____
e)   rain – _____
f)   write – _____
g)   ride – _____
h)   do – _____
i)   know – _____
j)   finish – _____
k)   be – _____
l)   eat – _____
m)   make – _____
n)   see – _____
o)   call – _____

2. Putting verbs in the present perfect

Complete the following sentences putting the words in brackets in the form of the present perfect

(I, meet) I have met your client before.

a)   (I, fly)   _____ to New York to work on the file with my client.
b)   (you, stay)   _____ in that hotel many times.
c)   (he, finish)   _____ talking to his client, he can see you now.
d)   (they, go)   _____ to Singapore in order to negotiate the deal with the bank.
e)   (she, ring)   _____ her client on a number of occasions but he has not replied.
f)   (we, represent) _____ that company in court many times.

3. Practicing contractions

*When speaking, **have** or **has** in the present perfect is often contracted with the preceding noun. Practice the contraction in each sentence written in italic*

a)   The weather has been beautiful all summer.
      The weather's been beautiful all summer.
b)   My colleagues have moved to a new office.
      My colleagues've moved to a new office.
c)   He has worked for the same client for the last two years.
      He's worked for the same client for the last two years.
d)   She has asked the court for an adjournment.
      She's asked the court for an adjournment.
e)   Frank has been in a meeting for the last two hours.
      Frank's been in a meeting for the last two hours.

4. Complete the sentences

Fill in the blanks

    Example: Have you ever been to Japan?

Yes I have. I (be) have been to Japan several times. In fact I (be) was in Japan just last year.

a) Have you ever eaten in that restaurant? Yes I _____. I (eat) _____ there many times. In fact, I (eat) _____ there with a client there last night.

b) Have you ever spoken to the senior partner about receiving a raise? Yes I _____. I (talk) _____ with him about getting a raise a couple of times. In fact, I (talk) _____ to him about it after the meeting yesterday.

c) What American states have you visited? I (visit) _____ Delaware and Texas. I (visit) California in 2005. I (be, not)_____ in New York since 2002.

d) Have you worked in that law firm? Yes, I _____ (work) there just after I qualified. I (work, not)_____ there for many years.

e) Have you finished working on that file? No I _____. I (be) _____ working on it for a number of days but I (not, finish) _____ yet.

PART 3 – AUDIO – LISTENING AND SPEAKING

Comprehension

Listen to the following conversation, make notes of all the relevant facts and then answer the questions below. If you have trouble understanding, follow the conversation while also reading the text.

Class discussion between Professor Bob and his students

Professor Bob: "So does anyone want to tell me what they understand by the theory of selective incorporation? Nobody? … How about you Frank?"

Frank: "You may recall Professor; I was unable to attend class last week because of a stomach ache."

Professor Bob: "How inconvenient for you Frank. OK someone else; who was here last week? James?"

James: "Selective incorporation is an example of judicial activism."

Professor Bob: "You still haven't told me what it is."

James: "Doesn't it have something to do with the Bill of Rights?"

Professor Bob: "Yes it does, but I'm the one asking the questions here, not you. Let's begin from another angle; what is the Bill of Rights?"

James: "The Bill of Rights is the charter of civil liberties guaranteed to all US citizens by the first ten amendments to the US Constitution."

Professor Bob: "Excellent James and can you give me an example of the protection set out in the Bill of Rights?"

James: "Well, let's see … it covers most basic civil liberties …."

Professor Bob: "C'mon James don't make me beg …! Can you give me some specific examples?"

James: "Oh OK like the freedom to speak, I mean to express yourself to hold opinions and to state them publicly or the freedom to practice your religion, the freedom of the press and the freedom to have a gun to defend yourself … and my favorite, the freedom for the state to execute murderers."

Professor Bob: "Does the Bill of Rights actually give this specific freedom to the government?"

James: "No not really, it was the Supreme Court that gave the states this power through its interpretation of the "cruel and unusual punishment" clause in the Eight Amendment."

Professor Bob: "Would you care to develop that some more?"

James: "Sure OK … by stating that the death penalty does not necessarily amount to cruel and unusual punishment, the Supreme Court gave the green light to the federal and states governments that wanted to apply a policy of capital punishment in their criminal justice system."

Professor Bob: "So in fact, it was the Court that legalized the death penalty in the United States?"

James: "Well by not preventing it, it gave the states the right to have such a policy."

Professor Bob: "Very good James. Now can you tell me to whom the Bill of Rights applies?"

James: "I guess it applies to all US citizens, as I said before."

Professor Bob: "Yes OK, it is true that US citizens benefit from its application, but who has to provide the protection?"

James: "Well that depends on the theory of selective incorporation."

Professor Bob: "Very good, so we are back to the theory of selective incorporation. Maybe now you can tell me what it is."

James: "Yes, it is the theory by which the Supreme Court applies some of the rights set out in the Bill of Rights to the State governments, where such rights are considered to come within the due process guarantee of the Fourteenth Amendment."

Professor Bob: "So to whom does the Bill of Rights apply?"

James: "The entire Bill of Rights applies to the federal government and many of its provisions also apply to the state governments under the theory of selective incorporation and all US citizens benefit from its provisions."

Professor Bob: "Very good James. Frank did you understand any of that? Frank …. Will somebody wake him up please?"

PART 3 – AUDIO COMPREHENSION – EXERCISES

1. Comprehension

From the notes you have taken of the conversation, answer the following questions

a)   Why was Frank unable to answer the question Professor Bob asked him?

b)   Is James in favor of the death penalty?

c)   Does the Bill of Rights apply to the state governments?

d)   Did Frank understand any of the explanation given by James?

e)   Does the Bill of Rights authorize the death penalty?

f)   What examples of the Bill of Rights did James give?

2. Speaking practice

In the following series of conversation couplets, develop suitable responses to the questions asked

   a)   Professor Bob: "For what period of time are justices appointed to the Supreme Court?"
        James: "_____."
   b)   Professor Bob: "Could you explain to me the relationship between state law and federal law in the United States?"
        James: "_____."
   c)   Professor Bob: "What do I mean when I talk about the cases and controversies clause?"
        James: "_____."
   d)   Professor Bob: "Can you give me an example of some civil liberties enjoyed by US citizens?"
        James: "_____."
   e)   Professor Bob: "What do I mean when I talk of the standing requirement?"
        James: "_____."
   f)   Professor Bob: "Does the Bill of Rights apply at federal level or at state level?"
        James: "_____."
   g)   Professor Bob: "What do we mean when we talk about judicial activism?"
        James: "_____."
   h)   Professor Bob: "What does due process mean?"
        James: "_____."
   i)   Professor Bob: "If a judge sitting on the Supreme Court is an instrumentalist, in what way will he interpret the Constitution?"
        James: "_____."
   j)   Professor Bob: "What amendment of the Constitution guarantees the right to bail and what does it mean?"
        James: "_____."

3. Speaking practice continued ......

Create five other conversation couplets using in each couplet at least one word from the vocabulary found in Part 1, Text 1 and Text 2.

4. Speaking practice continued ......

Listen to the suggested replies and repeat

   a)   Professor Bob: "For what period of time are justices appointed to the Supreme Court?"
        James: "Supreme Court justices are appointed for life and enjoy security of tenure."
   b)   Professor Bob: "Could you explain to me the relationship between state law and federal law in the United States?"

James: "Well in theory there is no relationship between them at all. Where federal law is applicable, it is applied and takes supremacy over state law."

c) Professor Bob: "What do I mean when I talk about the cases and controversies clause?"

James: "You are referring to article 3 of the US Constitution that limits federal judicial power to deciding cases that involve an issue arising under the Constitution or the laws adopted thereunder."

d) Professor Bob: "Can you give me an example of some of the civil liberties enjoyed by US citizens?"

James: "Well the First Amendment grants US citizens freedom of speech, freedom of religion, freedom to assemble and freedom of the press."

e) Professor Bob: "What do I mean when I talk of the standing requirement?"

James: "Under the standing requirement a person must be directly concerned by the problem at the origin of their action. They cannot bring an action on behalf of someone else."

f) Professor Bob: "Does the Bill of Rights apply at federal level or at state level?"

James: "The entire Bill of Rights applies at federal level. Moreover, some rights under the theory of selective incorporation apply at state level."

g) Professor Bob: "What do we mean when we talk about judicial activism?"

James: "Judicial activism refers to the tendency of Supreme Court justices to create law when exercising their power of judicial review."

h) Professor Bob: "What does due process mean?"

James: "Due process is a general notion that requires that the state must treat its citizens fairly."

i) Professor Bob: "If a Supreme Court judge is an instrumentalist, in what way will he interpret the Constitution?"

James: "Instrumentalist judges interpret the Constitution in a very dynamic way and do not limit themselves to a literal interpretation of its provisions."

j) Professor Bob: "What amendment of the Constitution guarantees the right to bail and what does it mean?"

James: "The right to bail is established in the Eight Amendment and gives the accused a right to be freed from detention, while he is awaiting his trial."

5. Associated questions

Discuss the following questions

a) Why do you think civil liberties were guaranteed so early in the United States?

b)   Do you think it is appropriate to have unelected judges making law, as occurs in the case of the United States Supreme Court?
c)   Do the courts in your jurisdiction enjoy a power of judicial review?
d)   Which branch of the federal US government is the most powerful in your opinion?

PART 4 – TRANSLATION EXERCISES

When carrying out the translations it is not necessary to translate directly word for word; rather the emphasis should be on translating the sense of the text. Language is not directly interchangeable and so direct translations do not always convey the meaning in the text.

Translate the following texts from English to French

A. Supreme Court Justices

The Constitution places no restrictions on who may be appointed to the Supreme Court; however, all Presidential nominees must be approved by the Senate. Normally, eminent legal scholars are appointed, for example Louis Brandeis or Thurgood Marshall, who was the lead lawyer in Brown v Board of Education (which brought about the end of racial segregation in education). They have often occupied important positions in the judicial structure, for example, a judge in one of the lower federal courts, a member of a state Supreme Court or a member of the Department of Justice. Earl Warren was a former governor of the State of California before becoming Chief Justice of the Supreme Court. Only three women have sat on the Court: Sandra Day O'Connor, Ruth Bader Ginsburg and Sonia Sotomayor. Only two judges have been of Afro-American background, Thurgood Marshall appointed in 1967 and Clarence Thomas who succeeded him and who continues to sit on the court to this day.

B. The appellate jurisdiction of the Supreme Court

Apart from some limited exceptions provided for in Article III of the Constitution, the Supreme Court above all enjoys an appellate jurisdiction. This power is a discretionary one, whereby the Court may accept or refuse to issue a writ of certiorari, an order that requires the court that had previously ruled on the matter to send the case file to the Supreme Court. In practice barely 1% of requests are accepted, representing a little over 100 out of 7,000. The Court specifies in its rules (rule 10) the criteria governing the acceptance of an appeal. It is necessary that the matter concern an important question of law involving the Constitution or a law of the United States (in other words a federal matter) and that this issue has not been previously ruled upon, or that the lower court has gone against previously decided case law.

C. Nominating judges to the Supreme Court

The President confirmed today that he was in favour of nominating a Supreme Court justice that represented the diverse character of the United States, whether on the basis of sex, racial origin, social background or religion. Questioned by the Wall Street Journal during his visit to Mexico, the President considered that *"the diversity of our country is a good thing (...) the more opinions and different experiences we can bring to the table, the better the result"*. He confirmed that he was going to carry out the nomination process in the same meticulous and careful way in which he had chosen the last Supreme Court judge.

Translate the following texts from French to English

A. Le XIV ème Amendement

Le XIV ème Amendement établit deux règles importantes :
- il garantit à tous une procédure régulière ;
- il assure qu'aucun État [...] ne refusera à quiconque relève de sa juridiction l'égale protection des lois.

Ces deux garanties trouvent leur origine dans la volonté des pouvoirs fédéraux d'empêcher les États du sud de rétablir l'esclavage. Elles permettent d'empêcher les discriminations raciales ou politiques. L'assurance d'une procédure régulière s'applique à tous les cas où l'individu se voit opposer une décision défavorable. Cette clause a permis à la Cour suprême de se doter d'une véritable compétence pénale, puisqu'elle ne s'applique pas seulement aux actes administratifs et législatifs mais aussi aux décisions des divers tribunaux, y compris les décisions de droit pénal. C'est aussi à travers cette clause que la Cour a développé la théorie de « l'incorporation sélective ».

B. Le pouvoir discrétionnaire de la Cour suprême : sa compétence d'appel

La Cour peut être aussi amenée à autoriser un appel/accorder le bénéfice de l'appel si plusieurs cours inférieures (fédérales ou dans les États) ont décidé une question de façons divergentes. La Cour peut alors répondre à une question ou choisir de se saisir de toute l'affaire. La partie qui souhaite faire appel à la Cour Suprême y dépose une demande écrite (pétition for certiorari) pour lui demander de statuer sur l'affaire en appel. La requête présente une synthèse de l'affaire, en précisant les questions du domaine fédéral qui sont en jeu, et les arguments qui l'amènent à contester la décision de la cour inférieure. L'examen de la requête est accepté si quatre juges votent en ce sens. Sinon, l'arrêt de la cour inférieure se trouve confirmé.

C. Les juges de la Cour suprême

Le Congrès a déterminé par la loi le nombre de juges siégeant à la Cour suprême : sept à l'origine, neuf depuis 1869, dont un qui est le Président. Celui-ci est appelé en anglais *Chief Justice*, les autres *Associate Justices*, ou simplement *Justices*. L'article III fixe leur mode de nomination et leurs privilèges. Ils sont nommés par le Président, avec le consentement du Sénat (l'approbation du Sénat peut être refusée, mais peu de candidats sont ainsi rejetés). Ils occupent leur fonction aussi longtemps qu'ils le souhaitent et ils peuvent seulement être destitués après jugement par le Congrès, selon cette même procédure d'*impeachment* qui peut s'appliquer au Président des États-Unis ; ce qui n'est jamais arrivé à aucun juge de la Cour suprême.

PART 5 – ADVANCED READING

Judicial imperialism – is the federal Supreme Court too powerful?

The Supreme Court has sometimes been criticized for acting beyond its powers by engaging in judicial activism, i.e. creating law rather than merely interpreting it.

Take for example the decision of the Supreme Court in *Roe v Wade*. In this case, the Supreme Court recognized a limited right to abortion, based in part on the Supreme Court's interpretation of the mother's "right to privacy", as guaranteed by the Constitution. No doubt privacy is an important issue in the abortion argument. However, in the opinion of many US citizens it remains a doubtful argument to be used as a central foundation for the legalization of abortion. Many in the US would argue that the rights of the unborn go beyond a narrow consideration of the mother's privacy rights and that the issue should be decided by the legislative power, reflecting the views of the general population.

Indeed, the US constitutional system, in allowing the Supreme Court to decide public policy issues such as abortion, has passed significant power to an unelected body. Moreover, judges exercise this power subjectively, applying vague constitutional provisions to specific factual situations. It is said that *"judges have wrought a coup d'état, – slow-moving and genteel – but a coup d'état nonetheless"*. Such allegations become all the more worrying if one considers that:
-   much of the Supreme Court's influence results from its power of judicial review, a power that is not expressly provided for in the Constitution and that judges *created* for themselves;
-   judges have frequently used that power to increase the power of the federal state at the expense of the state powers, at times probably in contradiction to the intentions of many of the framers of the Constitution.

The all-powerful character of the Supreme Court is only reinforced by the almost dictatorial character of the lifetime tenure that Supreme Court justices enjoy. Given that Supreme Court judges are often appointed at a relatively young age, the result is that they can be *in power* for decades, with next to no control being exercised over the manner in which they wield their considerable powers. Justices may be impeached before the Senate for abuse of their power but this has only occurred once in the history of the US federal state and thus cannot really be considered an effective control. The introduction of term limits or a mandatory retirement age would help to solve this issue. Moreover, given the political character of the Court, a mandatory retirement age would remove the arbitrary manner by which certain Presidents get to nominate a significant number of justices to the Supreme Court and others none at all. Some Presidents, because no vacancies arise during their time in office, are denied any possibility of exercising this power, whilst other Presidents may get to nominate a number of judges. In this context, presumably pressure is placed on judges not to retire in circumstances where they represent a different political philosophy to the sitting President. Were such justices to retire, the judge succeeding them would no doubt reflect the political philosophy of the President appointing them. Thus judges in some circumstances probably remain on the bench even longer than they might wish. Security of tenure brings one great benefit, namely impartiality and freedom from political pressure. However, it is possible to have security of tenure without it necessarily being for life.

Chapter seven

THE POLITICAL SYSTEM IN THE UNITED KINGDOM

PART 1 – TEXT 1 – INFORMATION

The organization of power in the United Kingdom

Power in the United Kingdom of Great Britain and Northern Ireland (UK) is **structured around** the monarchy and the political system is described as a **constitutional monarchy**. Power is divided at national level between the executive, legislative and judicial branches, with each of the **home countries**, Scotland, Wales and Northern Ireland, enjoying **varying** degrees of devolved power.

The Constitution of the United Kingdom

The UK Constitution is not **codified** into one single document and has many different sources.

- *Fundamental documents* **Magna Carta** is an example of a fundamental document making up the UK constitution and consequently the rights guaranteed in the Magna Carta have constitutional status[1]. By forcing King John to sign Magna Carta, the barons for the first time officially placed a limit on the exercise of power by the monarchy in the United Kingdom.
- *The laws adopted by the UK Parliament* The laws adopted by Parliament are **referred to** as **statute law** and the more important texts are said to have constitutional **standing**. For example, the Act of Settlement (1701) establishes that only persons of the Protestant faith can accede to the British throne. This remains the law today.
- *The laws created by the judiciary* These laws are sometimes referred to as case law or common law. Important principles of law developed by the courts in their decisions are said to have constitutional effect.
- *European Union Treaties* The UK joined the European Union (EU) in 1973 signing the Accession Treaty and thereafter EU law is said to **take precedence** over UK law.

---

[1]   In reality, the rights set out in Magna Carta have for the most part little relevance today and, where they do, they have been set out again in more modern documents; thus Magna Carta is not relied on today. This does not detract from Magna Carta's status as a fundamental document making up UK constitutional law.

Political institutions in the United Kingdom

There are a number of different political institutions operating in the United Kingdom.

- *The monarchy* The Queen is the head of state, and power is said to **flow** from this **source**. The Queen has **nominal** powers, such as the right to summon and **dissolve** Parliament. On the advice of Parliament, she appoints the **Prime Minister** and **confers** public honors such as **knighthoods**. She is also the **nominal** or **titular** head of the Church of England.
- *The executive* The Prime Minister and his/her government exercise executive power on behalf of the **Sovereign**. The day-to-day business of government is carried out by a number of government departments, headed politically by a senior minister and administratively by a senior civil servant, called a **permanent secretary**.
- *The legislature* Parliament in the United Kingdom is made up of two houses, the House of Commons and the House of Lords and the Monarchy. The House of Commons is made up of publicly elected **Members of Parliament** (MPs).
- *The judiciary* The court system is divided between three separate jurisdictions, namely England & Wales, Scotland and Northern Ireland. Traditionally powerful, the power of the courts to make law has been on the **wane**, as more and more legislation is being adopted by the European Union, **thereby** limiting the power of the courts to make law[2].

VOCABULARY

Structured (to be) around something – *être structuré autour de quelque chose*
Constitutional monarchy – *monarchie constitutionnelle*
Home countries (England, Wales, Scotland and Northern Ireland) – *pays d'origine/nations constitutives du Royaume-Uni*
Vary (to) – *changer*
Codify (to) – *codifier*
Magna Carta – *Magna Carta, Grande Charte des libertés de 1215 (consacrant notamment des libertés telles que celle de ne pas être emprisonné arbitrairement)*
Refer (to) to something as – *qualifier quelque chose de*
Statute law – *lois adoptées par le parlement puis publiées dans le journal officiel*
Have (to) standing (constitutional) – *avoir qualité (valeur constitutionnelle) ; se dit également de quelqu'un qui, devant une juridiction, a qualité pour agir*
Take (to) precedence over – *prévaloir/primer sur*
Flow (to) – *dériver/découler/résulter*
Source – *source*
Nominal (power) – *nominatif (pouvoir)*
Dissolve (to) – *dissoudre*

---

[2] If an area is dealt with by EU legislation, the courts must apply it and may not make law in this area.

Confer (to) – *conférer*
Knighthood – *titre honorifique de chevalier*
Nominal head/titular head – *chef théorique/symbolique/honorifique*
Sovereign – *souverain*
Prime minister – *premier ministre*
Permanent secretary – *secrétaire permanent*
Wane (to) – *décliner/décroître*
Member of Parliament – *membre du parlement/député*
Thereby – *ainsi/par conséquent*

PART 1 – TEXT 1 – EXERCISES

1. Vocabulary test

Fill in the missing words using the vocabulary in Text 1

a) Pursuant to the Act of _____ , the Monarch must be _____ in order to accede to the throne.
b) There are two Houses of Parliament in the United Kingdom, the _____ and the _____; members of the latter House are called MPs.
c) The Monarchy has _____ powers that (s)he may only _____ on the advice of the prime minister.
d) In reality, although the Queen is the Head of State, _____ power in the UK is exercised by the government.
e) The UK _____ has many sources including fundamental documents, decisions adopted by the court and _____ law adopted by Parliament.
f) The United Kingdom joined the _____ in 1973 and _____ is said to take _____ over UK law.
g) _____ was signed by King John, placing a _____ on the exercise of royal power.

2. Vocabulary test

Write sentences with the following pairs of words. Your sentence should demonstrate the relationship between the words

a) Statute law/Parliament
b) Permanent secretary/government department
c) Magna Carta/fundamental rights
d) Queen/Church of England
e) Home countries/power
f) Precedence/EU law

3. Knowledge test

Each of the following statements is false; do you know why? Write a sentence stating why it is false

a) All government in the UK is centralized nationally.
b) The United Kingdom is governed by a single constitutional document, referred to as the UK Constitution.

c)   The Queen has the exclusive right to confer public honors, such as knighthoods.
d)   The power of the UK judiciary to make law is diminishing because the executive power is becoming too powerful.
e)   In the United Kingdom a person can be appointed as Monarch, no matter their religion.

PART 1 – TEXT 2 – MORE INFORMATION

Organization of power in the United Kingdom

The political organization in the United Kingdom of Great Britain and Northern Ireland is **structured** around the monarchy, and the political system is referred to as a **constitutional monarchy**. The ceremonial role of **head of state** is vested in the monarchy but real power is divided between the executive, legislative and judicial branches of government. Executive power is exercised nationally on behalf of the Queen by the UK government, **headed** by the **Prime Minister**, representing all of the United Kingdom. Limited executive power is also found at the level of the devolved governments of Scotland, Wales, and Northern Ireland. Legislative power is **vested** nationally in two **chambers**, the House of Commons and the House of Lords, and regionally in the Scottish Parliament and the Welsh and Northern Ireland Assemblies. Judicial power is also expressed both nationally and regionally. At national level there is the Supreme Court of the United Kingdom and the courts at regional level are found in three separate **jurisdictions**: England & Wales, Scotland and Northern Ireland. The UK is a multi-party system and two main parties dominate Parliament at national level, namely the Labour Party on the left and the Conservative Party on the right. The system of government in the UK is known as the **Westminster**[3] **system of government** and has been adopted in various forms by many of the UK's former colonies such as India, Canada and Australia.

The Constitution of the United Kingdom

It is often said by non-jurists that England has an *unwritten* constitution. Strictly speaking this statement is, however, incorrect. The UK Constitution, which is made-up of written texts and court decisions, is certainly at least partly recorded in writing. However, it is true to say that the rules making up the UK Constitution have not been codified into one single constitutional document.

It is this lack of codification that makes the UK Constitution unusual at a time when most other western democratic countries have adopted a codified constitution. As there is no single codified constitutional document, the Constitution is said to come from a number of different **sources**, for example:
*   *fundamental documents* **Magna Carta** is a fundamental document of UK constitutional law. The importance of the charter is found in the

---

[3]   Westminster is the geographical location of the UK Parliament and thus, when speaking of Parliament, frequently people just say Westminster, it being understood that they are referring to Parliament.

fact that it forced the then King to accept that sovereign power could not be exercised in a completely arbitrary way and was thus subject to control. Under the heading of fundamental documents also comes the 1689 **Bill of Rights,** vesting sovereignty in Parliament and setting out the rights UK citizens enjoy under the system of constitutional monarchy created thereunder[4];

- *laws adopted by the UK Parliament* The laws adopted by the Parliament are **referred to** as **Acts of Parliament** and once published are known as **Statute law**. The more important statutes are said to have constitutional **standing**.
    - Act of Settlement (1701) – establishing the manner of **accession** to the UK throne and providing that non-Catholics or persons married to Catholics cannot accede to the throne. Interestingly, despite its overtly discriminatory character, there is no movement to have the Act repealed and members of the royal household that marry or become Catholic continue to be removed from the line of succession even today.
    - Acts of Union, (1707) and (1801) – whereby Scotland and Ireland respectively were annexed to the United Kingdom and lost their independent parliaments. The effect of the 1701 Act of Union with Scotland was partially overturned by the Scotland Act, 1998. Under this Act, Scotland was granted limited **self-determination**, whereby it can now elect its own parliament and government. The 1801 Act was repealed when southern Ireland became independent from the United Kingdom; Northern Ireland continues to remain part of the Union. Devolved government has to a lesser extent also been conferred on Northern Ireland and Wales (see discussion immediately below).
    - Parliament Act (1911) – restricting the power of the House of Lords. In 1911, the House of Lords' power to veto bills coming from the House of Commons was **done away with**. The Act thus confirmed that the House of Commons is the most powerful of the two parliamentary chambers.
    - Statute of Westminster (1931) – whereby the UK **effectively** granted independence to some of its former **colonies**. Although **retaining** the Crown as their official Head of State, under the Statute of Westminster these states were **nonetheless** given an **effective right** to self-determination[5].
    - EEC Act (1972) – providing for the UK's admission to the European Economic Community (EEC, hereafter the European Union).
    - Human Rights Act (1998) – incorporating the European Convention on Human Rights (1950) directly in UK law.
    - Government of Wales Act (1998)/Northern Ireland Act (1998)/

---

[4] Created thereunder – created under that, i.e. the system of constitutional monarchy created under/by the Bill of Rights.

[5] Namely Canada, Australia, Newfoundland, New Zealand, South Africa and the then Irish Free State.

> Scotland Act (1998) – providing for **varying degrees** of devolved government for the home countries of Wales, Northern Ireland and Scotland.
>
> – House of Lords Act (1999) – whereby the House of Lords saw its membership radically altered. In particular, the number of **hereditary peers** was reduced to ninety-two.

- *laws created by the judiciary* These laws are sometimes referred to as case law or common law. Perhaps one of the most important common law rules is that of **habeas corpus**. Under this principle, every prisoner has a right to **appear** before the courts to have the legality of their imprisonment **reviewed**. As is often the case with good case law, this rule was later **confirmed** by the adoption of an Act of Parliament, the Habeas Corpus Act 1679;

- *European Union treaties* As we have seen, the UK joined the European Union (EU) in 1973 (at that time called the European Economic Community (EEC)). The EU is **constructed** on the basis of a number of different treaties under which the UK has surrendered part of its **sovereignty**. It is this **loss** of sovereignty and a **feeling** that *foreigners* are deciding the content of UK law that explains the unpopularity of the European Union **amongst** British citizens. EU law is considered by the UK courts to take **precedence** over UK law;

- *constitutional convention* Convention refers to certain political customs or understandings that exist between the different branches of power, as regards the manner in which they co-exist together. For example, the Queen's *royal assent* is needed before legislation adopted by Parliament can pass into law. However, there is an understanding or a *convention* between the Parliament and the monarchy that the latter will not refuse to give the royal assent. This convention, although unwritten, is considered constitutional in status.

The different branches of power in the United Kingdom

Scotland, Wales and Northern Ireland each have their own **respective** executive and legislative powers, each with responsibility for the differing varying devolved powers granted to them by the national government in Westminster. Thus, Scottish, Irish[6] and Welsh people are represented both in their own national parliaments/assemblies and also in the national parliament. England is the only home country without its own regional assembly and is ruled directly from Westminster. Thus, Scotland, Northern Ireland and Wales are ruled partly from Westminster and partly at regional national level[7].

As in the United States of America, power in the United Kingdom is organized pursuant to Montesquieu's theory of the separation of powers. However, there

---

[6] Irish here refers to Northern Irish; Ireland is divided into the Republic of Ireland, which is an independent state but which is also a member of the European Union, and Northern Ireland, which is part of the UK.

[7] Each of the home countries has received different degrees of devolved power, reflecting the wishes of their national populations at the time devolution was introduced.

are significant differences between the two systems. For example in the United States the President exercises executive power. This cannot happen in the UK, as the Queen is not a publicly elected official. Thus, the *de facto* exercise of executive power in the UK **rests** with the Prime Minister, the leader of the legislative branch, and not with the Queen. Another difference has to do with the power of the UK courts under the heading of **judicial review**. In the UK, as sovereignty vests in Parliament, in theory it may adopt any law it wishes and, once adopted, the courts cannot review the constitutionality of that law. This is known as the **doctrine of parliamentary sovereignty** and limits the UK Supreme Court's power of judicial review compared with the system in place in other common law democracies, such as the United States.

There are a number of different branches of power in the United Kingdom.

- *The monarchy* The Queen is the head of state and **titular** head of the executive. Sovereignty however does not **reside** in the monarchy but is **instead**, pursuant to the provisions of the Bill of Rights, 1689, vested in the national UK Parliament in Westminster, elected by national vote. The Queen has **nominal** powers, such as the right to call and **dissolve** Parliament, which she exercises on the advice of the Prime Minister. Also on the advice of the Prime Minister, the Queen **confers** public honours such as **knighthoods**. As we have seen, the Queen must also give her royal assent before proposed legislation can pass into law. She holds weekly meetings with the Prime Minister at which she expresses her views, if any, on government policy. She is also the titular head of the Church of England, which explains why the Monarch must be a member of the Protestant Church. The monarchy plays mainly a consultative role in UK politics but, although primarily a **figurehead**, the Sovereign still retains some **influence** over the exercise of power.
- *The executive* Her Majesty's Government, on behalf of the Sovereign, exercises executive power at national level. As in the case of Parliament, executive power is based in Westminster and is headed by the Prime Minister, also referred to as the Head of the Government and **leader of the House of Commons**. Appointed by the Queen on the advice of Parliament, the Prime Minister then appoints the other Ministers, who together form the national government of the United Kingdom. Senior ministers meeting together with the Prime Minister are referred to as the **Cabinet** and together make up the inner government. The day-to-day business of government is carried out by a number of government departments, each headed politically by senior ministers and administratively by a senior civil servant, referred to as a **permanent secretary**. The **latter reports to** his/her senior Minister.
- *The legislature* Parliament in the United Kingdom is made up of the Queen and the two Houses of Parliament, the House of Commons and the House of Lords. The House of Commons is made up of publicly elected Members of Parliament, referred to as MPs. The House of Lords is made up of two types of members: the **Lords Temporal** and the **Lords Spiritual**. The Lords Temporal are made up of either:

- life peers, appointed by the government, with no hereditary right for their descendants to sit in the house; or
- ninety-two hereditary peers, enjoying a right to a **hereditary seat** in the House of Lords. Reform of the mode of election to the House of Lords is being discussed and any change that is introduced will probably bring to an end the role of hereditary peers in the legislative process.

Lords Spiritual are **bishops**, i.e. senior members of the Church of England, and enjoy an automatic right to sit in the House of Lords. This is open to criticism, as being an official in the Church of England is hardly the most **pluralist selection base** for a modern democracy made up of many different religions. Together with the House of Commons, the Lords are responsible for the adoption of legislation. However, the House of Commons dominates the legislative process and the House of Lords may only hold up or delay the adoption of legislation passed by the House of Commons. Thus, the House of Lords has no right of **veto** as regards the adoption of legislation. Generally, it can be observed that the power of Parliament has been in decline over the last number of years, with the executive branch playing an increasingly dominant role.

- *The judiciary* Judicial power in the UK is divided between the different jurisdictions of England & Wales, Scotland, and Northern Ireland. Thus, England and Wales share the same courts, whilst a separate court system exists in both Scotland and Northern Ireland[8]. Appeals from each of these jurisdictions are heard before the UK Supreme Court operating at national level. Judicial power in the United Kingdom is divided into two basic jurisdictions, the civil courts and the criminal courts. Although traditionally powerful, the ability of the courts to make law has been on the **wane,** as more and more legislation is being adopted, both by the national and regional parliaments and by the European Union, thereby limiting the scope of the UK courts to make law[9].

VOCABULARY

Structured (to be) around something – *être structuré autour de quelque chose*
Constitutional monarchy – *monarchie constitutionnelle*
Headed (to be) – *être dirigé par*
Prime minister – *premier ministre*
Head of State – *chef d'état*
Vested – *conféré/assigné/attribué*
Chambers (of Parliament) – *chambres du Parlement*

---

[8] Moreover, the legal system in Scotland employs elements of the Civil law system developed on the Continent, i.e. mainland Europe.
[9] If an area is covered by legislation adopted by Parliament or the EU, the courts may not make law in this area, due to the notions of parliamentary sovereignty and the supremacy of EU law over UK national law.

Jurisdiction – *juridiction*
Westminster system of government – *système de gouvernement de Westminster*
Source – *source*
Magna Carta – *Magna Carta/Grande Charte des libertés de 1215 (consacrant notamment des libertés telles que celle de ne pas être emprisonné arbitrairement)*
The Bill of Rights, 1689 – *proclamation des droits de 1689, de statut constitutionnel, définissant les principes de la monarchie parlementaire (les pouvoirs du Parlement, les droits fondamentaux des sujets etc.)*
Refer (to) to something as – *qualifier quelque chose de/dénommer*
Act of Parliament – *loi du Parlement non promulguée*
Statute law – *lois votées par le Parlement et promulguées*
To have standing (constitutional) – *avoir qualité (constitutionnelle) ; se dit également de quelqu'un ayant qualité pour agir devant une juridiction*
Self-determination – *auto-détermination*
To be done away with – *être éliminé/supprimé*
Colony – *colonie*
Effectively – *effectivement*
Retain (to) – *conserver*
Nonetheless – *néanmoins*
Given (to be) an effective right to something – *se voir conférer un droit effectif à quelque chose (l'autodétermination)*
Varying degrees – *à des degrés divers*
Hereditary peers – *pairs héréditaires (au sein de la Chambre des Lords)*
Habeas Corpus – *Habeas Corpus*
Appear (to) – *apparaître (ici, comparaître)*
Review (to) – *contrôler/examiner (la légalité)*
Confirm (to) – *confirmer*
Construct (to) – *fonder/bâtir*
Sovereignty – *souveraineté*
Precedence – *primauté*
Respective – *respectif/propre (possessif)*
De facto – *de facto*
Power is said to rest with someone – *le pouvoir repose sur une personne donnée*
Judicial review – *contrôle juridictionnel de légalité*
Doctrine of parliamentary sovereignty – *théorie de la souveraineté parlementaire (impossibilité de saisir les cours du Royaume-Uni pour contester la constitutionnalité d'une loi préalablement adoptée)*
Titular – *honorifique*
Reside (to) – *résider (au sens d'appartenir)*
Instead of – *au lieu de*
Nominal – *théorique/symbolique*
Dissolve (to) – *dissoudre*
Confer (to) – *conférer*
Knighthood – *titre honorifique de chevalier*
Figurehead – *figure de proue*
Influence – *influence*
Leader of the House of Commons – *Chef du House of Commons (premier ministre)*

Cabinet – *cabinet*
Permanent secretary – *chef d'un département gouvernemental*
The latter – *ce dernier*
Report (to) to someone – *rapporter à quelqu'un*
Lords Temporal – *Lords temporels*
Lords Spiritual – *Lords spirituels*
Hereditary seat – *siège héréditaire*
Bishop – *evêque*
Pluralist selection base – *corps représentatif pluriel*
Veto – *veto/opposer un veto*
On (to be) the wane – *être sur le déclin*

PART 1 – TEXT 2 – EXERCISES

1. Definitions

Write a sentence defining each of the following terms

- a)   *Magna Carta*
- b)   *Habeas Corpus*
- c)   Constitutional standing
- d)   Self-determination
- e)   Lords Spiritual
- f)   Permanent secretary
- g)   Cabinet

2. Sentences

Write sentences with the following pairs of words demonstrating the relationship between the words

- a)   Sovereignty/Parliament
- b)   Queen/Prime Minister
- c)   House of Lords/Lords Spiritual
- d)   Act of Parliament/European Union
- e)   Constitution/sources
- f)   Judicial review/UK courts
- g)   Judicial power/jurisdictions
- h)   Figurehead/nominal powers
- i)   Knighthood/Prime Minister
- j)   Permanent secretary/Minister

3. Fill in the missing words

Fill in the missing words using the vocabulary in Text 2

- a)   The UK is often described as a _____ monarchy whereby the Queen has only _____ powers and is above all a figurehead.
- b)   The UK is governed pursuant to the _____ system of government, with power being exercised at both national and _____ level.
- c)   The UK Constitution is made up of a number of different elements

such as _____ documents, statute law and _____ established by the courts.

d) Judicial power in the UK is divided between three jurisdictions: England & Wales, _____ and _____. The latter jurisdiction employs a hybrid system blending elements of both the common and civil law systems.

e) Meetings involving senior _____ and the Prime Minister are referred to as _____ meetings.

4. Knowledge test

The following questions may be answered in writing or by way of discussion

a) Why do you think the UK Constitution requires that the Monarch be Protestant?

b) Do you think that the monarchy should be abolished? Why do you think the British chose to have a monarchy?

c) Do you think home nations such as Scotland will remain part of the United Kingdom?

d) Do you think the UK ought to have a single constitutional document? What arguments can be made in support of having a vague constitutional organization of government as in the UK?

PART 2 – QUICK LOOK GRAMMAR REVISION

Using SINCE and FOR with the present perfect

For and *since* can both be used with the present perfect to talk about something that continues up until the present.

1. Since

Since is used with the present perfect tense to express the idea that an activity:
- *began at a specific time in the past;* and
- *continues up until the present.*

Example:
I have been here *since* 9:00 am, where have you been?
I have been here *since* Tuesday and the weather is dreadful.
I have lived here *since* May.
I have been working here *since* last November.

Note:

*The following are incorrect, as **SINCE takes the present perfect when the intention is to show that something true in the present started in the past.***
I *am living* here *since* May – incorrect
I *live* here *since* May – incorrect
I *lived* here *since* May – incorrect

I *have lived* here *since* May/I *have been living* here *since* May –
CORRECT[10]

If the specific moment in the past is not expressed by a noun but by a verb,
the tense used after since will be the past simple.

Example:
I *have worked* with the client *since* he *came (= since 10 o'clock, etc.)*.
I *have made* many friends in the firm *since* I *joined (= since 2012, etc.)*.

2. For

Using **for** with the present perfect indicates a period of time running up to the
present.

Example:
I have worked on the file *for two hours*.
I have worked here *for two years*.
I have worked here *for too long*!

> **Note:**
>
> Using the present perfect in a sentence with *for* means that the action
> began in the past and continues to the present day.
> If you do not use the present perfect but the simple past + *for*, then it
> means that the action has come to an end.
>
> *Example*
> John *has worked* with the firm *for* two years – this sentence means
> that John is still working with the firm.
> John *worked* with the firm *for* two years – this sentence means that
> John no longer works with the firm.

PART 2 – GRAMMAR EXERCISES

1. Since *or* For

Fill in the spaces using since or for ......

I have been working here ......

a) _____ two months.
b) _____ April.
c) _____ 2005.
d) _____ last month.
e) _____ one year.
f) _____ two hours.

---

[10] I have been living here – is an example of the present perfect progressive and is discussed
later in the book.

g) _____ 9:15 this morning.

h) _____ about three months.

2. Since *or* For continued …

Complete the following sentences with your own words using "since" and "for"

> *Example*:
> *I have been in the office since 9:00 am this morning.*
> *I have been in the office for 37 minutes exactly.*

a)   I have been in New York since ...
     I have been in New York for ...
b)   I have been a qualified lawyer since ...
     I have been a qualified lawyer for ...
c)   I have worked on this case since ...
     I have worked on this case for ...
d)   I have been in prison since ...
     I have been a prisoner for ...

3. Forms of the present perfect

Complete the sentences using the words in brackets

a)   I (only/know) _____ Jim since I (be) _____ in law school.
b)   John (have) _____ a lot of problems since David (become) _____ head partner.
c)   Since the third semester (begin) _____, we (have) _____ five different exams to sit.
d)   I (be) _____ friends with Jules ever since I (live) _____ in Paris.
e)   Julie (be) _____ in law school since she (be) _____ twenty-two years old.
f)   Since we (begin) _____ to do this exercise, I (complete) _____ nearly five sentences.
g)   John and I are very old friends. I (know)_____ John since he (be) _____ at university.

4. Simple past and past participle

Write the simple past and past participles of the following verbs

		Simple past	Past Participle
a)	Fall	_____,	_____.
b)	Give	_____,	_____.
c)	Bite	_____,	_____.
d)	Wear	_____,	_____.
e)	Grow	_____,	_____.
f)	Get	_____,	_____.
g)	Drink	_____,	_____.

PART 3 – AUDIO – LISTENING AND SPEAKING

Comprehension

Listen to the following conversation, make notes of all the relevant facts and then answer the questions below. If you have trouble understanding, follow the conversation while also reading the text.

Conversation between Andrew and Philippe in a Scottish pub about the constitutional organization of the United Kingdom

Philippe: "Hello Andrew, thanks for agreeing to meet with me."

Andrew: "Not at all, on the phone you said you wanted to better understand the constitutional organization of the United Kingdom."

Philippe: "Yes, as you know I am a visiting law student and before arriving in the United Kingdom I thought that it was just one country but since I have been living here in Scotland I am no longer sure of this."

Andrew: "Ah, that probably is all the talk you have been hearing from Scottish nationalists like myself."

Philippe: "Yes, it is difficult to understand. On one hand, we are in the United Kingdom but yet up here in Scotland, you seem to have your own executive, parliament and people don't seem to pay any attention to what is happening in London. Yet on the other hand, the national press is constantly complaining about the fact that real decision-making power in the United Kingdom now seems to be located in Brussels, with the European Union. I frankly have difficulty understanding the role of the United Kingdom in all this."

Andrew: "Well, we here in Scotland are not quite as independent as you might think Philippe, but you are right, there have been some significant changes over the last few years giving more power to Scotland. And yes it is true, that at the same time, increasingly many national issues do seem to be decided by Brussels instead of Westminster."

Philippe: "This is what I want to try and understand; what is the United Kingdom today? Is it disappearing?"

Andrew: "No it is not disappearing but it is definitely changing and for the better in my point of view; but of course I would think that because I'm a Scottish nationalist."

Philippe: "Can you explain to me what is happening?"

Andrew: "Well, I'll give you my point of view but perhaps it is best to begin with a short history lesson. The modern entity referred to as the United Kingdom can trace its origins back to 1066 with the invasion of the Normans. The Normans and their successors first took control of the south of England but gradually their presence spread throughout Wales, Scotland and Ireland. This conquest occurred slowly but by the 1800's Wales, Scotland, Ireland and England were unified as one kingdom and all ruled directly from Westminster in London. However, although unified, some people in the different home countries continued to remain attached to their own separate identities."

Philippe: "So, is Ireland a member of the United Kingdom?"

Andrew: "Yes and No. Ireland always retained a strong nationalist identity and many in the country resented being ruled from London. No doubt this separate identity was reinforced by the fact that the Irish live on a separate island and were predominantly Catholic when the remainder of the United Kingdom was predominantly protestant and fearful of Catholicism. As a result, the Irish rebelled against Westminster rule and finally in 1922 the country was partitioned, with the south of Ireland eventually becoming an independent republic, completely separate from the United Kingdom in 1949. However, Northern Ireland is still ruled from London and this explains much of the struggle that has been occurring in cities like Belfast since the 1970's. So only the north of Ireland is now part of the United Kingdom."

Philippe: "What is the condition of the United Kingdom today?"

Andrew: "Well in response to the nationalist struggle in the north of Ireland and increasing calls for self determination in Scotland and to a lesser extent in Wales, the United Kingdom government decided to give limited devolved powers to Scotland, Wales and northern Ireland. However, not every region wanted the same degree of independence and so the powers of the Welsh assembly are not as extensive as those powers enjoyed by the Scottish Parliament."

Philippe: "So Scotland is the most independent of the home countries?"

Andrew: "Yes probably, and at the moment there seems to be increasing momentum towards eventual Scottish independence, despite defeat in the last referendum on the question. However, given that soon we will all be ruled from Brussels, I often wonder if it really makes any difference."

Philippe: "You mean by the European Union … so what is the role of Brussels in all this?"

Andrew: "Well that is another story; buy me another whisky and I'll tell you all about it Philippe."

PART 3 – AUDIO COMPREHENSION – EXERCISES

1. Comprehension

From the notes you have taken answer the following questions

a) Is Ireland a member of the United Kingdom?
b) What does Andrew mean when he says that soon "we will all be ruled by Brussels"?
c) What does Andrew mean when he refers to "Westminster"?
d) What home countries now make up the United Kingdom?
e) Which home country in the United Kingdom does Andrew consider to be the most independent?
f) What drink does Andrew prefer?

2. Speaking practice

In the following series of conversation couplets, develop suitable responses to the questions asked

a) Andrew: "Hello Philippe, so do you speak English well?
    Philippe: "_____."
b) Andrew: "Tell me Philippe, where are you from?"
    Philippe: "_____."

c)   Andrew: "So Philippe you rang because you want to learn about the constitutional organization in the UK?"
      Philippe: "_____"

d)   Andrew: "Philippe, do you know the name of the different home countries making up the United Kingdom?"
      Philippe: "_____."

e)   Andrew: "What is the status of Ireland, is it a member of the United Kingdom?"
      Philippe: "_____."

f)   Andrew: "If you want me to tell you about the European Union, you will have to buy me another whisky."
      Philippe: "_____."

g)   Andrew: "Do you understand what a Scottish nationalist is?"
      Philippe: "_____."

h)   Andrew: "Do you like Scotland Philippe?"
      Philippe: "_____."

i)   Andrew: "Why did you decide to come to study in the United Kingdom?"
      Philippe: "_____."

3. Speaking practice continued ......

Create five other conversation couplets, using in each couplet at least one word from the vocabulary found in Part I – Text 1 or Text 2

4. Speaking practice continued ......

Listen to the suggested replies and repeat

a)   Andrew: "Hello Philippe, do you speak English well?
      Philippe: "I guess my English is average, it has certainly improved since I have come to Scotland."

b)   Andrew: "Tell me Phillippe where are you from?"
      Philippe: "Originally I am from France."

c)   Andrew: "So Phillippe you rang because you wanted to learn about the constitutional organization in the UK?"
      Philippe: "Yes, I want to understand how the United Kingdom is organized."

d)   Andrew: "Do you know the name of the different home countries making up the United Kingdom?"
      Philippe: "Yes, there is England, Scotland, Wales and the Northern Ireland."

e)   Andrew: "What is the status of Ireland, is it a member of the United Kingdom?"
      Philippe: "Well Northern Ireland is a member of the United Kingdom but the south of Ireland is a separate country."

f)   Andrew: "If you want me to tell you about the European Union, you will have to buy me another whisky."

Philippe: "OK but I don't think I will join you, I am already feeling a little light headed."

g)   Andrew: "Do you understand what a Scottish nationalist is?"
Philippe: "Yes, I think so, it means you want Scotland to be a separate country, independent from the United Kingdom."

h)   Andrew: "Do you like Scotland Philippe?"
Philippe: "I love the country and the people, but the weather is dreadful, it never seems to stop raining; I miss the sunshine!"

i)   Andrew: "Why did you decide to come to study in the United Kingdom?"
Philippe: "To improve my English of course."

5. Associated questions

Discuss the following questions

a)   Do you think that nationalism is a good thing? Can it ever be dangerous?

b)   Why do you think some people in Scotland want independence from the United Kingdom?

c)   Do some research on Scotland and consider whether it could function as a separate entity.

d)   Do you think it is normal that Catholics or people who marry Catholics cannot accede to the throne in the UK?

PART 4 – TRANSLATION EXERCISES

When carrying out the translations it is not necessary to translate directly word for word; rather the emphasis should be on translating the sense of the text. Language is not directly interchangeable and so direct translations do not always convey the meaning in the text.

Translate the following texts from English to French

A. What exactly is the Magna Carta?

Magna Carta was signed in June 1215 by the barons of medieval England and King John. The term *Magna Carta* is Latin, meaning *Great Charter*. It was signed at Runnymede near Windsor Castle, where members of the British royal family continue to live to this day. The charter was an attempt by the barons to stop the King abusing his power, especially his power of taxation. King John, by signing the document, demonstrated the relative weakness of the monarchy in medieval England. Why would a king – who was meant to be all powerful in his own country – agree to the demands of the barons, who were meant to be below him in authority? Because the King had little or no choice in the matter.

B. The House of Commons

The House of Commons was developed during the 14th century and has been sitting in near continuous existence ever since. After political union with Scotland and Ireland under the Acts of Union, members of the House of Commons were drawn from all over the United Kingdom and not from just England & Wales. The House of Commons was originally far less powerful than the House of Lords, but today its legislative powers are greater than those of the Lords. Under the Parliament Act (1911) the Lords' power to veto legislative bills was reduced to a delaying power. Lords can now hold up the adoption of legislation, but only for a limited period. The Government of the country is primarily responsible to the House of Commons and the Prime Minister stays in office only as long as the Commons' support is retained. Almost all government ministers are drawn from the House of Commons, although ministers may also be appointed from the House of Lords.

C. What is Habeas Corpus?

Habeas Corpus is an ancient common law right[11]; in other words, it was a right first developed by the courts. Under this right, the courts are empowered to issue an Extraordinary Writ of Habeas Corpus commanding the Crown, if it is restricting the liberty of a person, to forthwith produce the detainee before the court and show just cause as to why the liberty of that person is being so restrained. Absent[12] sufficient justification, the court is duty bound to order the person discharged. Habeas Corpus is fundamental to common law systems of jurisprudence and it is remarkable that, even in medieval England, the Crown power could be controlled in this way.

Translate the following texts from French to English

A. « House of Lords » (La Chambre des Lords)

Depuis le 14ème siècle, la Chambre des Lords siège dans une chambre séparée de celle des Communes. La Chambre des Lords est composée de Lords temporels et de Lords spirituels nommés par le roi. A partir du 15ème siècle, les Lords temporels ont également été connus sous le titre de pairs. Historiquement, la Chambre des Lords pouvait rejeter et exercer son droit de veto à l'encontre de toute loi proposée par la Chambre des communes mais, progressivement, ce pouvoir fut réduit avant d'être aboli. Ce changement intervint en 1909 quand la Chambre des Lords refusa d'approuver le budget préparé par David Lloyd George. D'orientation socialiste, le budget posait les fondements qui aboutirent plus tard à la création de l'Etat providence. Le rejet du budget par les Lords conduisit à l'adoption de la loi sur le Parlement de (1911), en vertu de laquelle les Lords gardaient le droit d'examiner et de suspendre l'adoption de propositions de lois approuvées par la Chambre des communes mais perdaient le droit d'exercer son veto à l'encontre de telles lois.

---

[11] This sentence can mean two things, that:
- habeas corpus is a remedy of the common law that has existed for a long time, i.e. we give the term *common law* its general meaning;
- habeas corpus is a remedy developed by the common law courts, i.e. we give the term *common law* its more specific meaning, as law developed by the common law courts; see discussion concerning the common law, Chapter 3, Vol. 1 of this edition.

[12] Absent – in the absence of.

B. Qu'est-ce-que la décentralisation?

La décentralisation implique la création d'assemblées régionales élues dans chacune des régions constituant le Royaume-Uni. Chaque région a fait l'objet d'une loi sur la décentralisation définissant les différents pouvoirs qui lui sont conférés par le gouvernement central. Les compétences transférées garantissent à l'Ecosse, au Pays de Galles et à l'Irlande du Nord un droit limité à l'autonomie ; ces transferts n'incluent cependant aucune compétence majeure telles que la collecte de l'impôt, le contrôle des forces armées ou encore la politique étrangère. Ces domaines continuent de relever du contrôle de l'Etat central. Aussi, pour certains, la décentralisation n'a pas permis d'apporter le degré d'autonomie souhaité par une partie de la population vivant dans ces régions.

C. D'où vient l'habeas corpus?

Bien que développé par les tribunaux, la Magna Carta prévoit également explicitement le droit de soumettre une requête en habeas corpus. Selon la Magna Carta : *« Aucun homme libre ne sera arrêté ou emprisonné (...) ou exilé sauf en vertu d'un jugement légal de ses pairs, conformément à la loi du pays »*. Préalablement à l'adoption de la Magna Carta, le droit à l'habeas corpus faisait déjà l'objet d'une pratique jurisprudentielle constante et constituait donc un élément fondamental du droit non écrit du pays. Le recours en habeas corpus est un exemple de principes développés par les tribunaux médiévaux et qui continuent, aujourd'hui, de présenter un intérêt constitutionnel.

PART 5 – ADVANCED READING

Is the executive too powerful in the United Kingdom?

Pursuant to the doctrine of parliamentary sovereignty, power in the United Kingdom is vested in the Westminster Parliament on behalf of the people of the United Kingdom. Thus, out of the three branches of power, the legislative power, as it is predominantly elected through the vote of the citizens of the United Kingdom, should be the dominant power. However, many commentators feel that an increasingly powerful executive is undermining the role of the legislative branch. If this is true, why is power shifting away from parliament to the government? There are in fact a number of reasons.

- *The system of direct vote relied on in parliamentary general elections* One reason behind the increasing power of the executive branch, and in particular the power of the office of prime minister, results from the UK's reliance on the *first past the post electoral system* for national general elections. Reliance on such a system has in the past frequently resulted in very large parliamentary majorities. The result of this is that the leader of the majority party, i.e. the prime minister, can force government policy through both Houses of Parliament, without having to make any compromises as to its content.
- *Absence of a credible upper parliamentary house* No matter how laudable New Labour's intentions to democratize the House of Lords, in reality the reform process appears to have become a means

of reinforcing executive power. By removing most of the hereditary peers and leaving the Lords dominated by government appointed life peers, prime ministerial control over the upper house has, if anything, actually been reinforced.

- *An increasing reliance on secondary legislation* The increase in the power of the executive branch at the expense of its legislative partner has been reinforced by the increased trend toward the use of secondary delegated legislation. Such legislation in effect grants a minister power to effectively legislate in a specific area. Frequently secondary legislation[13] is adopted in the form of "skeleton acts" which, in place of specifying limits on how executive power may be used, give government ministers the power to act as they consider necessary in a given circumstance; thus there is little or no control exercised by parliament.
- *The ceremonial status of the monarchy* Any powers the UK monarchy might enjoy are in reality limited by convention. This is understandable; and it is difficult to imagine the Queen, given her unelected status, refusing to give the royal assent and blocking legislation adopted by parliament. However, it is necessary that some institution exist as a balance to the power of the executive branch.

That the UK constitutional system is to be commended for having achieved a gradual and mostly peaceful handover of power from absolute monarchy to parliament is not being questioned; however, in reality much of this power has now passed from the House of Commons to the government and in particular to the office of prime minister. Any such concentration of power in one individual cannot be considered good for democracy or for the prime minister!

---

[13] Secondary legislation, also called delegated legislation or subordinate legislation, is law made by ministers on the basis of a specific grant of power by parliament, contained in a primary legislative instrument.

Chapter eight

COURT STRUCTURE IN THE UNITED KINGDOM

PART 1 – TEXT 1 – INFORMATION

The court structure in the United Kingdom

The United Kingdom (UK) is effectively **made up of** four separate *home* nations or countries similar to the regions that one finds in other countries. The home nations are England, Wales, Scotland and Northern Ireland. Each of these areas is **governed** at national level by the monarch (Queen Elizabeth), a legislature (Houses of Parliament – the House of Commons and the House of Lords), an executive (prime minister and his government) and a judiciary. However, each home country, with the exception of England, also has its own regional parliament or **assembly** and executive. **Like** the United States, the UK has more than one legal system. In fact, there are three separate jurisdictions, namely England & Wales, Scotland and Northern Ireland.

Court structure in England and Wales

Law courts in England and Wales are divided into courts of criminal jurisdiction and courts of civil jurisdiction.

a) Courts of Criminal Jurisdiction in England and Wales
Original criminal jurisdiction in England and Wales is exercised in the Magistrates' Court or the Crown Court, **depending on** the **gravity** of the criminal **offence** involved. The large majority of smaller criminal matters, often referred to generally as summary offences, are **dealt with** by the Magistrates' Court; they are also referred to as **minor offences** or **non-indictable offences**[1]. Serious crimes, referred to as **indictable offences,** are tried in the Crown Court; these offences are also referred to as **felonies**. A third category of offence, known as a **triable-either-way** offence, **allows** the **accused** to **choose** either a **summary trial** before the Magistrates' Court or a **trial by jury** in the Crown Court[2]. Appeals from the Magistrates' Court on **questions of fact** go to the Crown Court, whilst the Administrative Court, a specialist court within the Queen's Bench Division, deals with appeals on **questions of law/points of law**. Appeals

---

[1] For a more in-depth discussion of criminal proceedings, the reader is recommended to read Chapter 6 on Criminal law, Vol. II of this series.

[2] This choice has to be confirmed/approved by the judiciary but is not normally withheld. Triable-either-way offences are also known as dual offences; hybrid offences are also referred to as "wobblers" in certain US jurisdictions.

from the Crown Court on questions of law also go to the Administrative Court. **Thereafter**, appeals on points of law may be **brought before** the Supreme Court. Appeals on conviction or sentence from the Crown Court **lie to** the Criminal Division of the Court of Appeal. The Supreme Court does not hear appeals on conviction or sentence.

b) The Civil Law Courts of England and Wales

The first instance civil jurisdiction **trial court** in England and Wales is the **County Court** and it has very wide jurisdiction, dealing with **claims** involving substantial amounts of money. However, a limited part of the County Court's civil jurisdiction has been **transferred** to the Magistrates' Court, for example **debt collection**. Thus, the Magistrates' Court has some **crossover** civil **jurisdiction**, although it remains primarily a criminal court. There is also a Family Court that hears family law cases, such as child custody, **maintenance** and **separation** orders. The next level of civil jurisdiction, after the County Court, is the High Court. The High Court has both a first instance jurisdiction for complex civil claims and an appellate jurisdiction from both the Magistrates' Court and the County Court. In certain limited circumstances appeals from the County Court go directly to the Civil Division of the Court of Appeal. The Court of Appeal also hears appeals from the High Court; appeals from decisions of the Court of Appeal lie to the Supreme Court.

There is no right to appeal to the **Court of Justice of the European Union** at any stage in UK court proceedings[3]. However, appeals may be brought before the **European Court of Human Rights** in Strasbourg for matters **arising** under the **European Convention on Human Rights**, established by the **Council of Europe** in 1950. Even so, before an action can be brought before the European Court of Human Rights, it is necessary that **domestic remedies be first exhausted**.

VOCABULARY

Made up of – *être constitué de*
Governed – *gouverné/dirigé*
Assembly – *assemblée (corps législatif aux prérogatives limitées)*
Like – *comme*
Original criminal jurisdiction – *compétence de première instance en matière pénale*
Depend (to) on – *dépendre de/varier selon*
Gravity – *gravité*
Offence – *infraction/délit*

---

[3]   There is the possibility for the UK national courts, if the trial concerns a question of EU law, to refer a question to the European Union courts; however, this only concerns questions as to the interpretation to be given EU law provisions. Once the correct interpretation is established by the European Court of Justice, the case is referred back to the national UK jurisdiction.

Deal (to) with something – *s'occuper de (ici, au sens de traiter quelque chose)*

Minor/summary/non-indictable offence – *infraction mineure (ne pouvant être jugée que suivant une procédure simplifiée, c'est-à-dire par une Magistrates' Court)*

Felony – *infraction grave*

Indictable offence – *infraction grave*

Triable-either-way offence – *infraction de gravité intermédiaire*

Allow (to) – *autoriser*

Accused – *accusé*

Choose (to) – *choisir*

Summary trial – *procès sommaire/simplifié*

Trial by jury – *procès devant jury*

Questions of fact – *questions de fait*

Appeal on questions of law – *appel fondé sur des questions de droit*

Lie (to) to – *être examiné par/relever de la compétence de*

Thereafter – *par la suite*

Brought (to be) before – *être porté devant*

Trial Court – *tribunal de première instance*

County Court – *tribunal de Comté*

Claim – *demande/réclamation*

Transfer (to) – *transférer*

Liquor licensing applications – *demandes de licence pour la vente de boissons alcoolisées*

Debt collection – *recouvrement de créance*

Maintenance order – *ordonnance d'entretien/de paiement d'une pension alimentaire*

Separation order – *ordonnance de séparation de corps*

Cross-over jurisdiction (having both criminal and civil jurisdiction) – *compétence mixte*

Court of Justice of the European Union (made up of the Court of Justice, the General Court and the Civil Service Tribunal) – *Cour de justice de l'Union européenne (composée de la Cour de justice, du Tribunal de première instance et des tribunaux spécialisés adjoints au Tribunal)*

European Court of Human Rights – *Cour européenne des droits de l'homme*

Arise (to) under – *relever de*

European Convention on Human Rights – *Convention européenne de sauvegarde des droits de l'homme et des libertés fondamentales*

Council of Europe (a pan-European organization, separate from the European Union, established to deal with social and human rights issues on a pan-European basis (1949)) – *Conseil de l'Europe (Organisation pan européenne, créée en 1949, distincte de l'Union européenne, et instituée afin de traiter différentes problématiques à caractère social et liées aux droits de l'homme)*

Domestic remedies be first exhausted (that no further right to appeal the decision exists at national level) – *règle procédurale de l'épuisement des voies de recours internes*

PART 1 – TEXT 1 – EXERCISES

1. Vocabulary test

Fill in the missing words using the vocabulary in Text 1

a) Unlike many legal systems, the UK has only two courts systems concerning _____ law and _____ law.
b) The first _____ civil law court in England and Wales is called the county court; however, the _____ court also enjoys limited civil law jurisdiction for small matters, such as debt collection.
c) Criminal offences in the UK are divided into indictable offenses and _____. Jurisdiction for the former is enjoyed by the _____.
d) Non-indictable offences also referred to as _____ offences are subject to _____ trial in the Magistrates' Court.
e) In civil law, appeals from the High Court _____ to the Civil Division of the Court of Appeal and thereafter to the _____.
f) Appeals concerning violations of human rights can be made to the _____ in Strasbourg; however, the matter must concern an issue coming within the _____.
g) The Magistrates' Court primarily has jurisdiction for _____ matters but because it also has limited responsibility for civil matters, it is said to have a _____ jurisdiction.

2. Vocabulary test

Write sentences with the following pairs of words. Your sentence should demonstrate the relationship between the words

a) Indictable/non-indictable
b) Triable-either-way offence/accused
c) Claims/County Court
d) Appeal/Supreme Court
e) Debt collection/County Court
f) Non-indictable/summary trial

3. Knowledge test

Each of the following statements is false; do you know why? Write a sentence stating why it is false

a) The Magistrates' Court only has jurisdiction over civil law matters.
b) The Supreme Court has the right to hear appeals from all criminal law decisions adopted by the Criminal Division of the Court of Appeal.
c) Minor offences can be tried either as indictable or non-indictable offences.
d) There is no court that has jurisdiction over the whole of the United Kingdom.
e) Appeals from the Supreme Court can be brought to the Court of Justice of the European Union.

PART 1 – TEXT 2 – MORE INFORMATION

The court structure in the United Kingdom

The United Kingdom is **made up of** four separate nations or home countries, effectively taking the form of regions: England, Wales, Scotland and Northern Ireland. Each of these areas is **governed** at national level by a monarch, a legislature (Houses of Parliament – the House of Commons and the House of Lords), an executive power (headed by a prime minister and his government) and a judiciary. Some executive and legislative powers have been devolved to the home countries of Scotland, Wales and Northern Ireland. At judicial level, both Scotland and Northern Ireland each have their own court system, whilst England and Wales together make up another separate jurisdiction. However, the UK Supreme Court acts as the final court of appeal for all three jurisdictions.

Court structure in England and Wales

Jurisdiction in England and Wales is divided between criminal law and civil law and the organization of the courts follows this basic division. The distinction between criminal and civil law is important, as each **fundamentally** serves a different function. In civil law matters, a **claimant/ complainant sues** another person seeking **compensation** for what has **occurred**. In criminal law, the state **prosecutes** the defendant, in order to punish him and **thereby deter further** crime. The **burden of proof** in criminal law matters requires that the prosecution prove that the accused is **guilty beyond all reasonable doubt**. In civil law matters, the burden of proof is **less high** and the claimant is only **required** to **prove** his case **on the balance of probabilities**. **Obviously**, this is an easier **standard** to satisfy. There is no separate administrative court system, **as is the case** in civil law countries.

> *a) Courts of Criminal Jurisdiction in England and Wales*
> **Original criminal jurisdiction** in England and Wales is exercised in the Magistrates' Court or the Crown Court, **depending on** the **gravity** of the criminal **offence** involved[4]. The Magistrates' Court, under the heading of minor or non-indictable offences, deals with the large majority of criminal matters. Serious crimes, referred to as **indictable offences** (also known as **felonies** in some common law jurisdictions), are tried in the Crown Court[5]. Some indictable offences, known as **triable-either-way** offences[6], **allow** the **accused** to **choose** between either a **summary trial** before the Magistrates' Court or a **trial by jury** in the Crown Court. The judge in the Magistrates' Court must confirm the choice of the defendant and thus the

---

[4] For a more in-depth consideration of criminal proceedings, the reader is recommended to read the Chapter 6 on Criminal law.

[5] Indictable offences are serious crimes that require a preliminary hearing, referred to as an indictment hearing, to establish whether there is sufficient evidence against the accused to justify his being tried by jury in the Crown Court. Non-indictable offences or minor offences, as their name suggests, do not require such a hearing.

[6] Also known as dual offences, hybrid offences are also referred to as "wobblers" in certain US jurisdictions.

process remains under the control of the state. By choosing to go before the Magistrates' Court, the defendant will probably receive a more lenient sentence, and this saves the state money and time, as it will not have to organize a jury trial. An example of a triable-either-way offence is theft. However, statistically, juries are less inclined to find someone guilty and thus some defendants prefer to opt for a jury trial.

Appeals from the Magistrates' Court on **questions of fact** go before the Crown Court, whilst the Administrative Court, a specialist court within the Queen's Bench Division, deals with appeals on **question of law/points of law**. Appeals from the Crown Court on questions of law also go to the Administrative Court. **Thereafter**, an appeal on a point of law may be **brought before** the Supreme Court. Appeals on conviction or sentence from the Crown Court **lie to** the Criminal Division of the Court of Appeal. The Supreme Court does not hear appeals on conviction or sentence.

b) The Civil Law Courts of England and Wales
b) i) The civil law courts
The civil jurisdiction trial court in England and Wales is the County Court, established by the County Courts Act of 1846. The County Court in England and Wales enjoys **jurisdiction over** disputes in most civil law areas such as contract law, **tort law**, land disputes, family law etc. County Court judges are either **district justices**, qualified to hear small claims, or circuit judges who hear more important matters. Appeals from decisions of County Court district justices are heard in the County Court by circuit judges. Appeals from County Court circuit judges are either heard by the High Court or the Court of Appeal. As a result of a **backlog** of cases, a limited part of the County Court's civil jurisdiction has been **transferred** to the Magistrates' Court, which is, as we have seen, **primarily** a court of criminal jurisdiction, for example for **debt collection**. Family law issues such as **maintenance and separation orders** are heard in the recently established Family Court.

The next level of civil jurisdiction is the High Court. The High Court has both a first **instance/original jurisdiction** for complex or civil law claims and also an appellate jurisdiction. At first instance, the High Court's **original jurisdiction** extends to civil law matters, which will be heard in one of its three divisions:
-   actions concerning the **common law** matters, for example tort or contract law, are heard by the Queen's Bench Division (based on the original Court of King's Bench);
-   questions involving **trusts**, company law, etc. are heard by the Chancery Division (based on the former Court of Chancery, created by the **Chancellor**); and
-   family law questions are heard by the Family Law Division.

The Civil Division of the Court of Appeal hears appeals from the High Court and decisions from the Court of Appeal go before the Supreme

Court. Exceptionally, it is possible to appeal a case directly from the High Court to the Supreme Court, by **leapfrogging** the Court of Appeal. This can occur if the Court of Appeal is already:
- **bound by precedent** to rule in a certain way on the issue; and
- if the Supreme Court has already **indicated its intention**, through an **obiter dictum**[7] to reconsider the precedent in question.

In such circumstances, rather than bringing the action before the Court of Appeal, which will be bound by precedent as to the decision it can take, the matter can be brought directly before the Supreme Court. The Supreme Court only hears appeals on questions of law of significant public importance and the 12 justices of the Supreme Court, like their US Supreme Court **colleagues**, severely limit the number of appeals they hear.

b) ii) Jurisdiction of the civil law courts
Civil law cases are **categorized** into different *tracks* on the basis of the amount of **damages** the complainant is **claiming** and on **whether** the case is complicated or not:
- ***small claims track*** Where the complainant is seeking less than £10,000 in damages, the action is brought in the County Court and will be dealt with under **simplified procedural rules**;
- ***fast track claims*** The **fast track procedure** applies to claims over £10,000 but less than £25,000. Again simplified procedural rules are applied and **expert testimony** is limited so as to **ensure** the matter is dealt with quickly, i.e. normally in one or two days;
- ***multi track claims*** This track involves claims of over £25,000. With such claims a **case manager** is **appointed** and a decision is taken whether the case, based on its complexity, should be heard in the County Court or the High Court. Normally, only very **complex** cases are heard in the High Court.

The High Court, sitting as the Administrative Court, has in addition a power of **judicial review**, whereby it reviews the legality of decisions taken by tribunals, local authorities and other administrative bodies. In this role, it fulfils the function of a separate administrative court.

c) Other courts
The Judicial Committee of the Privy Council takes its origins from the circle of **advisors** on which the King relied in medieval times. It is one of the oldest of the UK's institutions and nowadays it hears appeals from the Supreme Court decisions of certain **Commonwealth** countries, such as the Bermuda, the British Virgin Islands and the Cayman Islands. Decisions of the Privy Council are final and cannot be appealed to the Supreme Court. The Privy Council also has a limited domestic jurisdiction over disputes concerning the **Church of England**. In addition to the Privy Council, there is also an **array** of tribunals, whose function is to deal with specialist

---

[7] See discussion in Chapter 3.

issues such as employment law, tax law etc. Appeals from the decisions of these tribunals lie to the Administrative Court, under the heading of judicial review.

d) The relationship between the European Court of Justice (European Union) and the European Court of Human Rights (European Convention on Human Rights)

There is no right to appeal at any stage in UK court proceedings before the European Union (EU) courts, which are only empowered to apply EU law. However, questions concerning the interpretation to be given EU law, when a matter is before the UK courts, may be referred to the EU Court of Justice for a **determination, pursuant** to article 267 of the Treaty for the Functioning of the European Union. **Thereafter**, the matter is referred back to the UK trial court that made the request, which then decides the case based on the interpretation it received from the ECJ[8]. In its decision in the Factortame case (1990), the House of Lords[9] acknowledged that EU law takes precedence over UK law.

Appeals may be brought from the UK court system before the **European Court of Human Rights** in Strasbourg, for issues **arising** under the **European Convention on Human Rights**, established by the **Council of Europe** in 1950. However, before an appeal may be brought before the Court of Human Rights, it is necessary that all **domestic remedies be exhausted**.

VOCABULARY

Made (to be) up of – *être constitué de*
Govern (to) – *gouverner/diriger*
Categories – *catégories*
Fundamentally – *fondamentalement/essentiellement*
Complainant/claimant/plaintiff – *plaignant*
Sue (to) someone – *poursuivre quelqu'un en justice*
Compensation – *dédommagement*
Occur (to) – *se passer/se produire*
Prosecute (to) – *poursuivre/engager des poursuites pénales*
Thereby – *ainsi*
Deter (to) – *dissuader*
Further – *plus/additionnel*
Burden of proof – *charge de la preuve*
Guilty – *coupable*
Beyond all reasonable doubt – *au delà de tout doute raisonnable*
Less high – *moins élevé (idée de complexité)*
Required (to be) – *être exigé*

---

[8]   See first translation text for more information.
[9]   The former name of the Supreme Court.

Prove (to) – *démontrer/établir/prouver*
On the balance of probabilities – *balance/prépondérance des probabilités*
Obviously – *évident/manifeste*
Standard – *norme*
As is the case – *comme c'est le cas*
Original criminal jurisdiction – *compétence de première instance en matière pénale*
Depend (to) on – *dépendre de/varier selon*
Gravity – *gravité*
Offence – *infraction*
Deal (to) with something – *s'occuper de (au sens de traiter quelque chose)*
Minor/summary/non-indictable offence – *infraction mineure (ne pouvant être jugée que suivant une procédure simplifiée, c'est-à-dire par une Magistrates' Court)*
Felony – *crime sérieux (terme générique)*
Indictable offence/felony – *infraction grave*
Triable-either-way offence – *infraction de gravité intermédiaire*
Allow (to) – *autoriser*
Accused – *accusé*
Choose (to) – *choisir*
Summary trial – *procès sommaire/simplifié*
Trial by jury – *procès devant jury*
Questions of fact – *questions de fait*
Appeal on a point/question of law – *appel fondé sur une question de droit*
Lie (to) to – *être examiné par/relever de la compétence de*
Thereafter – *par la suite*
Brought (to be) before – *(être) porté devant*
Tort law – *droit de la responsabilité civile extracontractuelle*
District justice – *juge de district/magistrat*
Backlog – *accumulation (d'affaires non jugées)*
Transfer (to) – *transférer*
Primarily – *principalement/avant tout*
Liquor licensing applications – *demandes de licence pour la vente de boissons alcoolisées*
Debt collection – *recouvrement de créance*
Maintenance order – *ordonnance d'entretien/de paiement d'une pension alimentaire*
Separation order – *ordonnance de séparation de corps*
Original jurisdiction – *compétence de première instance*
Common law – *domaine de droit développé par les cours établies par le roi*
Trust – *fiducie*
Chancellor – *chancelier/premier ministre du roi*
Leapfrogging – *saute-mouton (bruler/sauter une étape)*
Bound (to be) by precedent – *être lié par un précédent*
Indicate (to) its intention – *indiquer son intention*
Obiter dictum – *obiter dictum (opinion émise par les cours supérieures sur un point de droit non déterminant pour l'affaire jugée en l'espèce et permettant*

d'indiquer une direction à suivre à l'avenir (la règle du stare decisis ne s'applique pas))

Colleague – *confrère/collègue*
Categorize (to) – *classifier*
Damages – *dommages et intérêts*
Claim (to) – *revendiquer/demander*
Whether – *si*
Small claims track – *règlement de litiges ne dépassant pas une somme modique*
Simplified procedural rules – *règles procédurales simplifiées*
Fast track procedure – *règlement rapide des litiges d'un montant intermédiaire*
Expert testimony – *témoignage/avis d'expert*
Ensure (to) – *garantir*
Multi track claims – *système de règlement des différends à voies multiples de résolution*
Case manager – *juge nommé pour gérer l'affaire*
Appoint (to) – *nommer/désigner*
Complex – *complexe*
Amount – *montant*
Judicial review – *contrôle juridictionnel de légalité*
Advisor – *conseiller*
Commonwealth countries – *pays du Commonwealth*
Church of England – *Eglise anglicane*
Array – *multitude/ensemble*
Preliminary determination/ruling – *question préjudicielle*
Pursuant to – *en vertu de/sur la base de*
European Court of Human Rights – *Cour européenne des droits de l'homme*
Arise (to) under – *relever de*
European Convention on Human Rights – *Convention européenne de sauvegarde des droits de l'homme et des libertés fondamentales*
Council of Europe – *Conseil de l'Europe*
Domestic remedies (must) be exhausted – *règle procédurale de l'épuisement des voies de recours internes*

PART 1 – TEXT 2 – EXERCISES

1. Definitions

Write a sentence defining each of the following terms

    a)   Indictable offence
    b)   Triable-either-way offence
    c)   Burden of proof
    d)   Appeal
    e)   Jurisdiction
    f)   Commonwealth

2. Sentences

Write sentences with the following pairs of words demonstrating the relationship between the words

   a)   Multi track claims/case manager
   b)   Appeal/European Court of Human Rights
   c)   Original jurisdiction/High Court
   d)   To leapfrog/Supreme Court
   e)   Civil law/criminal law
   f)   Chancery division/equity
   g)   Triable-either-way offence/Magistrates' Court
   h)   Non-indictable offence/indictable offence
   i)   Court of Justice of the European Union/appeal
   j)   County Court/criminal law

3. Fill in the missing words

Fill in the missing words using the vocabulary in Text 2

   a)   In the United Kingdom civil law claims are divided into three
        categories: the small claims track, _____ or multi track claims. As
        regards the latter track, a _____ will decide which court will hear
        the matter.
   b)   Criminal law offences are divided into two categories: _____ offences
        and _____.
   c)   Appeals from the Magistrates' Court on questions of _____ are
        heard in the Crown Court and appeals on points of law are heard by
        the _____.
   d)   The function of criminal law is to punish an offender in order to_____
        further crime, while the aim of civil law is to _____ the victim.
   e)   Appeals from the UK courts system to the European Court of Human
        Rights are possible once all _____ remedies have been _____.

4. Knowledge test

The following questions may be answered in writing or by way of discussion

   a)   Do you think the UK system of justice would operate better if it had a
        separate administrative system? Why do you think an administrative
        system has not developed?
   b)   In your jurisdiction, are crimes divided up on the basis of indictable
        and non-indictable offences?
   c)   Normally jury members have no experience or technical ability; why
        do we continue to rely on juries? Are they a relic from the past or are
        they necessary to ensure the fairness of the system?
   d)   Is it right that the basic function of criminal law is to punish the guilty
        party rather than help the victim?

Court structure in the United Kingdom

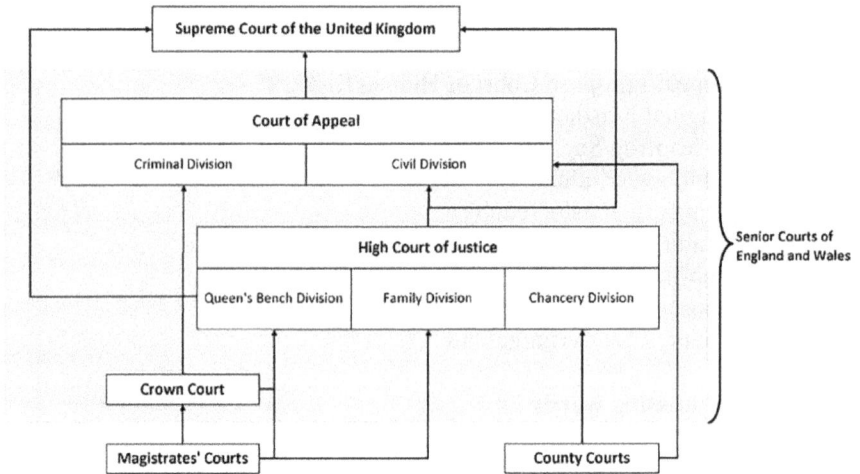

PART 2 – QUICK LOOK GRAMMAR REVISION

Frequency mid-sentence adverbs

The position of adverbs

Adverbs can be placed at the beginning of a sentence, mid-sentence, or at the end of the sentence.

Adverbs of frequency are usually placed mid-sentence.

Examples

Always
Ever
Almost never
Occasionally
Never
Usually
Rarely
Frequently
Seldom
Sometimes
Hardly ever

Using mid-sentence adverbs

Rule: *The adverb comes directly after the first auxiliary or before the verb if there is no auxiliary.*
Example:

He *always* **drafts** his contract like that.
He has *finally* **finished** drafting the brief.

When the verb "to be" is used other than as an auxiliary, it is common to place the adverb after the verb:
Example:
He **is** *always* on time for meetings.
He **was** *probably* in court yesterday.

If the adverb is placed after the verb "to be", it carries more weight. Compare to the above:
He *always* **is** on time. Why are you so surprised to see him?
He *probably* **was** in court yesterday. Why do you think he is lying?

The rule is similar for questions. The adverb is placed before the main verb.

In the negative ....

Rule: *Normally in a negative sentence, adverbs of frequency come in front of the verb.*

In a negative statement, the adverb can be placed before the main verb or before the negative auxiliary:
He does not *usually* **draft** contracts.
He *usually* **does** not (**doesn't**) **draft** contracts.

Exceptions ......

Rule: ***Always*** *and* ***never*** *follow a negative "helping verb" or the verb "to be" in negative form*
Example:
He **does** not (**doesn't**) *always* **draft** the contracts.
He **is** *never* on time for court.

PART 2 – GRAMMAR EXERCISES

1. Form the sentence

Add the word in brackets in its correct place in the sentence ....

(always) In this law firm Frank drafts the contracts for oil companies.
In this law firm Frank *always* drafts the contracts for oil companies.

a) (always) Frank is in his office at nine o' clock.
b) (usually) Frank sees clients in the afternoon.
c) (probably) The client will be here soon.
d) (already) The client is here.
e) (finally) Frank wrote back to the client.

f) (finally)   Frank is in the office.
g) (always)   Does Frank work from home?
h) (always)   Can you find Frank at work in the evenings?
i) (usually)   When does Frank leave his office?
j) (already)   Frank has read the contract.
k) (occasionally) Frank stays overnight in his office.

2. Form the sentence continued......

Add each of the adverbs to the sentence putting them in their mid-sentence position. Make changes to the sentence if you think it is necessary

A. Sentence: Jack does not arrive at work until 12 o'clock.
    usually   Jack usually does not arrive at work until 12 o' clock.

    Words: i) often, ii) frequently), iii) generally, iv) never, v) rarely.

B. Sentence: I do not draft contracts.
    Words: i) generally, ii) hardly ever, iii) occasionally, iv) usually, v) never, vi) seldom.

C. Sentence: Jack is not in the office in the afternoon.
    Words: i) usually, ii) generally, iii) ever, iv) seldom, v) frequently, vi) always.

3. Finish the sentence

Complete the sentences using the words in brackets.

a) (often)   The office is too hot.
b) (usually)   Frank does not take his car to work.
c) (always)   I do not stay up to watch the TV.
d) (never)   Frank does not take his car to work.

PART 3 – AUDIO – LISTENING AND SPEAKING

Comprehension

Listen to the following conversation, make notes of all the relevant facts and then answer the questions below. If you have trouble understanding, follow the conversation while also reading the text.

Discussion between John, a solicitor and James ....

John: "So James, tell me what can I do for you?"
James: "Well, I have had some difficulty with a company called Frank's Furniture Removals and I want to make them pay for what they have done to me."
John: "Right James, let's go back to the beginning. What happened exactly?"
James: "Oh OK. Last month my wife and I moved house. As part of the move

we hired Frank's Furniture Removals to transport our furniture from our old house to our new house."

John: "And you had an agreement with Frank's Furniture Removals? Did you actually sign a contract?"

James: "No, ah Frank came recommended by a friend and so we just reached an oral agreement. Is that a problem?"

John: "No not necessarily, but normally it is better to have a written agreement. Obviously it makes things clearer but it is possible to have an oral agreement and the most important thing is the agreement itself I guess. What exactly did you agree with Frank's Furniture Removals?"

James: "To move the furniture of course, what do you think?"

John: "Yes, I guessed that James, but under what conditions. Presumably he agreed to be there at a certain time and you agreed to pay him. What were the details of the agreement?"

James: "Well, he agreed to come to my house on the 4th of July at 9:00am and to transport all my furniture to my new address. In return I agreed to pay him £5,000. I have a good deal of furniture and so he needed to use a number of trucks and removal men. He said it would take all day to get the job done and a team of six removal men, not including Frank himself."

John: "Ok, so what happened?"

James: "Well, he turned up at 10 o'clock in the morning, an hour late and only had two workers with him. When I asked him where the other workers were, he said that they would be there later; in the meantime he suggested that I give them a hand."

John: "And did you?"

James: "No, I'm not in the habit of paying someone £5,000 to move my furniture and then moving it myself, what do you think?"

John: "I'm just trying to find out what happened. So what went wrong apart from the fact that he did not have a team of six men? Did he actually promise you that there would be six men there?"

James: "No not exactly, but he said six men would be necessary to do the job and judging by what happened he was right."

John: "So the removal did not go as planned?"

James: "You could say that. First, the removal ended up taking two days and not one day and secondly the furniture was damaged. There was a piano that was obviously dropped because one of the legs is damaged and it no longer stays in tune. Also an old bureau that is an heirloom from my wife's family was scratched and some pieces seem to have gone missing."

John: "OK, well there seems to be both civil and criminal liability here. You can sue Frank's Furniture Removals for the damage done to the furniture. However, for the furniture that is missing you are going to have to go to the police and make out a report stating that you have been robbed."

James: "I've done that, but the police don't seem to be too interested. They went to his address and there is no one there. Moreover, apparently there is no actual company called Frank's Furniture Removals. They rang the number that I had but no one answered and apparently it is registered to an old lady who knows nothing about it."

John: "OK, well it does not look good James. If you wanted to bring an action against Frank's Furniture Removals you would first have to have an address for Frank. You said a friend recommended him? Have you talked to your friend?"

James: "Well it was not so much a friend. In fact it was a guy I met in a bar and I don't know his name."

John: "Well that is not great and even if we found Frank, if that is even his name, you would have to decide the amount of your claim."

James: "Oh I have decided that alright. I had the furniture and the piano valued. I've lost close to £15,000 thanks to that guy."

John: "OK well that would allow us to decide what kind of action to bring. In a matter like this we would probably bring a fast track claim. It is faster as the name suggests and cheaper as a result."

James: "Good, well that is what I want to do so."

John: "Yes but as I said before, prior to bringing the action, we need to know who Frank really is. How did you pay him, by check or credit card?"

James: "No, I paid him in cash. He offered me a reduction of £1,000 if we kept the transaction under the table[10] and so I paid him in cash and I did not get a receipt."

John: "Oh no .....!"

PART 3 – AUDIO COMPREHENSION – EXERCISES

1. Comprehension

From the notes you have taken of the conversation, answer the following questions

    a)   Why has James come to see John?
    b)   What deal did John make with Frank's Furniture Removal?
    c)   Why did James agree to pay cash?
    d)   What loss did James suffer?
    e)   What happened when James went to the police?
    f)   What kind of civil action did John suggest that James bring?

2. Speaking practice

In the following series of conversation couplets, develop suitable responses to the questions asked

    a)   John: "So James, did you agree to pay by check or by cash?"
          James: "_____."
    b)   John: "Could you tell me what losses you suffered as regards your furniture?"
          James: "_____."
    c)   John: "Did you go to the police?"
          James: "_____."
    d)   John: "Why did you contact Frank's Furniture Removals?"
          James: "_____."

---

[10] Under the table: a transaction under the table is one that is not formally registered and is normally done so as to avoid paying tax on the transaction.

e)   John: "Why did you agree to pay by cash?"
     James: "_____."
f)   John: "What are the advantages of bringing a *fast track claim*?"
     James "_____"
g)   John: "Have the police being able to find anything out?"
     James: "_____."
h)   John: "So how long did the actual move take?"
     James: "_____."
i)   John: "Who recommended Frank's Furniture Removals to you?"
     James: "_____."

3. Speaking practice continued ......

*Create five other conversation couplets using in each couplet at least one word
from the vocabulary found in Part 1, Text 1 and Text 2*

4 . Speaking practice continued ......

Listen to the suggested replies and repeat

a)   John: "So James, did you agree to pay by check or by cash?"
     **James: "No I paid in cash, so the whole transaction was under
     the table."**
b)   John: "Could you tell me what losses you suffered as regards your
     furniture?"
     **James: "Well, some furniture went missing; they dropped the
     piano and damaged a valuable piece of furniture belonging to
     my wife."**
c)   John: "Did you go to the police?"
     James: "Yes, but they don't seem to be doing anything about it."
d)   John: "Why did you contact Frank's Furniture Removals?"
     James: "They came recommended."
e)   John: "Why did you agree to pay by cash?"
     **James: "Because he agreed to give me a reduction if it was a cash
     transaction."**
f)   John: "What are the advantages of bringing a *fast track claim*?"
     **James: "Well, if you bring a fast track claim, the costs will be
     reduced and you'll get a judgment more quickly."**
g)   John: "Have the police being able to find anything out?"
     James: "Nothing I'm afraid, they don't seem to be interested."
h)   John: "So how long did the actual move take?"
     James: "It took two days."
i)   John: "Who recommended Frank's Furniture Removals to you?"
     James: "Some guy in a bar, unfortunately I don't know his name."

5. Associated questions

Discuss the following questions

a)   Is any legal system capable of effectively dealing with companies like Frank's Furniture Removals?
b)   What crimes would Frank's Furniture Removals be guilty of in your country?
c)   If you were the lawyer in this situation, what advice would you give?
d)   If the police caught Frank and you were his lawyer, what advice would you give Frank?

PART 4 – TRANSLATION EXERCISES

When carrying out the translations it is not necessary to translate directly word for word; rather the emphasis should be on translating the sense of the text. Language is not directly interchangeable and so direct translations do not always convey the meaning in the text.

Translate the following texts from English to French

A. What is the article 267 procedure under European Union law?

The preliminary reference procedure is used when proceedings before a national court involve an element of EU law. If the national court is unsure of how to apply the EU law, the court may refer a question on the matter to the Court of Justice. The national court is said to ask the ECJ for a preliminary ruling, so as to enable it to correctly apply the relevant EU provision to the case before it. The function of the preliminary reference procedure is to ensure the effective and uniform application of EU law across all the Member States.

B. Judicial independence

The judiciary plays a vital part in British society and to perform its role it must be apolitical. Decisions and judgments adopted have to be made without any form of political bias. Indeed, judicial independence is seen by many as being the most important part of the Westminster system. So what is judicial independence? The courts of Great Britain are referred to as Crown courts, in that their jurisdiction is derived from the executive power of the Crown. However, although managed by the executive, the courts are required to be independent from both the executive and the legislative power. Thus, the executive is not allowed to delay or divert the course of justice. Moreover, the executive is also not allowed to force judges into acting in a manner that is anything other than impartial. Finally, judges have security of tenure whereby they can only be removed from office if they are guilty of serious misconduct.

C. Small claims actions in civil law actions before the UK courts

If the value of a case is £5,000 or less, it will generally be allocated to the small claims track. However, if it is a personal injury claim, it will be allocated to the small claims track only if the value of the claim for the personal injuries is not more than £1,000. In some cases, even if the value of the case is more than £5,000, should both parties agree, the court may allocate the case to the small claims track, so as to allow for a quick resolution of the matter. District justices hear small claims actions and decisions are taken by the judge sitting alone and not with a jury.

Translate the following texts from French to English

A. L'organisation de la Haute Cour

La Haute Cour comprend trois divisions distinctes. La première est connue sous le nom de division du Banc de la Reine. Elle est compétente pour les matières de *common law* telles que le droit des contrats, de la responsabilité civile extracontractuelle ou encore le droit foncier. La division du Banc de la Reine est composée de tribunaux qui agissent en tant que sous-divisions spécialisées : à titre d'exemple, la Cour Commerciale et la Cour de l'Amirauté (compétente en affaires maritimes). La division suivante est connue sous le nom de division de la Chancellerie et est compétente en matière de testaments, de fiducies, de faillites, de droits fonciers, de droit de propriétés intellectuelles (droit d'auteur et brevets) ainsi qu'en droit des sociétés. La Cour des sociétés, une sous-division spécialisée de la Chancellerie juge la plupart des litiges concernant les entreprises. Enfin, il existe une division des affaires familiales qui s'occupe des divorces, des affaires relatives aux mineurs ainsi que de l'administration des testaments.

B. La Cour d'appel

La Cour d'appel d'Angleterre et du Pays de Galles est la seconde plus haute juridiction du système juridique au Royaume-Uni. Les divisions criminelles et civiles de la Cour d'appel sont compétentes pour entendre les appels en matière criminelle et civile et sont respectivement présidées par le *Lord Chief Justice* et le *Master of the Rolls*. La division criminelle de la Cour d'appel entend les appels interjetés contre l'ensemble des condamnations et des peines prononcées par la Cour de la Couronne ; la division civile entend les appels interjetés contre les décisions de la Haute Cour de justice et des tribunaux de comté. Ce droit d'interjeter les appels n'est pas automatique et une autorisation préalable doit être obtenue, soit de la juridiction inférieure, soit de la Cour d'appel elle-même. Pour qu'une demande soit acceptée, un appel doit avoir de réelles chances de succès ou bien il doit exister une raison impérieuse qui justifie qu'il soit entendu.

C. La Cour suprême

La Cour suprême du Royaume-Uni entend les appels relatifs à tout litige jugé par les juridictions d'Angleterre et du Pays de Galles, de l'Irlande du Nord et de l'Ecosse. C'est la juridiction de dernier ressort et la plus haute cour d'appel dans le Royaume-Uni. La Cour suprême est également compétente pour résoudre les litiges relatifs à la décentralisation. Instituée par la loi de 2005 sur la réforme constitutionnelle, la Cour suprême a remplacé la Chambre des Lords en tant qu'instance judiciaire d'appel de dernier ressort. Avant cette réforme constitutionnelle, la Chambre des Lords était constituée d'une branche législative, ainsi que d'une branche judiciaire. L'une des raisons expliquant la création de la Cour suprême était la volonté d'établir une séparation claire entre les branches législative et judiciaire du pouvoir ; en réalité, ces liens n'étaient que symboliques.

PART 5 – ADVANCED READING

Differences between the common law and civil law systems

The major difference between common and civil law methodology is that the civil law system is primarily developed by technocrats and legislators and is based on detailed codes, the secondary role of the courts being to apply this law. In comparison, lawyers and judges developed the common law, and thus a primary role was given to case law with a secondary role played by legislation/doctrine. This basic divergence leads to fundamental differences in the administration of justice in common and civil law countries.

- *The significance given to the role of public law* Under the civil law system, private law is considered as almost a gift by the legislator to private citizens; the real role of the state being one of *control* and *generalized protection* as opposed to the *affirmation of individual rights.* Thus, the development of the civil law necessarily required not only a distinction to be drawn between public and private law but also a prioritization of public interests over those of the private citizen. In comparison, the common law awards the state far less prerogatives and consequently the state is frequently subject to the same laws as its citizens. Consequently, there has been no real need to create a separate court system to accommodate it.

- *The civil law is interested in who you are; the common law in what happened to you* The civil law system is structured on the creation of legal categories in which people are filed according to their classification: some are automatically granted protection, others automatically owe duties. As a result, the civil law courts are less interested in the facts of a case and more interested in defining the nature of the parties, so as to determine the law to be applied to them. Traditionally, the common law, rather than creating categories of protection and corresponding duties, tended to treat everyone the same. Thus, even today, it is less interested in *who people are* and concentrates more on *what has happened to them,* and it is by reference to the facts of the situation that rights are distributed. The common law adopts a fact-based analysis of what actually happened to the parties and, as the facts change, so too does the nature of the law. To the contrary, the civil law applies a legal analysis to a situation, and the facts of the matter are of secondary interest.

- *Adversarial v inquisitorial trial procedure* The above difference has in turn led to a different approach as regards the administration of justice. The common law is said to adopt an adversarial approach; the civil law, on the contrary, operates by way of an inquisitorial system. In the adversarial system the parties to a legal action compete, and the state is involved above all to ensure that both parties receive a fair hearing. In contrast, the inquisitorial system requires the judge to become directly involved in the trial, whereby (s)he acts as an inquisitor seeking to reveal the truth of what occurred.

- *Binding precedent* As regards the operation of the common law case law system, binding precedent is a central element of the system. Under the *stare decisis* rule, courts on the same level, and all courts of lower jurisdiction, must follow previously adopted decisions. Common law court precedent can concern either a rule of law developed by the court itself or a binding interpretation of a legislative provision.

In the civil law system, the primary source of law is written codified texts and the role of case law and binding precedent is less important, remaining primarily a secondary and persuasive source of law. That said, just as written law is taking on more importance in the common law system, case law is playing an increasingly significant role in civil law systems.

Chapter nine

THE HISTORY AND ORGANIZATION OF THE EUROPEAN UNION

PART 1 – TEXT 1 – INFORMATION

The creation of the European Union

The **aftermath** of World War II saw the creation of many international organizations in Europe. These organizations were established with the **aim** of avoiding future wars and also **sought** to ensure Europe's **future** economic and political survival. It was in this environment that a number of different treaties were entered into in the 1950s by some European countries, eventually leading to the establishment of what is now known as the European Union (EU).

The European Coal and Steel Treaty (1951)

The European Coal and Steel Treaty, signed in 1951, established the European Coal and Steel Community (ECSC). The Treaty **came into effect** in 1952, lasting for a **period** of fifty years, and its signatory states were Germany, France, Italy and the Benelux countries (Belgium, the Netherlands and Luxembourg). **Basically**, the Treaty recognized that **coal** and **steel** were the principal **ingredients** of war and that **placing** the **management** of these **raw materials** under the ECSC member states' **joint control** would ultimately help to ensure peace between these states. **Although** the **scope** of the Treaty was limited to the coal and steel industries, the Treaty is of **vital** historical importance as it **sowed the seeds** for future European integration.

The European Economic Community Treaty (1957)

The **European Economic Community** was established in 1957 (EEC, later known as the **European Community** (EC)) by the EEC Treaty (later known as the EC Treaty). The European Union (EU) was subsequently created in 1992 by the Treaty on European Union (TEU or Maastricht Treaty). Finally, the Treaty on the Functioning of the European Union (TFEU) replaced the EC Treaty in 2009, and the EC has ceased to exist.

To achieve the aims of the EU, the TFEU Treaty adopted and developed the institutional structure previously put in place by the EC Treaty.
- **European Council** The European Council is made up of the Heads of State of each of the 28 EU member states and has a President elected by its members for a period of two and a half years. The Council normally meets at pre-scheduled meetings, a **set number of times** a year.
- **Council of the European Union** The Council is the main decision-

making body of the EU and is **composed** of **ministers** from the governments of each of the member states. It is the top tier legislative body in the EU.

- **European Parliament** The Parliament along with the Council represents the second member of the **two-tier** EU legislative structure. Members of the Parliament are elected by the direct vote of the European Union's citizens.
- **European Commission** If the Council and the Parliament represent the two-tiered legislative power of the Union, then the Commission in many ways comprises its **executive branch** and is the main initiator of EU policy.
- The **Court of Justice of the European Union** is made up of three courts: the **Court of Justice**, the **General Court** and the **Civil Service Tribunal**. Together these courts have jurisdiction over the interpretation of EU law.
- **European Central Bank** The European Central Bank is responsible for the management of the Union's single currency, the Euro.
- **Court of Auditors** The Court of Auditors is **tasked with** the **auditing** of the EU's finances.

The Treaty on European Union (TEU or Maastricht Treaty – 1992)

The Maastricht Treaty created a new organization called the **European Union, expanding** the **scope of European integration** beyond the economic aims of the EC to two new areas:
- common foreign and security policy;
- police and judicial cooperation.

Since the adoption of the Maastricht Treaty, other treaties such as the Treaty of Amsterdam, the Nice and the Lisbon Treaties have been signed, and the activities of the European Union now extend to social, political and economic matters. The European Union is the world's largest economic block with its own currency, the Euro, which is used by 19 of its 28 member states. It is a truly unique organization: part federal and part **intergovernmental**.

VOCABULARY

Aftermath – *à la suite de*
Aim – *objectif*
Seek (to) – *rechercher*
Future – *avenir*
Come (to) into effect – *entrer en vigueur*
Period – *durée*
Basically – *au fond*
Coal – *charbon*
Steel – *acier*
Ingredients – *ingrédients/facteurs*

Place (to) – *mettre*
Management – *gestion*
Raw materials – *matières premières*
Joint control – *contrôle commun*
Although – *bien que*
Scope – *portée*
Vital – *vital/capital*
Sow (to) the seeds – *semer les graines*
European Economic Community Treaty – *Traité instituant la Communauté européenne*
European Community (new name for the EEC after Maastricht Treaty in 1992) – *Communauté européenne*
Treaty on the Functioning of the European Union (TFEU) (new Treaty encompassing much of the former EC and Maastricht Treaty – *Traité sur le fonctionnement de l'Union européenne*
Council of the European Union – *Conseil de l'Union européenne*
Composed (to be) of Ministers – *être composé de ministres*
European Council – *Conseil européen*
Set number of times – *nombre déterminé de fois*
European Central Bank – *Banque centrale européenne*
European Parliament – *Parlement européen*
Two-tier – deux tiers
European Commission – *Commission européenne*
Executive branch – *pouvoir exécutif*
Court of Justice of the European Union (collective name for the institution containing three courts) – *Cour de justice de l'Union européenne (composée de trois institutions)*
Court of Justice – *Cour de justice*
General Court – *Tribunal*
Civil Service Tribunal – *Tribunal de la fonction publique*
Court of Auditors – *Cour des comptes*
Tasked (to be) with something – *être missionné/avoir pour fonction de*
Audit (to) – *auditer*
European Union (union of states in which integration occurs at economic, social and political level) – *Union européenne*
Pillars – *piliers*
Common Foreign and Security Policy – *politique étrangère et de sécurité commune*
Cooperation in the area of Justice and Home Affairs – *coopération dans le domaine de la justice et des affaires intérieures*
Since – *depuis*
Intergovernmental – *intergouvernemental*

PART 1 – TEXT 1 – EXERCISES

1. Vocabulary test

Fill in the missing words using the vocabulary in Text 1

a) The name of the _____ was changed to the European Community (EC) by the _____.

b) The _____ is sometimes referred to as the executive of the _____.

c) The _____ is said to have _____ the seeds for later European integration.

d) The _____ is made up of the Heads of State from each of the _____.

e) The Court of Auditors has the duty to _____ the European Union's _____.

f) The _____ created three different spheres of EU activity, namely economic union, the establishment of a common foreign and security policy and _____ and _____ cooperation.

2. Vocabulary test

Write sentences with the following pairs of words. Your sentence should demonstrate your knowledge of the relationship between the words

a) Period/fifty years

b) European Economic Community/European Community

c) Court of Justice of the European Union/General Court

d) Pillars/Maastricht Treaty

e) Raw materials/European Coal and Steel Treaty

3. Knowledge test

Each of the following statements is false; do you know why? Write a sentence stating why it is false

a) The European Coal and Steel Treaty is the most significant EU Treaty still in force as it laid the grounds for later EU integration.

b) The Council of the European Union is made up of the Heads of State of each of the member states.

c) The Maastricht Treaty officially brought the European Community to an end.

d) The Euro is made up of the twenty-eight European Union member states.

PART 1 – TEXT 2 – MORE INFORMATION

The creation of the European Union

The **aftermath** of World War II saw the creation of many organizations **seeking** to **improve** international relations. For example, in order to **prevent future wars**, the **United Nations** (UN) was established in 1945. On the economic **front**, the **General Agreement on Trade and Tariffs** (GATT) and subsequently the **World Trade Organization** (WTO) were created to promote **trade** and commerce between states. Finally, as regards social **issues**, the **Council of Europe** established in 1949 sought to **ensure** respect for human rights through the adoption of the **European Convention on Human Rights** in 1952. The countries of Western Europe in particular realized the **need** for transnational cooperation between them. This was not only to **avoid** future wars but also to ensure Western Europe's economic and political future, in a post World War II world dominated by the United States of America (USA) and the **Union of the Soviet Socialist Republics** (USSR). The **later** arrival of Japan as a major economic power only served to **confirm** this view, and it was in this global environment that the first **steps** towards the establishment of the European Union (EU) were taken.

What is the European Union?

The EU is a unique organization established **pursuant to** a number of different treaties **discussed below**. The EU does not quite seek to create a federation of states like the United States; yet, **as regards** the **scope** and **depth** of the integration it promotes between its member states, it goes much **further** than a typical international organization. **Membership requires** states to **surrender** part of their **sovereignty** to the EU's institutions in those areas coming within the EU's **remit**. In these areas the law of the European Union is given supremacy over national law **provisions**. This transfer of sovereignty is reinforced by the fact that many decisions adopted by the member states at European level may be adopted by way of **majority** voting. **Thus**, decisions can be adopted even when some of the member states do not agree. However, in more sensitive areas such as tax harmonization and foreign policy, unanimity between the member states is required. In these areas, member states are said to enjoy a **right of veto** as regards the adoption of policy. Consequently, the EU is a hybrid organization, **part intergovernmental** and part federal.

The key treaties establishing the European Union

The European Union has been created through the adoption of different treaties, each one **reinforcing** and **extending** the **level** and scope of integration between its member states. The **project** began with the establishment of the **European Coal and Steel Treaty** in 1951 and the later establishment of the EEC in 1957, until finally the European Union (EU) was created in 1992. **Throughout** this time, the membership of the Union expanded, as did the role and power of the European institutions established to run it.

*a) The **European Coal and Steel Treaty (1951)***
The first treaty promoting European integration was the European Coal and Steel Treaty, signed in 1951. It established the European Coal and Steel Community (ECSC) and came into effect in 1952, lasting for fifty years. The aim of the European Coal and Steel Treaty was to prevent war **occurring** between its member states, namely Germany, France, Italy and the Benelux countries (Belgium, the Netherlands and Luxembourg). Recognizing that member state coal and steel industries were the **main**

ingredients of war, the ECSC sought to place the exploitation of these materials beyond the control of its member states and thus **ensure** peace between them. Under the Treaty, a number of institutional bodies were established to **manage** the exploitation of these two resources on behalf of the member states, which in return gave up control or **sovereignty** over their national coal and steel **reserves**. The Treaty, which had a **lifespan** of 50 years, came to an end in 2002; however, it remains significant as it **sowed the seeds** for future European integration. Indeed, the **preamble** of the Treaty made it clear that it was only the first step towards the establishment of greater economic and social cooperation between its member states.

b) The *European Economic Community Treaty (1957)*

The European Economic Community Treaty was signed in 1957 and established the European Economic Community (EEC), later referred to as the European Community (EC), before being incorporated into the newly created European Union (EU) in 1992 under the Maastricht Treaty. In 2009 the EC Treaty was replaced by the **Treaty on the Functioning of the European Union** (TFEU), pursuant to the terms of the Lisbon Treaty, also adopted in 2009 and at this time the EC ceased to exist. One of the main aims of the EU is to establish a **single market/internal market** between its twenty-eight member states, whereby goods, services, workers and capital can circulate freely.

c) The *Single European Act* (*1986*)

Prior to the creation of the EU, the Single European Act (SEA) was introduced to improve the functioning of the EEC. To do this, SEA sought to achieve three main aims.

- *Accelerate the creation of the Single Market* Under the institutional regime established by the EEC Treaty, the Commission's proposals regarding the single market had to be adopted unanimously by all the member states meeting at Council level. The result was that very few legislative initiatives creating the Single Market were actually **passed**. To **overcome** this, the SEA expanded the use of **qualified majority voting** (QMV) as regards single market **legislative proposals,** thereby removing the right of veto enjoyed by member states. Under QMV, directives establishing the internal market can be adopted where 55% of the Council's members, representing 65% of the Union's population, are in favour of the proposal.
- *Increase the role of the European Parliament* As the activities of the EEC grew, it was considered necessary to democratize the process of European integration and to increase the role of the European Parliament in the legislative process.
- *Formalize certain practices that had grown up since 1957* Although at the time of its creation the EEC was primarily an economic organization, it was created **in the context of** a general move by European countries towards greater political and social integration. Thus, as member states brought their economies closer together, they

had also begun to take **tentative** steps towards establishing better political and social cooperation between them. The SEA sought to confirm this new approach by **creating** an official **framework,** promoting member state cooperation in the development of foreign policy.

To some extent the SEA was the **bridge** between the economic integration established by the EEC Treaty and the subsequent political and social integration introduced by the **Treaty on European Union**.

*d) The **Treaty on European Union** (TEU or Maastricht Treaty, 1992)*
The Maastricht Treaty extended the scope of European integration beyond economic matters into areas of a more political and social character. It created a new organization called the European Union, which effectively encompassed three separate areas of activity.

* *Economic union* Following the adoption of the Maastricht Treaty, the EEC was incorporated into the newly created European Union and its name was changed to the EC (European Community).
* *Common foreign and security policy* Member states increased efforts aimed at **coordinating** their individual foreign policies.
* *Police and judicial cooperation* Under this heading member states agreed to begin taking measures to coordinate policy between them, in areas such as **money laundering, asylum and refugees, customs cooperation** etc.

e) Treaties adopted after Maastricht
After the Maastricht Treaty, other treaties such as the Amsterdam, Nice and Lisbon Treaties were signed, extending the scope of the Union and reforming its structure so as to allow increased membership. As we have seen, the Lisbon Treaty, also known as the Reform Treaty, amended the TEU and replaced the EC Treaty with the TFEU, thereby officially bringing the EC to an end. The Lisbon Treaty also extended the role of QMV and the European Parliament as regards the adoption of legislation. It created the position of High Representative of the Union for Foreign Affairs and Security Policy in a bid to better coordinate EU member states' foreign policy. Finally, in recognition of increasing EU unpopularity, it put in place, for the first time, a procedure whereby member states could leave the EU.

The European Union now comprises twenty-eight member states all working together in the areas of activity outlined above. It is a major economic superpower, which has allowed the countries of Western Europe to overcome the economic hardships of war. It has also facilitated the peaceful transformation of central European countries from communist states into modern European economies founded on common democratic values.

The economic aims of the European Union

At economic level the EU aims to promote integration between member states in different areas.

- *Internal market* One of the fundamental aims of the EU is the creation of a single market between its member states, i.e. the creation of a single **trading block** allowing for the **free movement** of goods, workers, services and capital between member states. It has also established a **customs union** between its members by applying a **common customs tariff** for the importation of goods into the EU from non-EU states.

- *CAP/TRANS* The EU sought to develop common policies in the areas of agriculture and transport by establishing a **Common Agricultural Policy (CAP)** and a **Common Transport Policy (TRANS)**. The purpose behind the CAP is to develop a mechanized, efficient agricultural industry, so as to ensure that Europe can produce enough food for its own needs. The Common Transport Policy seeks to establish pan-European transport routes (road, rail, air and maritime) between member states, from north to south and east to west.

- *EU-wide competition policy* Alongside the Single Market, the EU has established a common **competition policy** to ensure a competitive European industrial and services base. Competition policy is a mechanism **whereby** businesses are **prevented** from acting in a non-competitive manner towards each other. Non-competitive behaviour can involve a **company** in a **monopoly position** abusing its **market power**, for example by forcing another company to pay excessive prices for its services. Alternatively, if a number of separate companies come together and form a cartel and fix prices for their products, they will also be considered to be in breach of EU competition law. Responsibility for the application of competition policy has been given to the European Commission, one of the EU's most important institutions.

The institutions of the European Union

To achieve its aims the Union has a number of different institutions

- **European Council** Composed of the Heads of State of each of the member states, the European Council became a formal institution of the European Union, pursuant to the reform introduced by the Lisbon Treaty adopted in 2009. It is headed by a President appointed for a period of two and a half years and meets a number of times a year at pre-scheduled meetings, referred to as summits. The European Council has the power to introduce policy and generally gives political direction to the Union.

- **Council of the European Union** The Council, along with the European Parliament, is the dominant legislative power of the EU and is **composed of** ministers from each of the member states.

- **European Parliament** The European Parliament represents the democratic face of the European Union and is elected by the direct vote of the Union's citizens. The Parliament is the second member of the Union's **two-tier** legislative structure.

- **European Commission** If the Council and the Parliament represent the legislative power of the Union, the Commission can be considered to act as its **executive branch**[1]. As the Union's executive power, the Commission is responsible for proposing EU laws that are later adopted or rejected by the Council and the Parliament. The Commission is also responsible for the day-to-day administration and implementation of EU policies and programs.
- **European Central Bank** The European Central Bank (ECB) also became an official institution of the European Union pursuant to the terms of the Lisbon Treaty. Its function is to govern the EU's single currency, the Euro.
- **Court of Justice of the European Union** The Court of Justice of the European Union is responsible for the application of the Treaties making up the EU, as well as the laws and decisions established **thereunder**. The **judicial branch** is made up of the **General Court**, a **Civil Service Tribunal** for ruling on **staff** disputes within the organization's institutions and the **Court of Justice.** The Court of Justice has both an appellate and original first instance jurisdiction.

VOCABULARY

Aftermath – *à la suite de*
Seek (to) (sought) – *rechercher (recherché)*
Improve (to) – *améliorer*
War – *guerre*
United Nations – *Nations Unies*
Front – *front*
General Agreement on Trade and Tariffs – *Accord général sur les tarifs douaniers et le commerce*
World Trade Organization – *Organisation Mondiale du Commerce*
Trade – *commerce/échange commercial*
Issues – *problèmes/questions*
Council of Europe – *Conseil de l'Europe*
Ensure (to) – *garantir/assurer*
European Convention on Human Rights – *Convention européenne de sauvegarde des droits de l'homme et des libertés fondamentales*
Need – *besoin*
Avoid (to) – *éviter*
Union of the Soviet Socialist Republics (USSR) – *Union des républiques soviétiques socialistes*
Later – *plus tard/ultérieurement*

---

[1] Here reference is made to Montesquieu's theory of the separation of powers. The EU institutions are not formally organized pursuant to this theory and reference is made here to facilitate an understanding of the relationships between the different institutions.

Confirm (to) – *confirmer*
Step – *étape*
Pursuant to – *conformément à*
Discussed below – *analysé ci-dessous*
Further – *plus loin*
Membership – *être membre*
Require (to) – *exiger*
Surrender (to) – *céder*
Sovereignty – *souveraineté*
Remit – *attribution/compétence (champs de)*
Provisions – *dispositions*
Majority – *majorité*
Thus – *ainsi*
Right of veto – *droit de veto*
Part intergovernmental – *partiellement intergouvernemental*
Reinforce (to) – *renforcer*
Extend (to) – *élargir/étendre*
Level – *niveau*
Project – *projet*
European Coal and Steel Treaty – *traité de Paris instituant la Communauté européenne du charbon et de l'acier*
Throughout – *tout au long de/pendant ce temps*
Occurring – *se produisant*
Main ingredients – *ingrédients/facteurs principaux*
Ensure (to) – *garantir*
Manage (to) – *gérer*
Reserves – *réserves*
Lifespan – *durée de vie*
Sow (to) the seeds – *semer les graines*
Preamble – *préambule*
European Economic Community Treaty – *Traité instituant la Communauté économique européenne*
Treaty on the Functioning of the European Union – *Traité sur le fonctionnement de l'Union européenne*
Single market – *marché unique*
Single European Act – *acte unique européen*
Accelerate (to) – *accélérer*
Pass (to) a law – *adopter une loi*
Overcome (to) – *surmonter*
Legislative proposal – *proposition législative*
Formalize (to) – *formaliser*
In the context of – *dans le cadre de*
Tentative – *tentative*
Create (to) – *créer*
Framework – *cadre*
Bridge – *pont*
Treaty on European Union – *Traité sur l'Union européenne*
Coordinate (to) – *coordonner*

Money laundering – *blanchiment d'argent*
Asylum and refugees – *asile et réfugiés*
Customs cooperation – *coopération douanière*
Trading block – *bloc commercial*
Free movement – *libre circulation*
Customs union – *union douanière*
Common customs tariff – *tarif douanier commun*
Common Agricultural Policy (CAP) – *Politique Agricole Commune (PAC)*
Trans-European-Network (TEN) – *Politique Commune des Transports*
Competition policy – *politique de la concurrence*
Whereby – *en vertu duquel*
Prevent (to) – *prévenir*
Company – *société*
Monopoly position – *position de monopole*
Market power – *pouvoir de marché*
Council of the European Union – *Conseil de l'Union européenne*
Composed (to be) of – *composé de*
Qualified majority voting – *vote à la majorité qualifiée*
European Council – *Conseil européen*
European Central Bank – *Banque centrale européenne*
European Parliament – *Parlement européen*
European Commission – *Commission européenne*
Two-tier legislative – *pouvoir législatif ayant deux chambres*
Executive branch – *pouvoir exécutif*
Court of Justice of the European Union (collective name for the institution containing three courts) – *Cour de justice de l'Union européenne (composée de trois cours)*
Court of Justice – *Cour de justice*
General Court – *Tribunal*
Civil Service Tribunal – *Tribunal de la fonction publique*
Staff – *personnel*

PART 1 – TEXT 2 – EXERCISES

1. Definitions

Write a sentence defining each of the following terms – one sentence per term

    a)   Intergovernmental
    b)   Remit
    c)   Lifespan
    d)   Framework
    e)   Legislative proposal

2. Sentences

Write sentences with the following pairs of words. Your sentence should demonstrate your knowledge of the relationship between the words

    a)   Court of Justice of the European Union/Court of Justice

b)   Free movement/customs union
c)   Treaty on European Union/European Union
d)   Reform Treaty/Treaty on the Functioning of the European Union
e)   Aftermath/TEU
f)   Competition policy/single market
g)   European Central Bank/euro

3. Fill in the missing words

Using the vocabulary in Text 2, fill in the missing words

a)   The purpose behind the _____ is to allow for the development of a mechanized and efficient European _____ industry.
b)   If the political organization of the EU was to be compared to Montesquieu's theory of the separation of powers, the European Commission is its _____ branch and the Parliament along with the _____ represent its legislative branch.
c)   Membership of the European Union involves a partial _____ of sovereignty from _____ to the organization.
d)   The _____ is the body responsible for the adoption and application of the European Convention on Human Rights adopted in _____.
e)   The function of EU competition policy is to prevent companies in a _____ position from _____ their market _____.

4. Knowledge test

The following questions may be answered in writing or by way of discussion

a)   Why do you think the European Union has become unpopular?
b)   Should the European Union in your opinion, stop taking in new member states and limit its future activity to economic matters?
c)   Do you believe that the Euro will continue to be the currency of EU member states?
d)   List the positive things that the EU has achieved for Europe.

PART 2 – QUICK LOOK GRAMMAR REVISION

The Past Perfect – *had done something*

The past perfect expresses an activity or event that *occurred **before another activity or event also situated** in the past.*

The past perfect is formed by the auxiliary had + past participle of the main verb

For example:
I was not tired at dinner time because *I had already slept* in the plane.

Note:

Distinguishing the past perfect from the present perfect

Unlike the past perfect, *the present perfect expresses an activity that gives information about the present*; the past perfect gives information about the past

For example:
Past perfect: I *was* not hungry at 12:00pm, I *had already* eaten.
Present perfect: I *am* not tired now, *I have already slept* in the plane.

Note:

Distinguishing the past perfect from the past progressive

The past progressive expresses an activity that was in progress at a particular time in the past.

Both the past perfect and the past progressive are frequently coupled with the past simple.

When the past progressive is coupled with the past simple, it illustrates that one event was in progress when another occurred.

When the past perfect is coupled with the past simple, the past perfect expresses something that happened before the event related in the past simple.

For example:
Past perfect: I *had* already *eaten* when my client arrived.
Past progressive: I *was eating* when my client arrived.

1. Forms of the past perfect

a) When making a statement:
The auxiliary HAD + the past participle of the verb:
   – I, you, he, she, it, we, they HAD SLEPT/EATEN/WORKED by the time the plane arrived;
      or in spoken form
   – I'd, you'd, he'd, she'd, it'd, we'd, they'd SLEPT/EATEN/ WORKED by the time the judge arrived.

b) When negating, the word NOT is placed after the auxiliary HAD:
   – I, you, he, she, it, we, they HAD NOT SLEPT/EATEN/WORKED by the time the plane arrived;
      or in spoken form
   – I, you, he, she, it, we, they HADN'T SLEPT/EATEN/WORKED by the time the plane arrived.

c) When asking a question:
   – Had I, you, he, she, it, we, they SLEPT/EATEN/WORKED by the time the plane arrived?

d) When answering a question:
  – Yes, I, you, he, she, it, we, they HAD SLEPT/EATEN/WORKED by the time the plane arrived.
  – No, I, you, he, she, it, we, they HAD NOT/ HADN'T SLEPT/ EATEN/WORKED by the time the plane arrived.

PART 2 – GRAMMAR EXERCISES

1. The past perfect v the present perfect

Complete the sentence with the word in brackets using either the present or the past perfect

(Eat already) I am not hungry
I am not hungry. I have already eaten

a) *(Finish, already)* It is twelve o' clock I _____ my work, so I am going home to bed.
b) *(Finish, already)* By twelve o' clock I _____ my work, so I went home to bed.
c) *(Start, already)* I was late. The case _____ by the time I got to court.
d) *(Start, already)* I'm late. The case _____.
e) *(Leave, already)* John missed his meeting yesterday because of a traffic jam.

By the time he reached the airport, his plane _____.

2. The past perfect v the past progressive

Complete the sentence with the word in brackets using either the past perfect or the past progressive

a) *(Rain)* When I left for the office this morning it _____, so I bought an umbrella.
b) *(Stop)* By the time the case was over this evening, the rain _____.
c) *(Finish)* Last night I started to work at 8:00pm. The meeting in the office next door _____ by that time.
d) *(Wash)* When I walked into the office kitchen after the meeting, someone _____ all the dishes.
e) *(Wash)* When I walked into the office kitchen, someone _____ the dishes.

3. Ask and answer the question

Complete the questions and answers with the words in brackets

(You, enjoy) Did you enjoy the meeting last night?
Yes, *(go, not)* I had not/hadn't gone to a meeting in a long time.

a) *(You, see)* _____ the client yesterday?

Yes I did. It *(be)* good to see him after all these years. I *(see, not)* him for such a long time.

b)   *(You recognize)* me?
Oh hello John, I *(see)* _____ you in ages. I *(speak, not)*_____ to you in years.

c)   *(You, go)* _____ out to eat last night? No, by the time I *(arrive)* _____ home my husband *(make, already)* _____ dinner.

d)   How *(be)* _____ your dinner last night? Fine I *(have)* _____ fish. While I (eat) a client rang and I had to go back to the office.

e)   What *(do, you)* _____ after dinner? I *(want)* _____to go to a movie but my husband *(already, see)* _____it.

PART 3 – AUDIO – LISTENING AND SPEAKING

Comprehension

Listen to the following conversation, make notes of all the relevant facts and then answer the questions below. If you have trouble understanding, follow the conversation while also reading the text.

Discussion between Professor Bob and his student James

James: "Hi Professor, I'm here for my four o'clock appointment. Remember you were going to explain to me how the European Union functions."
Professor Bob: "Ah yes, so I was, come in James and please take a seat. So what is it you want to know?"
James: "Well I want to understand what is the European Union exactly. I mean is it a country or is it just another international organization?"
Professor Bob: "It is a bit of both I guess. It is certainly more than an international organization and yet the European Union is certainly not a country. Yes it has a flag, an anthem of sorts and its own currency, and so it has many of the attributes of a country."
James: "But that's my point exactly; in reality it's just like a country."
Professor Bob: "Yes, but the majority of European citizens continue to think of themselves in national terms. Moreover, the Union does not have any tax raising powers of its own. The money that it spends is given to it by the member states. However, although EU law takes precedence over national law, the scope of EU law is limited and so many areas are still governed by way of national legislation, for example tax policy. Finally, the European Union does not have its own foreign policy and does not have the power to declare war; rather it seeks to coordinate the independent foreign policy of each of its twenty-eight member states and believe me, it is not easy."
James: "Why?"
Professor Bob: "Because different member states have different priorities. The United Kingdom claims to have a special relationship with the United States, whilst France and Germany certainly do not. The interests of the Baltic Republics are obviously very different to the concerns of the Greeks."
James: "Is there a European army?"
Professor Bob: "Not yet but the French, British and Germans are beginning to

pool their resources a little and over time you can expect to see the development of a European army of some kind. However, member states such as Sweden and Ireland, which are traditionally neutral will probably not want to participate in any such developments."

James: "So it is possible for a member state to choose the European projects in which it wishes to participate?"

Professor Bob: "In principle no, but certain member states have negotiated opt outs for certain activities, such as the euro or the Schengen Agreement. Normally, this is not allowed but sometimes because of a member state's special circumstances an exception may be made. When this occurs, the situation is referred to as a *two-speed Europe*."

James: "Oh OK .... And is it the intention of the European Union to become a unified state?"

Professor Bob: "Well, that is a tough question to answer. Some member states have not hidden their desire for ever-closer union. States such as France and Germany are committed to some form of European Union I believe. However, other states such as the United Kingdom or Denmark are more *Eurosceptic*[2] and probably want to see a union of nation states, where national governments retain sovereignty."

James: "Are you a Eurosceptic?"

Professor Bob: "I wouldn't say that I am a eurosceptic but I don't believe in Union just for the sake of it. Obviously, European countries need to group together if they are to influence events in the world and survive economically. However, there probably are also benefits for each of the states retaining some independence. Certainly, there should be no Union unless national voters are committed to the program."

James: "So what will happen here in the United Kingdom?"

Professor Bob: "I think that United Kingdom citizens will continue to think of themselves as separate from other Europeans and will probably continue to look toward the United States. Culturally and linguistically the two countries are natural allies. However, I also believe that over time, the differences between the United Kingdom and the US on social and economic questions, which are already present, may become greater. If this occurs, the United Kingdom may have no choice but to throw its lot in with Europe."

James: "Can you tell me, what does the European Union do?"

Professor Bob: "Oh it does an awful lot; I could not begin to explain all that it does. Well for example it has established the largest trading block in the world made up of twenty-eight different member states. Consequently, a UK firm producing goods in Scotland can market and sell those goods in any one of the other member states, without the imposition of any charges or customs duties. There is a common transport policy promoting the creation of high-speed traffic links between each of the member states. The Schengen Area has been created allowing for free movement of people throughout most of the member states. Legislation has been harmonized in many areas ensuring better protection for employees, the environment, children etc. In fact, the list is nearly endless ..."

---

[2] Eurosceptic is the name given to people who do not believe that European integration is a good thing.

James: "So the European Union is a good thing?"

Professor Bob: "Yes, it probably is."

James: "Why is it that people do not like it?"

Professor Bob: "It is not necessarily a question of good and bad. A lot of it has to do with people's preference. Europe's past history is founded upon patriotism and centuries of nationalist propaganda. Thus it is natural that some people retain a patriotic stance; moreover, there are the recurrent fears of *big government* and *big business* high-jacking the integration process."

James: "Are not people justified in being afraid that big business and big government will take over the world?"

Professor Bob: "But James, maybe they already have!"

James: "And do you think that as time passes people will probably become more European in their thinking, in the way they see themselves?"

Professor Bob: "Yes, probably and as they begin to cooperate, they will begin to see that their supposed enemies were not their enemies at all. For example, it is now difficult to imagine the French and the Germans going to war, yet prior to the creation of the European Union, they were constantly at war and worse dragged the rest of the world into their disputes. Perhaps the biggest success of the European Union is the relative peace it has brought to Western Europe."

James: "Thanks Professor Bob, you have cleared up a lot of issues for me."

Professor Bob: "My pleasure James. Don't forget to shut the door on the way out."

PART 3 – AUDIO COMPREHENSION – EXERCISES

1. Comprehension

From the notes you have taken of the conversation, answer the following questions

a)   Name some of the things that in Professor Bob's opinion the European Union has accomplished.

b)   What examples of a two-speed Europe does Professor Bob give?

c)   What is the biggest success of the European Union in Professor Bob's point of view?

d)   What states does Professor Bob identify as being Eurosceptic?

e)   Does Professor Bob say that there is a European Army?

f)   What are the reasons that Professor Bob gives for justifying his conclusion that the European Union is not a state?

2. Speaking practice

In the following series of conversation couplets, develop suitable responses to the questions asked

a)   Professor Bob: "So can you name any successful programs carried out by the European Union?"
     James: "_____."

b)   Professor Bob: "Do taxation and fiscal policy come within the competence of the European Union?"

James: "_____."
c)   Professor Bob: "What do you think has been the European Union's biggest success?"
     James: "_____."
d)   Professor Bob: "Why do you think some member states and their citizens are Eurosceptic?"
     James: "_____."
e)   Professor Bob: "What does the term Single Market mean exactly?"
     James: "_____."
f)   Professor Bob: "What do we mean when we talk about a *two speed Europe* and could you give me an example?"
g)   Professor Bob: "Is there likely to be a European Army in the future?"
     James: "_____."
h)   Professor Bob: "Is the European Union a country or an international organization?"
     James: "_____."
i)   Professor Bob: "Can the European Union raise its own taxes?"
     James: "_____."
j)   Professor Bob: "Does the European Union have its own flag? If yes, what is it like?"
     James: "_____."

3. Speaking practice continued ......

Create five other conversation couplets, using in each couplet at least one word from the vocabulary found in Part 1, Text 1 and Text 2.

4. Speaking practice continued ......

Listen to the suggested replies and repeat

a)   Professor Bob: "So can you name any successful programs carried out by the European Union?"
     James: "Yes, for example the Single Market program or the development of the Schengen Area."
b)   Professor Bob: "Do taxation and fiscal policy come within the competence of the European Union?"
     James: "No, the European Union does not have its own power of taxation."
c)   Professor Bob: "What do you think has been the European Union's biggest success?"
     James: "Well, perhaps the greatest success of the European Union is that it has led to peace between European countries."
d)   Professor Bob: "Why do you think some member states and their citizens are Eurosceptic?"
     James: "I guess that they do not want to share their national sovereignty with other states."
e)   Professor Bob: "What does the term Single Market mean exactly?"

James: "I guess a single market is a zone in which goods, workers, services and capital can move freely between states."

f)   Professor Bob: "What do we mean when we talk about a *two-speed Europe* and could you give me an example?"
      James: "A two speed Europe refers to the phenomenon whereby some member states choose to integrate more closely."

g)   Professor Bob: "Is there likely to be a European Army in the future?"
      James: "Probably in some form or other, although it is likely that some member states such as Ireland and Sweden will choose not to participate."

h)   Professor Bob: "Is the European Union a country or an international organization?"
      James: "You could say it has characteristics of each. For example, although it has a flag and an anthem, it does not have many of the powers normally enjoyed by an independent country or state."

i)   Professor Bob: "Can the European Union raise its own taxes?"
      James: "No, it receives its revenue from the member states."

j)   Professor Bob: "Does the European Union have its own flag? If yes, what is it like?"
      James: "Yes, there is a European Union flag; it is blue with twelve yellow stars forming a circle."

5. Associated questions

Discuss the following questions

a)   Why do you think independent European states decided to create the European Union? What advantages does such an organization bring to its member states?

b)   Why have Eurosceptic European Union member states such as the United Kingdom remained in the organization?

c)   Do you believe that the European Union will eventually evolve into a separate state like the United States of America?

d)   Do you think the European Union is a good thing? Should South American or Asian countries seek to establish the same type of organization?

PART 4 – TRANSLATION EXERCISES

When carrying out the translations it is not necessary to translate directly word for word; rather the emphasis should be on translating the sense of the text. Language is not directly interchangeable and so direct translations do not always convey the meaning in the text.

Translate the following texts from English to French

A. The European Parliament

The European Parliament is elected by the citizens of the European Union to represent their interests. Its origins date back to the 1950s and the founding treaties, and since 1979 its members have been directly elected by universal suffrage. Elections are held every five years, and every EU citizen is entitled to vote and to stand as a candidate. The EP thus expresses the democratic will of the Union's citizens, more than 490 million people, and represents their interests when negotiating with the other EU institutions. The present Parliament has 736 members from all 28 EU member states. Members of the European Parliament (MEPs) do not sit in national blocks but in seven European-wide political groups representing the full-spectrum of political views, right and left.

B. The Council of the European Union

The Council is the EU's main decision-making body. The founding treaties established the Council in the 1950s. It represents the member states, and its meetings are attended by a government minister from each of the EU's member state national governments. If the matter before the Council involves economic policy, then the finance ministers of each of the member states will attend and the Council is referred to as the ECOFIN Council. In the same way, if the Council is to discuss environmental issues, the meeting will be attended by the Environment Minister from each EU member state and sitting together they are known as the Environment Council. The External Relations Council deals with the EU's relations with the rest of the world.

C. The European Commission

The Commission is the European Union institution that is the most independent of the governments of the member states. Its job is to represent and uphold the interests of the EU as a whole. It drafts proposals for new European laws, which it presents to the European Parliament and the Council. It is also the EU's executive arm – in other words, it is responsible for implementing the laws adopted by the Parliament and the Council. Like the Council, the European Commission was set up in the 1950s under the EU's founding treaties. The term 'European Commission' is used in two senses:

- first, it refers to the team of European Commissioners – one from each EU member state – appointed to run the institution and represent it in its dealings with the other institutions;
- secondly, the term refers to the institution itself and all of its administrative staff.

Translate the following texts from French to English

A. La Cour de justice de l'Union européenne

La Cour de justice de l'Union européenne comprend trois juridictions : la Cour de justice, le Tribunal et le Tribunal de la fonction publique. La fonction de la Cour de justice de l'Union européenne est d'assurer le respect du droit dans l'interprétation et l'application des traités de l'UE. Dans le cadre de cette mission, la Cour de justice de l'Union européenne :

- contrôle la légalité des actes des institutions de l'Union européenne ;

– veille au respect, par les États membres, des obligations qui
  découlent des traités ; et
– interprète le droit de l'Union européenne à la demande des juges
  nationaux.

B. Le budget de l'Union européenne et la Cour des comptes

L'Union européenne a un budget d'environ 120 milliards d'euros, ce qui
représente environ 1% du revenu national brut (RNB) des 28 Etats membres.
Comparé aux budgets nationaux des Etats membres, ce montant demeure
relativement modeste. Toutefois, pour les Etats membres les plus pauvres, les
fonds de l'UE jouent un rôle important dans le financement d'activités publiques
telles que le développement d'infrastructures. Les recettes de l'Union européenne
proviennent principalement des contributions des Etats membres qui sont basées
sur leur RNB d'une part et sur une mesure annexée sur le montant de la taxe
sur la valeur ajoutée recouvert par les différents Etats membres d'autre part.
Le budget est déterminé annuellement par le Conseil et le Parlement européen.
Le rôle de la Cour des comptes est de veiller à ce que l'argent soit dépensé
correctement et que les citoyens de l'UE bénéficient d'une utilisation bénéfique
de leurs euros difficilement gagnés.

C. Qu'est-ce que le vote à la majorité qualifiée?

Dans certains domaines sensibles comme la politique étrangère et de sécurité
commune ou la fiscalité, le Conseil statue à l'unanimité. Autrement dit, chaque
Etat membre dispose d'un droit de veto. Cependant, dans la plupart des cas le
Conseil statue à la majorité qualifiée. Le système fonctionne ainsi : entre le 1er
décembre 2009 et 1er novembre 2014, la majorité qualifiée est acquise lorsqu'un
texte recueille 255 voix sur 345, représentant au moins 50% des Etats membres.
À partir de 2014, les règles de la majorité qualifiée changeront pour mettre en
œuvre le nouveau système d'une double majorité. Selon les nouvelles règles
établies par le traité de Lisbonne, pour être adopté, un texte devra recueillir 55
% des voix des Etats membres du Conseil et représenter des Etats membres
réunissant au moins 65 % de la population de l'Union. Ce système garantit que
les Etats membres les plus peuplés ne dominent ou ne bloquent pas le processus
législatif.

PART 5 – ADVANCED READING

The rejection of the European Constitution and Lisbon Treaty

In 2004 a new constitutional treaty, popularly named the European Constitution,
was presented for approval before the populations of the different EU member
states. However, it was withdrawn after the traditionally pro-European member
states of France and the Netherlands voted against its adoption. In its place the
member state governments drafted a replacement treaty, the Lisbon Treaty, and
adopted it at parliamentary level, bypassing the need for a popular vote on the
issue. However, in Ireland this sleight of hand was not constitutionally possible
and, when asked, the Irish people voted No; so sometime later they were simply

asked to vote again. This time, under economic pressure, they voted Yes and the European ship of integration steamed ahead into its next iceberg, the Euro crisis.

In the opinion of some commentators, the ratification process surrounding both the European Constitution and its replacement, the Lisbon Treaty, was a travesty of democracy: not just because of the failure by the European authorities to accept the vote of the people but also because of the conditions in which the vote took place. In this regard, the vote concerned documents that nobody really understood. As a result, the pro-treaty campaigns were centred not so much on the Treaties themselves but rather on the grounds that Europe had been very good for the European people and thus, in principle, they should trust their leaders and blindly vote Yes. Incredibly, some of Ireland's leaders publicly acknowledged that they did not understand the Treaty, admitting that they had not read all of it contents. However admirable their honesty, as an argument to vote Yes, this was hardly convincing. Indeed, over 46% of Irish "No" voters justified their No vote on the basis that they did not understand what they were being asked to vote on. The No vote campaigns were equally disappointing, representing a ragged and sometimes illogical coming together of all sides of the political spectrum, from the extreme right to the extreme left. Reflecting their disparate origins, their arguments against the Treaty were equally disparate and sometimes downright wrong. In Ireland it was claimed by the No vote campaign that the European Constitution would promote the right to abortion; in France it was claimed that it would limit this right; whilst in reality the Treaty was totally silent on the issue.

Then there is the issue of the Irish electorate being asked to vote repeatedly on the question, presumably up until the moment they agreed to vote Yes. The process was described by no less a person than Jean-Claude Juncker, President of the European Commission, as a: *"(S)ham, because when the result is not pleasing, the vote is simply ignored and the legislation introduced in another way, or if not possible, this having already been done, the population is asked to vote again with an economic gun held to its head"*. Still something had to be done; a small majority of Irish voters could not be allowed to become an Irish tail wagging the giant European Union dog. Expediency won out and they were quite simply steamrolled by the European juggernaut. However, given that 46% of Irish voters voted "No" because they could not understand the Treaty, and the fact that many voters in France, the Netherlands, the Czech Republic, the United Kingdom, Denmark, Poland etc. were also against the adoption of the Lisbon Treaty's predecessor document, the European Constitution, perhaps it would have been better to address these issues, rather than forcing through the adoption of the Treaty by questionable democratic means. Can we really be surprised that there is a resurgence of nationalist sentiment throughout the EU member states, if this is the approach of our European masters?

Chapter ten

THE INTERNAL MARKET

PART 1 – TEXT 1 – INFORMATION

The notion of free movement in the European Union

One of the primary **objectives** of the European Union is to create a fully **integrated and homogenous economic market** in which people, capital, products and services can move freely without the imposition of restrictions. A number of different terms are used to describe this market: the **common market**, the **single market** or the **internal market**. In EU law, the scope of the internal market applies to the four main **factors of production**, namely goods, workers, services and capital.

The scope of the internal market

Goods Article 28 of the TFEU Treaty calls for the elimination of restrictions on the free movement of goods, including:

- **customs charges** or **taxes** on goods coming from other EU member states;
- **quantitative restrictions**, i.e. restrictions on the amount of imported goods from other member states; and
- measures having the same or **equivalent effect** as quantitative restrictions.

Free movement of workers Article 45 of the TFEU Treaty requires that member states **abolish** restrictions or *"any discrimination based on nationality between member state workers as regards employment, **remuneration** and other conditions of work and employment"*. It is important to recall that the notion of free movement in article 45 only **extends** to workers and not to people in general.

Establishment and services Article 49 of the TFEU defines the **right of establishment** as: the right of any **natural** or **legal person** to set up a business in any member state and to pursue commercial activities in that state. Thus, a company established in one member state has the right to establish a **branch** or **agency** in any other member state and carry out business there. Pursuant to article 56 of the TFEU, a business is also free to **provide services** in other member states, without actually establishing a branch or agency in those states.

Free movement of capital The free movement of **capital** requires the **suppression** of **exchange controls** preventing the transfer of money from one member state to another.

The principles underlying the creation of the single market

To create the single market the European Union had to:
- remove direct **barriers** to free movement, for example **border controls** and **tariff systems**;
- remove indirect **barriers** to free movement caused by differences in the existing rules of each member governing the manner in which economic activity is pursued. For example, let us imagine that to **qualify** as a nurse in one member state, three years study is necessary, **whilst** in another member state four years study is required. Should a nurse that **fails to meet** the full-educational requirements of one state be prevented from working in that state? To prevent issues like this **arising,** the EU had to somehow **coordinate** member states' economic laws and regulations. In attempting to do this, the European Union had two basic choices; it could either:
- seek to **harmonize** all the regulatory rules existing in each member state and develop one single European-wide code; or
- apply the principle of **mutual recognition** as regards the different systems and laws in place in each member state, i.e. each state would recognize the **standards** in place in other member states.

The European Union decided to do something in between these two extremes, adopting a new **methodology,** referred to as the **new approach**. The new approach is above all based on the application of mutual recognition as regards the regulatory rules in place in each of the member states. Under the doctrine of mutual recognition the EU member states agree to mutually recognize the standards and rules in place in each other's state, as regards the areas coming within the definition of the internal market; they then agree on the basis of **reciprocity** to **permit** goods, businesses and services to **circulate** freely between them. Thus, under this system, the **granting** of a **license** to a business by the regulatory authorities of one member state works as a **single market passport,** allowing that business to establish and offer its services **throughout** the Union's twenty-eight member states. However, where matters of particular public importance are identified, involving issues such as consumer safety, the rules are harmonized at European level. Thus, the EU applies a system based on mutual recognition with limited harmonization.

VOCABULARY

Objectives – *objectifs*
Integrated – *intégré*
Homogenous – *homogène*
Common market/single market/internal market – *marché commun/marché unique/marché intérieur*
Factors of production – *facteurs de production*
Customs charges/taxes – *droits de douane/taxes*
Quantitative restrictions – *restrictions quantitatives*

Equivalent effect – *effet équivalent*
Abolish (to) – *abolir/supprimer*
Remuneration – *rémunération*
Extend (to) to – *étendre à (s'appliquer à)*
Right of establishment – *liberté d'établissement*
Natural person/legal person – *personne physique/personne morale*
Branch – *succursale*
Agency – *agence*
Provide (to) services – *fournir/prester des services*
Capital – *capital*
Suppression – *suppression*
Exchange controls – *contrôle des échanges*
Barriers – *barrières*
Border controls – *contrôle aux frontières*
Tariff systems – *systèmes tarifaires*
Qualify (to) – *obtenir un diplôme*
Whilst – *alors que/tandis que*
Fail (to) to meet – *ne pas réussir à atteindre*
Arise (to) – *émerger*
Coordinate (to) – *coordonner*
Harmonize (to) – *harmoniser*
Mutual recognition – *reconnaissance mutuelle*
Standard – *norme/règle/standard*
Methodology – *méthodologie*
New approach – *nouvelle approche*
Reciprocity – *réciprocité*
Permit (to) – *autoriser*
Circulate (to) – *circuler*
Controls – *contrôles*
Grant (to) – *accorder*
License – *permis*
Single market passport – *passeport pour le marché unique*
Throughout – *dans l'ensemble de*

PART 1 – TEXT 1 – EXERCISES

1. Vocabulary test

Fill in the missing words using the vocabulary in Text 1

    a)   The single market is also known as the _____ or the _____.
    b)   The free movement of _____ requires the removal of _____ as regards the transfer of money between member states.
    c)   The notion of free movement in the European Union extends to _____ of _____, _____, _____ and capital.
    d)   To create the _____ it was necessary to remove _____ to free movement.
    e)   Freedom of _____ allows any natural or _____ person to set up a business in another European Union member state.

f) Free movement of goods requires the _____ of customs charges and _____ restrictions.

g) Under the new approach, the single market was established through a combination of _____ and limited _____.

h) Under the application of mutual recognition, a business _____ to carry out business in one member state may offer its services in any other EU _____.

2. Vocabulary test

Write sentences with the following pairs of words. Your sentence should demonstrate your knowledge of the relationship between the words

a) Establishment/services
b) Free movement/tariff
c) Quantitative restrictions/goods
d) Factors of production/single market
e) Homogenous/internal market
f) Mutual recognition/new approach

3. Knowledge test

Each of the following statements is false; do you know why? Write a sentence stating why it is false

a) The creation of the single market required the harmonization of all the regulatory rules in each of the member states.

b) Under the rules governing the single market, member states can impose quantitative restrictions on the free movement of goods.

c) The notion of free movement in the European Union is confined to the free movement of goods.

d) A member state may prevent a worker from another member state entering its territory, when there is a high rate of unemployment in the host member state[1].

e) Mutual recognition means that each member state can prevent free movement of goods, persons, services or capital coming from other member states.

f) The expression *single market passport* describes a type of EU passport that is issued to EU nationals.

PART 1 – TEXT 2 – MORE INFORMATION

The notion of free movement in the European Union

One of the primary **objectives** of the European Union is to create a fully **integrated and homogenous economic market,** where free movement between member states as regards goods, people, services and capital is guaranteed. This is often referred to as the **common market**, the **single market** or the **internal**

---

[1]   Host member state is the name given to the member state to which the worker is going. The state from which the worker comes is referred to as the home member state.

market. Article 26 of the Treaty on the Functioning of the European Union (TFEU) describes the single market as:

> *"an area without internal frontiers in which the free movement of goods, persons, services and capital is possible."*

The scope of the Single Market

Thus, under EU law, the scope of the internal market extends to four main **factors of production**, namely goods, workers, services and capital; referred to collectively as the **four freedoms**. It is for this reason that the EU is said to approach the issue of creating a single market on a **sectorial basis**.

Goods Article 28 of the TFEU establishes the principle of free movement of goods between member states and calls for the elimination of all barriers to free movement of goods. In particular TFEU calls for an end to:

- **customs duties** and **charges** or **taxes** on goods coming from other EU member states;
- **quantitative restrictions**, i.e. restrictions on the amount of imported goods from other member states; and
- measures having the same or **equivalent effect** as quantitative restrictions.

Workers Article 45 of the TFEU Treaty requires that member states **abolish** restrictions on workers coming from other member states and in particular:

> *"any discrimination based on nationality between workers of the member states as regards employment, remuneration and other conditions of work and employment."*

It is important to recall that the notion of free movement in article 45 only **extends** to workers and not to people in general. This is because the TFEU Treaty was initially primarily concerned with economic questions and thus only provided for free movement of workers. It was only later, as the scope of the European Community evolved to cover social matters, that free movement was extended to people in general under the **Schengen Accord**[2]. The Schengen Accord is an example of a **two-speed Europe**[3], as it was only entered into by some of the EU member states and thus only extends to those member states that signed the Accord. Consequently, non-EU citizens travelling to non-Schengen member states (United Kingdom and Ireland) must satisfy the visa requirements of those countries.

More generally article 45 grants workers the right to:

- accept offers of employment and move to other member states for that purpose;
- stay in the member state to carry out the offer of employment;

---

[2]   See discussion in translation section.
[3]   See discussion in translation section.

- stay in the member state after the employment has terminated.

To render article 45 more humane, it has been interpreted by the Court of Justice as including family members and thus when a worker travels to another member state, members of his family may accompany him.

Establishment and services Article 49 of the TFEU defines the **right of establishment** as the right of any **natural** or **legal person** to set up a business in any member state and to pursue commercial activities there. Thus, a company established in one member state has the right to establish a **branch** or an **agency** in any other member state and carry out business there. Pursuant to article 56 of the TFEU, a business also has the right to **provide services** in other member states, without actually establishing a branch or agency in those states. Consequently, under article 56, a bank in the United Kingdom can, for example, ring clients in other member states and provide services for them; for example, invest money on their behalf.

Capital The free movement of **capital** requirement of article 63 TFEU calls for the **suppression** of **exchange controls** preventing the transfer of money from one member state to another. Free movement of capital was put in place prior to the establishment of the euro, as otherwise it would have been impossible to have a common currency.

The principles on which the single market was built

Thus, articles 28, 45, 49 56 and 63 of the TFEU establish free movement between member states as regards goods, workers, establishment, services and capital. However, the success of these articles was **undermined** by the fact that member states remain free to restrict free movement, where the restriction is justified on grounds of public policy or is non-discriminatory in effect.

At the time of the establishment of the EU, each member state had in place different rules governing the manufacture of goods and the exercise of professional activities, and these rules were normally considered to come under the heading of **public policy**. For example, imagine the twenty-eight member states have different rules in place regarding the period of time one has to study in order to become a nurse. In the absence of EU legislation **harmonizing** nurses' qualifications, nurses wishing to provide their services on a pan-European basis would have to respect twenty-eight different sets of member state rules. In this way, service providers and consumers were denied the benefit of a real single market, as free movement was restricted by secondary member state legislation. It is for this reason that the TFEU provides for the adoption of directives by the European Union, with the aim of **coordinating** the laws in the member states concerning the single market's areas of activity.

Initially when trying to adopt directives coordinating the different state legislation governing the free movement of goods, workers, services and capital, the Union authorities sought to establish harmonized European-wide rules. These rules would then be applicable in all of the member states. The project, which effectively sought to harmonize many of the regulatory rules in existence in each of the member states, failed for a number of reasons. Above all, it was far too ambitious. The number of regulatory rules governing the activities coming under the heading of the *four freedoms* is nearly endless. This situation was further complicated as:

- each member state has its own regulatory structure suitable for the economic, social and political system it put in place. At the moment of trying to adopt harmonizing legislation, each member state attempted to **champion** its own **regulatory system** as the applicable **model**. This problem was **exacerbated** as new member states continued to join the organization, further complicating the matter;
- prior to the adoption of the SEA, directives in the area of the single market were adopted through **unanimity**. Consequently, very few directives were in reality adopted, as it was unusual for *all* the member states to agree on a common set of rules for any given area.

As a result of these difficulties, progress as regards the development of the single market was very slow and by the 1980s much work remained to be done. Consequently, the Commission suggested that, instead of relying on harmonization, the Union authorities should apply the principle of **mutual recognition** as a means of coordinating member state legislation. Mutual recognition is a mechanism whereby states mutually recognize the standards and rules in place in each other's state and agree on the basis of **reciprocity** to permit goods, businesses and services to circulate freely between them. Under such a system, it would not be necessary to harmonize member state rules but rather to establish a process in which twenty-eight different sets of rules are applicable and recognized mutually.

Mutual recognition has been one of the principles relied on as a means of creating the single market economic system that exists in the United States. Pursuant to its application, a company established under the rules of one member state is free to establish or provide services in any other US state, and companies established in other states are free to provide services in its state. Such a system can lead to competition between the different member state regulatory systems and some European Union member states opposed its application, as they felt it would encourage a phenomenon referred to as **negative regulatory competition**. Negative competition occurs when member state regulatory authorities, in order to become an attractive location for business, begin to compete as regards the content of their regulatory systems. For example, they can do this by reducing the **prudential rules** they have in place regulating business. This will lead to a reduction in **compliancy costs** for businesses located in their state and thus make it a more attractive business location. The member state then benefits from increased employment and increased tax revenues. To compete with them, other member states will in turn lower their prudential standards, leading the system to **spiral** into a process of negative competition.

As a result of these worries the Union authorities developed the **new approach** as a system to create the single market. Under the new approach, the Union authorities rely on a mixture of harmonization and mutual recognition. Thus, when seeking to introduce free movement into an area, the Union will adopt an EU **directive** harmonizing those rules that it considers to be vital both for the sector and for EU citizens, for example the protection of consumers. Once the rules applicable in these areas are harmonized by directive, mutual recognition then remains the operative principle as regards free movement in this area. The harmonization of essential requirements is meant to prevent the excessive negative competition that can occur when relying solely on a system of mutual recognition. By harmonizing important regulatory rules throughout the member states, the standards in place in the EU, even in the competitive environment of the single market, cannot drop below the basic harmonized level established by EU directive. Finally, the Union established the principle of **home member state control** to operate alongside the principle of mutual recognition and limited harmonization. Under this system it is the **home member state** in which a business is established, and not the **host member state,** that regulates the business in question. In other words, regulation is carried out by the member state that granted the institution's **banking license**, i.e. control by the state of origin or home member state. Moreover, as we have seen, so as to **facilitate** the adoption of harmonizing directives, the SEA removed the unanimity requirement for the adoption of single market directives by the Council and the Parliament. Single market directives are now adopted by way of qualified majority voting and it is no longer possible for member states to exercise a right of veto and block their adoption.

Thus, under the EU single market system, the granting of a banking license to a **credit institution** by the regulatory authorities of one member state works as a **single market passport**. With this license, a bank may establish and offer its services throughout the Union's twenty-eight member states, while remaining under the control of its home member state regulatory authorities. This is possible because prudential issues such as the **capital adequacy** of banks have previously been harmonized at EU level through the adoption of directives, thereby preventing negative competition in regulatory standards within the EU single market.

VOCABULARY

Objectives – *objectifs*
Integrated and homogenous economic market – *marché économique intégré et homogène*
Common market/single market/internal market – *marché commun/marché unique/marché intérieur*
Factors of production – *facteurs de production*
Four freedoms – *quatre libertés*
Sectoral basis – *base sectorielle*
Customs charges/taxes – *droits de douane/taxes*
Quantitative restrictions – *restrictions quantitatives*

Equivalent effect – *effet équivalent*
Abolish (to) – *abolir/supprimer*
Extend (to) – *étendre (s'appliquer à)*
Schengen Accord – *Accord de Schengen*
Two-speed Europe – *Europe à deux vitesses*
Right of establishment – *droit d'établissement*
Natural person/legal person – *personne physique/personne morale*
Branch – *succursale*
Agency – *agence*
Provide (to) services – *fournir/prester des services*
Capital – *capital*
Suppression – *suppression*
Exchange controls – *contrôle des échanges*
Undermine (to) – *amoindrir/restreindre*
Coordinate (to) – *coordonner*
Public policy – *ordre public*
Harmonizing – *harmonisant*
Champion (to) – *soutenir/imposer*
Regulatory system – *système réglementaire/de réglementation*
Model – *modèle*
Exacerbate (to) – *exacerber*
Unanimity – *unanimité*
Mutual recognition – *reconnaissance mutuelle*
Reciprocity – *réciprocité*
Negative competition – *concurrence négative*
Prudential rules – *règles de prudence*
Compliancy costs – *coûts de mise en conformité*
Spiral (to) – *tournoyer*
New approach – *nouvelle approche*
Directive (there are three main types of EU legislative instrument: regulations, directives and decisions) – *directive*
Home member state control – *contrôle de l'état membre d'origine*
Home member state – *état membre d'origine*
Host member state – *état membre d'accueil*
Banking license – *permis/autorisation bancaire*
Credit institution – *institution de crédit*
Single market passport – *passeport pour le marché unique*
Capital adequacy – *adéquation des fonds propres*

PART 1 – TEXT 2 – EXERCISES

1. Definitions

Write a sentence defining each of the following terms – one sentence per term

    a)   Internal market
    b)   Exchange controls
    c)   Prudential rules
    d)   Host member state

e)   Home member state
f)   Mutual recognition
g)   Single market passport

2. Sentences

Write sentences with the following pairs of words. Your sentence should demonstrate your knowledge of the relationship between the words

a)   Quantitative restrictions/goods
b)   Regulatory system/harmonization
c)   Banking license/free movement
d)   Establishment/services
e)   Two-speed Europe/free movement
f)   Harmonize/recognition
g)   Goods/quantitative restrictions
h)   Compliance costs/regulatory rules
i)   Factor of production/workers
j)   New approach/mutual recognition

3. Fill in the missing words

Using the vocabulary in Text 2, fill in the missing words

a)   The _____ allowing for the free movement of persons is an example of a _____ Europe.
b)   The notion of _____ movement extends to the four main _____.
c)   Free movement of _____ requires the suppression of quantitative restrictions and any measures having _____.
d)   The New Approach adopted by the European Union provides for the application of _____ and limited _____ of important regulatory rules.
e)   The establishment of the single market allows a business _____ in one member state to sell its products in any of the other member states making up the _____.

4. Knowledge test

The following questions may be answered in writing or by way of discussion

a)   Do you think it is preferable to harmonize regulatory rules leading to the creation of a single market?
b)   What if any is the advantage of using mutual recognition as a means of establishing a single market?
c)   Does the creation of a single market unfairly advantage those EU member states with low manufacturing costs?
d)   Do you think that one day there will be a single market made up of the entire world? What are the obstacles to its establishment?

PART 2 – QUICK LOOK GRAMMAR REVISION

Adding *ing* and *ed* forms to verbs – how to spell it?

Although there is no fixed rule, the following chart indicates the spelling used when adding *ing* and *ed* to verbs.

1. "ing" endings

a) **When the verb ends in "e":**
When the verb ends in "e", normally simply drop the "e" and add "ing"
Example: smile = smil*ing*; hope = hop*ing*

b) **When the verb ends in two consonants**
When the verb ends in two consonants, just add "ing"
Example: help = help*ing*; learn = learn*ing*

c) **When the verb ends in two vowels and one consonant**
When the verb ends in two vowels and one consonant, just add "ing"
Example: rain = rain*ing*; heat = heat*ing*

d) **When the verb ends in one vowel and one consonant and is a one-syllable verb**
When the verb ends in one vowel and one consonant and is a one-syllable verb, double the consonant and add "ing"
Example: stop = stop*ping*; plan = plan*ning*

> **Note:**
>
> When the verb ends in one vowel and one consonant, the rule is to double the consonant and add "*ing*". However, there are exceptions to this rule.
>
> Exception: If the verb ends in one vowel and "w" or "x", then the consonant is not doubled.
>
> Example: fix = fix*ing*; snow = snow*ing*

e) **When the verb ends in one vowel and one consonant and is a two-syllable verb**
  • *If the first syllable of the two-syllable verb is stressed*
    When the first syllable of the two-syllable verb is stressed, do not double the consonant and add "ing".
    Example: visit = visit*ing*; offer = offer*ing*

  • *If the second syllable of the two-syllable verb is stressed, double the consonant*
    When the second syllable of the two-syllable verb is stressed, then the final consonant is doubled

Example: admit = admit*ting*; prefer = prefer*ring*

f) **When the verb ends in a "y"**
    When the verb ends in a "y", just add "ing"
    Example: play = play*ing*; worry = worry*ing*

g) **When the verb ends in "ie"**
    When the verb ends in "ie", change the "ie" to "y"
    Example: die = dying; tie = tying

2. *"ed" endings*

a) **When the verb ends in "e"**
    When the verb ends in "e", simply keep the "e" and add "d"
    Example: smile = smile*d*; hope = hope*d*

b) **When the verb ends in two consonants**
    When the verb ends in two consonants, just add "ed"
    Example: help = help*ed*; learn = learn*ed* *(learnt)*

c) **When the verb ends in two vowels and one consonant**
    When the verb ends in two vowels and one consonant, just add "ed"
    Example: rain = rain*ed*; heat = heat*ed*

d) **When the verb ends in one vowel and one consonant and is a one-syllable verb**
    When the verb ends in one vowel and one consonant, double the consonant and add "ed"
    Example: stop = stop*ped*; plan = plan*ned*

    Note:

    When the verb ends in one vowel and one consonant, the rule is to double the consonant and add "ed". However, there are exceptions to this rule.

    Exception: If the verb ends in one vowel and "w" or "x", then the consonant is not doubled.

    Example: fix = fix*ed*; snow = snow*ed*

e) **When the verb ends in one vowel and one consonant and is a two-syllable verb**
    •   *If the first syllable of the two-syllable verb is stressed*
        When the first syllable of the two-syllable verb is stressed, do not double the consonant but just add "ed".
        Example: visit = visit*ed*; offer = offer*ed*

- If the second syllable of the two-syllable verb is stressed, double the consonant before adding "ed"

When the second syllable of the two-syllable verb is stressed, then the final consonant is doubled

Example: admit = admit*ted*; prefer = prefer*red*

f) **When the verb ends in a "y"**
   - *When the verb ends in a vowel followed by "y", just add "ed"*
   Example: play = play*ed*; enjoy = enjoy*ed*

   - *When the consonant is followed by "y", change the "y" to "i" and add "ed"*
   Example: worry = worr*ied*; study = stud*ied*

g) **When the verb ends in "ie"**
   When the verb ends in "ie", just add "d" and not "ed"
   Example: die = die*d*; tie = tie*d*

PART 2 – GRAMMAR EXERCISES

1. Putting the verb in its "ing" and "ed" form.

(Note that some verbs are irregular)
Write the "ing" and "ed" forms of the following verbs

Start = *starting, started*

   a) Wait
   b) Quit
   c) Write
   d) Shout
   e) Swim
   f) Aim
   g) Open
   h) Help
   i) Sleep
   j) Tape
   k) Begin
   l) Occur
   m) Happen
   n) Refer
   o) Rain
   p) Run
   q) Win
   r) Explain
   s) Burn
   t) Charm
   u) Buy
   v) Try

w)   Tie
x)   Die
y)   Choose
z)   Ride

PART 3 – AUDIO – LISTENING AND SPEAKING

Comprehension

Listen to the following conversation, make notes of all the relevant facts and then answer the questions below. If you have trouble understanding, follow the conversation while also reading the text.

Discussion between Professor Frank and Edward

Professor Frank: "Ok Edward, for your exam I want you to tell me what is the single market."
Edward: "The European Union single market?"
Professor Frank: "Unless you know of another single market; yes of course the EU single market."
Edward: "Ah OK ....."
Professor Frank: "I have to examine twenty-five students today Edward, perhaps we could try and do this quickly."
Edward: "Yes of course ..."
Professor Frank: "OK so ... let's do it."
Edward: "The European Union single market is one of the fundamental ambitions of the Union."
Professor Frank: "Yes good. When was it established?"
Edward: "Well, it is a work in progress but the basic structure of the single market was established first in 1957 and later in 1992."
Professor Frank: "Very good and what treaty provides for the establishment of the single market?"
Edward: "Ah ..... the Treaty on European Union .... ?"
Professor Frank: "Are you asking me Edward? I thought I was meant to be asking the questions around here."
Edward: "Yes indeed, no it was not the Treaty on European Union .... that was also signed in 1992, that is why I got confused. In fact the single market was first spoken about in the European Economic Community Treaty in 1957."
Professor Frank: "Very good and does that Treaty exist today?"
Edward: "No, the Maastricht Treaty amended the name of the EEC Treaty to the EC Treaty, at which time the name of the European Economic Community was changed to the European Community."
Professor Frank: "So is the single market governed by the terms of the European Community Treaty?"
Edward: "No, I was just going to say that the European Community Treaty was changed to the Treaty on the Functioning of the European Union by the provisions of the Lisbon Treaty."
Professor Frank: "Ok, very good Edward... and what is the single market?

Edward: "The single market is a trading zone without internal barriers made up of the twenty-eight EU member states."
Professor Frank: "And what is the scope of the single market?"
Edward: "The scope?"
Professor Frank: "By scope I mean to say … what is the area of application of the single market … to what does it apply?"
Edward: "Ah yes, the single market applies to what is referred to as the four factors of production, namely goods, workers, services and capital."
Professor Frank: "Very good Edward …. And how has the single market been constructed?"
Edward: "The single market has been established by the European authorities."
Professor Frank: "Yes I know that Edward, but how did they do it?"
Edward: "Oh yeah … well they relied on the application of mutual recognition between the different EU member states regulatory models, while harmonizing important regulatory rules at EU level through the adoption of EU legislation referred to as directives. This has been called the New Approach."
Professor Frank: "Ok very good Edward ….. all over you can go now."
Edward: "Could you tell me my mark?"
Professor Frank: "No Edward, every student has to wait until the results come out and I cannot make an exception for you. However, it was not bad …OK?"
Frank: "OK …. I guess."

PART 3 – AUDIO COMPREHENSION – EXERCISES

1. Comprehension

From the notes you have taken of the conversation, answer the following questions

    a)   According to Edward, in what Treaty was the single market provided for?
    b)   In what year does Edward think that the single market was established?
    c)   How in Edward's opinion is the European Economic Community Treaty now called?
    d)   What does Edward say is the scope of the single market?
    e)   How does Edward say the single market was constructed?
    f)   When will Edward receive his mark for the exam?

2. Speaking practice

In the following series of conversation couplets, develop suitable responses to the questions asked

    a)   Professor Frank: "What is the single market?"
              Edward: "_____."
    b)   Professor Frank: "What does article 28 of the Treaty on the Functioning of the European Union provide?"
              Edward: "_____."
    c)   Professor Frank: "Does the TFEU provide for the free movement of capital?"

Edward: "_____."

d) Professor Frank: "Does the single market provide for the free movement of workers or persons?"
Edward: "_____."

e) Professor Frank: "The Schengen Accord is an example of what?"
Edward: "_____."

f) Professor Frank: "What is the scope of the single market?"
Edward: "_____."

g) Professor Frank: "Was the single market established in 1957?"
Edward: "_____."

h) Professor Frank: "What do we mean by the term mutual recognition?"
Edward: "_____."

i) Professor Frank: "Do directives establishing the single market have to be adopted unanimously?"
Edward: "_____."

j) Professor Frank: "What does the term *home member state control* mean?"
Edward: "_____."

3. Speaking practice continued ......

Create five other conversation couplets using in each couplet at least one word from the vocabulary found in Part 1, Text 1 and Text 2.

4. Speaking practice continued ......

Listen to the suggested replies for Edward and repeat

a) Professor Frank: "What is the single market?"
Edward: "It is an area without internal frontiers in which goods, workers, services and capital can move freely."

b) Professor Frank: "What does article 28 of the Treaty on the Functioning of the European Union provide?"
Edward: "Article 28 of the TFEU provides for the free movement of goods."

c) Professor Frank: "Does the TFEU provide for the free movement of capital?"
Edward: "Yes it does, article 63 of the Treaty specifically provides for the free movement of capital."

d) Professor Frank: "Does the single market provide for the free movement of workers or persons?"
Edward: "The single market provides for the free movement of workers and their families. It does not actually provide for the free movement of persons."

e) Professor Frank: "The Schengen Accord is an example of what?"
Edward: "It is said to be an example of a two-speed Europe."

f) Professor Frank: "What is the scope of the single market?"
Edward: "The scope of the single market extends to goods, workers, services, establishment and capital."

g) Professor Frank: "Was the single market established in 1957?"
Edward: "No, the single market was established as an aim of the European Economic Community in 1957."

h) Professor Frank: "What do we mean by the term mutual recognition?"
Edward: "Mutual recognition is a principle whereby the EU member states, on the basis of reciprocity, recognize the regulatory rules in other member states."

i) Professor Frank: "Do directives establishing the single market have to be adopted unanimously?"
Edward: "No, since the adoption of the Single European Act, directives establishing the single market are adopted by way of qualified majority vote."

j) Professor Frank: "What does the term *home member state control* mean?"
Edward: "The term home member state control means that it is the state in which a business is established that supervises the business."

5. Associated questions

Discuss the following questions

a) Why do you think the European Union authorities created the single market?

b) The 1957 EEC Treaty provided for the establishment of the single market; why did it take until 1992 for the single market to be actually established?

c) Do you consider that application of the principle of mutual recognition as regards the construction of the single market is a good thing?

d) Do you think that the European Union should be extended to include countries outside the European Union?

PART 4 – TRANSLATION EXERCISES

When carrying out the translations it is not necessary to translate directly word for word; rather the emphasis should be on translating the sense of the text. Language is not directly interchangeable and so direct translations do not always convey the meaning in the text.

Translate the following texts from English to French

A. What do we mean by a two-speed Europe?

Terms such as concentric circles, enhanced cooperation or two-speed Europe all refer to the same process, namely a situation where integration within the EU occurs at different speeds. It is said to occur when a limited number of EU member states choose to deepen cooperation between them, without the remaining member states participating. Examples of enhanced cooperation already exist, for example the Euro. Although the euro is the official EU currency,

not all member states are members of the Euro. Such cooperation is said to divide the EU into a number of concentric circles, the:
- first circle encompasses all of the EU member states;
- second circle would comprise the countries that have decided to further integrate their economies.

B. What is the Schengen Agreement (also known as the Schengen Accord)?

The Schengen Agreement is an example of a two-speed Europe. The Agreement is an accord between a number of the EU member states providing for free movement of people and the suppression of border controls between them. The borderless zone created by the Schengen Accord, referred to as the Schengen Area, currently consists of 25 European states[4], covering a population of 500 million people and a surface area of over 4,316,099 square kilometres. All European Union member states, with the exception of the United Kingdom and Ireland, have signed the Schengen Agreement. New EU member states do not have to sign the Schengen Agreement as it now forms part of the *acquis communautaire*[5].

C. Mutual recognition of professional qualifications between member states

The issue of how to treat qualifications obtained in third countries arises when considering the question of the free movement of workers. After all, it is worthless to have a right to free movement for workers if member states are allowed to use secondary issues, such as the non-recognition of foreign diplomas, as a way of protecting their national employment markets. The approach of the EU has not been to try to harmonize all the rules governing educational programs that lead to the granting of diplomas. This would have been too complicated to accomplish. Instead, the Union has introduced the principle of mutual recognition to the area, underwritten by a limited degree of harmonization where necessary.

Translate the following texts from French to English

A. Libre circulation des marchandises

Les Etats membres ne peuvent restreindre la libre circulation des marchandises que dans des cas exceptionnels : par exemple, lorsqu'il existe un risque pour la santé publique, l'environnement ou la protection des consommateurs. Afin de minimiser tout risque tout en protégeant la libre circulation des marchandises, l'UE a introduit des lois harmonisant les règlements techniques des Etats membres dans le domaine des secteurs produisant des marchandises dangereuses. A contrario, les secteurs qui ne sont pas « à risques » n'ont généralement pas fait l'objet d'harmonisation au niveau européen. Les échanges qui relèvent de secteurs non-harmonisés sont gouvernés par le principe de reconnaissance mutuelle en vertu duquel les produits qui sont légalement fabriqués dans un

---

[4] Some non-EU member states have signed the Schengen Agreement.
[5] The Community *acquis* is the body of common rights and obligations which bind all the Member States together within the European Union. Thus, the Schengen Agreement makes up an integral part of EU law, even if two member states have not signed it.

Etat membre doivent normalement être libre de circuler dans l'ensemble du marché unique européen.

B. La libre circulation des capitaux

Il n'y a pas si longtemps, les européens étaient obligés de gérer et d'investir leurs épargnes dans leur pays de résidence. Désormais, en vertu de la libéralisation des mouvements de capitaux et des paiements, les citoyens de l'UE peuvent entreprendre des opérations financières dans n'importe lequel des vingt-huit Etats membres de l'UE : par exemple, l'ouverture d'un compte bancaire, l'achat d'actions de sociétés étrangères ou l'acquisition de biens immobiliers. Ceci permet une meilleure allocation des ressources dans l'UE, facilite les échanges transfrontaliers, promeut la mobilité des travailleurs et permet aux entreprises de lever les capitaux dont elles ont besoin.

C. Le marché unique des services financiers et le reste du monde

La création d'un marché plus intégré pour les banques et les conglomérats financiers représente une ambition majeure de la politique de l'UE dans le domaine des services financiers. Cependant, les actions de l'Union dans ce domaine ne produisent pas seulement des effets internes mais ont également des conséquences externes. En effet, la dimension externe de la politique de l'UE en matière de services financiers joue un rôle essentiel dans son développement présent. Par exemple, cette politique se développe en principe dans le contexte d'un *dialogue réglementaire* avec les membres du *Comité de Bâle*. La politique de l'UE en matière de services financiers possède également une dimension externe lors de la négociation menée avec les Etats candidats à l'accession à l'UE : en effet, ces derniers ont l'obligation de rendre leur législation interne conforme au droit de l'Union.

PART 5 – ADVANCED READING

Member state social models and the single market

European Union member states have always employed different social models and consequently it is erroneous to speak of an EU social model. Whilst acknowledging that the social model of each member state has its own specific nature and is, as a result of the present financial crisis, in constant evolution, for the sake of simplicity the models existing inside the EU can be broadly broken up into four main groups, the:

- Continental model, typified by France. Briefly, this system is characterized by generous unemployment and pension benefits. Job protection laws in these states tend to be extensive and there is significant income redistribution;
- Scandinavian model, relied on by Sweden, Denmark, Finland, the Netherlands and increasingly Germany. As with the Continental model, large sums are spent on wealth redistribution, health and education. However, labor laws are not rigid and unemployment benefits are limited;

- Mediterranean model, developed in member states such as Greece and Italy. This model offers extensive job protection with rigid labor protection laws. Unemployment and pension benefits are limited, as is wealth distribution;
- Anglo model, developed in the United Kingdom. This model spends relatively little on wealth redistribution and offers only restricted job protection. However, unemployment benefits are adequate and significant funds are spent on job creation.
- Anglo-liberal model, relied upon by the member states of central Europe. The system uses flexible labor laws and pro-business tax laws with limited wealth redistribution.

If EU member states were not part of the EC single market established in 1992, the differences in these models would be of merely academic significance. However, the single market project has left member state economies open to competition from other member states, with the result that certain states have begun to perceive a need to protect themselves from outside competition, both economic and social. The existence of the single market can impact negatively on member states using the Continental or Mediterranean model in the following way: states with rigid job protection laws and extensive social protection tend, to a greater or lesser extent, to partly finance the resulting costs by the imposition of higher taxes on business. In this way, businesses in such member states lose competitiveness compared with member states employing a less comprehensive social model. The result can be a less competitive industry, the migration of businesses to other states, increased unemployment and reduced tax revenues, as the corporate and income tax base shrinks. Moreover, the reduction in tax receipts occurs at the very moment that there is increased demand on the social system resulting from the unemployment that the single market has provoked. The matter is further exacerbated by factors such as an increasingly aging society and greater global migration, placing further pressure on the public purse, as understandably refugees seek access to states with an attractive social model. As a result, the creation of a single market should, in the opinion of these member states, take into account the negative effect free movement can have on the integrity of the social model employed in these states. However, member states championing a more liberal economic model contend that any such limitations will rob the single market of the competitiveness it is meant to promote.

EXERCISE ANSWERS – INTRODUCTION TO THE COMMON LAW, VOL 1

CHAPTER 1 – THE ORGANIZATION OF THE COMMON LAW LEGAL PRACTICE

Answers Chapter 1 – Part 1 – Text 1 – Exercise 1

a) Full-service. b) Sole practitioner, partnership. c) Joint and several, limited. d) Partners, managing. e) Special counsel/of-counsel. f) Support, manager. g) Filing, research. h) Senior, junior. i) Diary; booking. j) Chief Executive Officer (CEO), directors.

Answers Chapter 1 – Part 1 – Text 1 – Exercise 3

Normally in a general partnership the partners have unlimited joint and severable liability; however, if they have formed a limited liability partnership or a limited liability company, they will enjoy limited liability. b) No, a sole-proprietorship is made up of only one lawyer and consequently cannot supply the full range of legal services provided by a full-service law firm. c) No, it is the partners who resemble the directors of a company and not the associates. d) No, paralegals make up part of the support staff of a law firm and are not lawyers. e) It is the associates and not the partners who are said to make up the rank and file lawyers in a law firm.

******

Answers Chapter 1 – Part 1 – Text 2 – Exercise 3

a) Jointly and severally, partners. b) Chief Executive Officer (CEO), directors. c) Full-service law firm, boutique. d) Practice, jurisdictions e) Appoint/hire, of counsel/special counsel.

******

Answers Chapter 1 – Part 2 – Exercise 1

a) The, I, Friday. b) Do, Frank Smith, Strawberry Fields. c) Professor Smith, Fake & Blake Solicitors, He, Boston. d) The, Danube, Atlantic Ocean, Black Sea. e) Alaska, Canada, Sao Paulo, South America, Antarctica. f) Dr. Smith, New York City. g) Canada, English, French. h) Frank, Plaza Building, Chicago. i) James, Bermuda, It, July, London City Airport.

******

Answers Chapter 1 – Part 4 – Translations

A. Cabinets d'avocats spécialisés dans un domaine – Boutique law firms

Un cabinet d'avocats peut être qualifié de « boutique » afin de désigner sa spécialisation dans un domaine spécifique du droit. A la différence d'un cabinet généraliste, dit « full service » (multidisciplinaire) au sein duquel sont pratiquées des matières juridiques très diverses, la « boutique » se spécialise dans un domaine spécifique. Les cabinets « boutique » sont généralement de petites structures mais quelques-uns peuvent, en fonction de leur succès, compter jusqu'à deux cents avocats. Le terme « boutique » fait avant tout référence à la spécialisation plutôt qu'à la taille des cabinets. Ces derniers ont tendance à se spécialiser dans des domaines tels que le droit de la propriété intellectuelle, le droit de la concurrence ou encore le droit du travail, domaines qui requièrent des connaissances professionnelles précises que les non-spécialistes pourraient ne pas détenir. Par exemple, un excellent avocat spécialisé en droit de la concurrence détiendra probablement également un diplôme d'école de commerce, par exemple un MBA : une bonne perception des théories économiques est essentielle dans ce secteur du droit.

B. L'histoire de J. Sullivan, fondateur de Sullivan, Jenkin & Freehold

L'histoire de Sullivan, Jenkins & Freehold est celle de l'imagination, de la volonté et d'un travail acharné. Durant plus de cent ans, le cabinet n'a eu qu'une seule ambition : être le plus grand et devenir une entreprise unique à l'échelle mondiale. Mais avant cela, il y eu un homme et un rêve. John Sullivan, né au milieu du 20ème siècle et issu du difficile milieu minier au Pays de Galles, fut lauréat d'une bourse pour Oxford. Il compléta sa maigre allocation d'études en travaillant dans différents bars étudiants, ainsi que comme videur dans une discothèque locale. Une fois diplômé, il a rejoint un cabinet de la « City » (de Londres), Shearer & Watson, avant de créer Sullivan, Jenkin & Freehold. Cette entreprise, qui était à l'origine une « boutique » spécialisée dans le droit bancaire, est devenue le plus grand cabinet au monde de droit commercial, avec une implantation sur les cinq continents. On a demandé à Sullivan, sur son lit de mort, le secret de sa réussite : « le nombre d'heures facturées » a-t-il répondu sur un ton sardonique.

C. L'organisation de la stratégie des cabinets d'avocats

Dans les cabinets juridiques, l'organisation des activités est différente de ce qu'elle est dans une entreprise industrielle ou commerciale ordinaire. En premier lieu, elle résulte de la nature des services offerts aux clients et de la façon dont ces services sont commercialisés. Le conseil juridique n'est pas un produit homogénéisé. Il existe néanmoins des ressemblances. Sans doute, les premières questions que tout avocat associé à la direction d'un cabinet poserait à ses associés sont:
  • Quel genre de travail veulent-ils faire ?
  • Quelle sorte de clients veulent-ils avoir ?

- A quelle taille d'entreprise aspirent-ils ?

Afin de mettre en place une organisation du travail cohérente et réalisable au sein du cabinet, il est essentiel de formuler des réponses claires à ces trois questions. A cet égard, des compromis devront être faits. Un cabinet qui souhaite travailler en priorité dans des domaines sociaux tels que le droit des réfugiés devra se faire à l'idée que sa capacité bénéficiaire ne sera jamais aussi importante que celle d'un cabinet œuvrant dans les services financiers.

A. Business law firms in France

France has close to 34,000 lawyers, 14,000 of whom are located in Paris. More and more are specializing in the area of business law. Linked to this growth is the emergence or even invasion of Anglo-Saxon firms operating on the French territory. In reality it is a market in constant transformation. For example, for the last number of years there has been a growing tendency for firms to merge, leading to an increased concentration of law firms. Important mergers have occurred as French firms try to cope with their Anglo-Saxon competitors. Further, the pace of such concentration has been accelerated as attempts are made to increase profitability and economies of scale.

B. The profession of in-house lawyer/legal adviser

The in-house lawyer/legal adviser is somebody who has studied law but who has not necessarily qualified as a lawyer. His role is to give legal advice and to ensure that the undertaking/business for which he works is in conformity with the laws *governing* the exercise of its activities. He is required to scrupulously track any legal actions brought against the business, defending and protecting its interests. Sometimes the legal adviser is also a qualified lawyer, especially in English-speaking countries. However, even if such a qualification is more and more usual, it is not actually necessary. In carrying out his/her work, the in-house lawyer is required to study the laws and regulations concerning the area in which his/her business is active. To succeed in this profession, it is necessary to be persuasive and convincing, to have good interpersonal skills and, needless to say, to be a good negotiator. It is a difficult profession but very interesting.

C. New qualification for paralegals

Soon the Quebec Bar will put in place a program whereby a license will be granted to those paralegals supplying services to the public. The law, which is soon to be adopted by the government, will make the Quebec Bar responsible for the standards and professional ethics of paralegals. The Quebec Bar will also be responsible for establishing a system governing the granting of licenses and the application of disciplinary measures as regards paralegals[1]. Moreover, paralegals will be required to follow an approved/recognized college course, pass an admission exam and have sufficient "moral fortitude" to be eligible to receive a license to practice. Special provision will be made for applicants

---

[1] Note that in English it is not desirable to have overly long sentences. The general rule normally is: one idea per sentence.

with acquired rights, i.e. having more than three years full-time experience in authorized practice areas during the last five years. Experienced paralegals and those who hold paralegal training diplomas from third level establishments will soon be able to apply to sit an examination for admission as paralegals in Quebec.

CHAPTER 2 – THE DIFFERENT KINDS OF LAWYERS IN THE COMMON LAW WORLD

Answers Chapter 2 – Part 1 – Text 1 – Exercise 1

a) Regulatory. b) Briefs. c) In-house lawyer/counsel, law firm. d) Plead, legal opinions. e) Drafting. f) Solicitor, probate. g) Attorney, transfer. h) Bound, legal opinion. i) Pleaded. j) Labor/Employment, competition.

Answers Chapter 2 – Part 1 – Text 1 – Exercise 3

a) No, solicitors do have limited rights of audience before the courts. b) No, attorney is a general term for a lawyer and consequently attorneys may work in any area of law. c) No, barristers may also issue legal opinions and work in-house for a company. d) No, unlike in civil law countries, an in-house lawyer in Anglo-Saxon countries will have normally qualified as a lawyer. e) No, succession law involves the transfer of property, including land upon someone's death; conveyancing involves the transfer of the title of land between living parties. f) No, legal opinions are issued by barristers.

******

Answers Chapter 2 – Part 1 – Text 2 – Exercise 3

a) Solicitor, pleads, jurisdiction. b) Convey/transfer, licensed conveyancer, mortgage. c) Solicitor advocate, jurisdictions, barrister. d) Probate, beneficiaries, will. e) Purchaser's, search, deed (contract of sale).

******

Answers Chapter 2 – Part 2 – Exercise 1

a) Is pleading. b) Understands. c) Working. d) Pleads. e) Is taking. f) Is working. g) Hates.

Answers Chapter 2 – Part 2 – Exercise 2

a) Reading. b) Does not understand. c) Needs. d) Does not know. e) Works. f) Is working. g) Does not think. h) Hopes. i) Knows.

Answers Chapter 2 – Part 2 – Exercise 3

a) Is Frank acting, represents, is hoping. b) Is it raining, is shining. c) Does John want, wants, prefers.

******

Answers Chapter 2 – Part 4 – Translations

A. Recours collectifs

L'arrivée en Europe des recours collectifs à la mode américaine ne fait pas que des heureux. Ce sont les hommes d'affaires qui pourraient être les premiers concernés. Il est clair qu'ils ont peur de se voir infliger des dommages et intérêts exorbitants du type de ceux qui sont accordés aux Etats-Unis. Récemment, par exemple, en Floride, un jury a contraint cinq groupes de l'industrie du tabac à verser $145 milliards de dédommagement, au nom de l'ensemble des fumeurs américains. Ahold, un détaillant néerlandais, a dû débourser $1.1 milliard pour le règlement d'une action collective menée en 2005 par des actionnaires. Et puis, l'an dernier, il y a eu les $65 millions qu'a coûtés à IBM le règlement d'un litige survenu en 2006 avec le personnel technique et administratif sur les heures supplémentaires. Nombreux sont ceux qui, en Europe, affirment que l'on peut se passer du système des recours collectifs, étant donné le haut niveau de réglementations déjà en vigueur. Ils redoutent un doublement des coûts : de mise en conformité réglementaire d'une part et de frais excessifs de justice d'autre part, ces actions à la mode anglo-saxonne entrainent une augmentation notable des procès intentés par les consommateurs.

B. Les transactions immobilières sur un mode réglementé sont de loin les plus onéreuses

La Commission Européenne a publié une étude réalisée par des consultants indépendants sur le marché des services juridiques de ventes de biens immobiliers et fonciers au sein de l'Union Européenne (marché des services de transfert de propriété immobilière). Cette étude révèle que dans le cadre de systèmes juridiques moins réglementés, les consommateurs disposent d'un plus large choix de services, en moyenne moins coûteux et d'une qualité qui n'en est pas diminuée pour autant. Le marché des services de transfert de propriété immobilière représente 17 milliards d'euros par an ; les économies, même marginales, découlant d'un mouvement de déréglementation permettraient donc aux consommateurs de thésauriser chaque année des millions d'euros. La Commission invite les Etats membres à prendre en considération ces conclusions, ainsi qu'à revoir et actualiser les législations nationales qui limitent la concurrence et la libre circulation des services au sein du Marché Unique. Le système notarial latin traditionnel, très réglementé, en vigueur dans la plupart des pays européens, se révèle être le plus onéreux sans nécessairement offrir un meilleur service aux clients. Un tel modèle se signale par :

- la participation obligatoire de juristes spécialisés pour toute transaction foncière ;
- des restrictions quantitatives sur le nombre de juristes qui peuvent se spécialiser dans ce domaine ;
- l'imposition de frais fixes définis par le gouvernement.

C. Quel est exactement le rôle des « barristers » ?

Les *barristers* sont des avocats qui travaillent essentiellement dans les tribunaux. D'ordinaire spécialisés dans un secteur particulier du droit, ils ont une connaissance approfondie des jurisprudences les plus récentes relatives à un domaine particulier. Cette connaissance, associée à leur parfaite maîtrise de la procédure devant les tribunaux, leur permet de faire nettement la différence quant à l'issue de l'affaire. Toutefois, ils ne mettent pas uniquement en œuvre leurs compétences devant les tribunaux. Une forte proportion d'affaires civiles fait l'objet d'un règlement à l'amiable et avoir recours aux services d'un *barrister* prestigieux renforcera sérieusement les chances du client dans la négociation. Si l'affaire est jugée devant les tribunaux, une bonne argumentation fera forte impression sur le juge : le *barrister* permettra ainsi à son client de maximiser les aspects positifs de l'affaire et d'en minimiser les négatifs. Dans le même ordre d'idées, une technique affûtée du contre-interrogatoire fera impression sur le jury. Si l'on considère l'importance de la jurisprudence dans le système dit de « common law », s'attacher les services d'un *barrister* de renom peut faire la différence sur l'issue d'une affaire.

A. The English are coming!

British and American lawyers are invading the French business/commercial law market. In an attempt to resist them, some French firms are developing new strategies. In fact, unbeknownst to the general public, there is an almost silent high stakes war being fought, the outcome of which will have a significant impact on the manner in which work is carried out in the world of business; as we speak, French lawyers are facing an Anglo-American landing. More than half the top twenty law firms specialized *in business* are now Anglo-Saxon. Even worse, many leading French lawyers are choosing to join large Anglo-Saxon firms, bringing with them their entire teams. "Their poaching here in France has had the effect of a double whammy", comments the boss of a large Parisian law firm. "They destabilize their French competitors, whilst at the same time buying their ability, their client lists and their market share."

B. Drop in unemployment forecast?

The new generation of Airbus A320 planes will be assembled in Hamburg, in the north of Germany, according to a press release of the German government that appeared on Monday. The finishing of the A320 at the present time is shared between Toulouse, in France and Hamburg. Other models will be assembled in China, specified the German government. The decision to assemble the aircraft in Hamburg is part of negotiations between Airbus and the German, French, British and Spanish governments concerning a possible loan of 3.3 billion from the latter to Airbus, so that it can ensure the delivery of its future long distance aircraft, the A350 by 2013.

C. So a solicitor is someone who ...

The term solicitor (legal counsel) refers to the type of lawyer that one finds in *common law* countries, such as the United Kingdom, Hong Kong, the Republic of Ireland, Australia, New Zealand, but not in the United States (where the word has a completely different meaning, referring to a chief legal officer of a city). In many common law countries, the profession of lawyer is divided between solicitors, who represent and give advice to their clients, and barristers (trial lawyers), working for the solicitor for the purpose of pleading before a judicial hearing or to supply a legal opinion. However, in a number of countries such as Canada or the United States, the profession of lawyer has seen these two activities merged. *In those jurisdictions* where such a merger has not occurred, when it is necessary to bring a case to trial the client first goes to see a solicitor, who will advise the client and later supply a file (brief) to a lawyer, whose function is to plead the case according to the instructions of the solicitor.

CHAPTER 3 – THE COMMON LAW – SOURCES OF LAW

Answers Chapter 3 – Part 1 – Text 1 – Exercise 1

a) Common, judicial, case law. b) King's Bench/Common Pleas, Exchequer. c) Chancellor, equitable/Christian. d) Corruption, damages. e) Common, local. f) Statute, Parliament. g) Source, immemorial. h) Statute, interpretation. i) Inadequacies, common, Chancery.

Answers Chapter 3 – Part 1 – Text 1 – Exercise 3

a) No, it was the common law and not equity that was too rigid and legalistic. b) No, the custom must exist from time immemorial or at least go back as far as living memory. c) No, once an Act of Parliament has been promulgated into law it becomes known as statute law. d) No, the Court of Common Pleas was established as a court of first instance. e) No, the Commonwealth is the name of the organization made up of the United Kingdom and of some of its former colonies. f) No, the most important source of law in the common law system is normally statute law adopted by the legislative branch of power.

******

Answers Chapter 3 – Part 1 – Text 2 – Exercise 3

a) Common, Chancellor. b) Custom, time immemorial, as of right. c) Act of Parliament, published/promulgated, statute. d) Regulations, directives, member state, implemented. e) Specific performance, injunction.

Answers Chapter 3 – Part 2 – Exercise 1

Got up; put; ate; read; fed; exercised; grabbed; ran; looked; saw; was; arrived; said; took; turned on; fixed; checked; opened; was working; worked; went; attended; took; said; returned; went; prepared; watched; went; dreamed/dreamt.

Answers Chapter 3 – Part 2 – Exercise 2

Began; built; came; drank; knew; made; quit; sold; shot; slept; struck; taught; understood; wore; wrote.

Answers Chapter 3 – Part 2 – Exercise 3

a) Was Frank acting, represented. b) Did John want, raining. c) Did John hope/

was John hoping, preferred. d) Did Frank take, failed. e) Was John studying, studied, passed.

Answers Chapter 3 – Part 2 – Exercise 4

a) Sat, wrote. b) Wanted, was raining. c) Hoped, asked. d) Took, failed. e) Was working, received. f) Was eating, called.

******

Answers Chapter 3 – Part 4 – Translations

A. L'Equity

La jurisprudence offre des remèdes (réparations/solutions juridiques) de deux origines différentes :
- la *common law*.
- l'*Equity*.

Le droit de common law n'offre qu'un unique remède : l'indemnisation financière sous forme de dommages et intérêts. L'Equity fournit des remèdes alternatifs tels que l'ordonnance d'exécution forcée ou encore l'injonction de ne pas faire. Un même préjudice peut donner droit à des solutions juridiques diverses. Par exemple, en cas de violation des dispositions d'un contrat, la partie lésée peut, dans le cadre de la *common law*, obtenir des dommages et intérêts ; elle peut également obtenir une solution en Equity et ainsi bénéficier d'une ordonnance d'exécution forcée obligeant le contractant responsable de l'inexécution à remplir ses obligations. Il convient cependant de rappeler que les voies de recours en Equity ont un caractère discrétionnaire. Normalement seuls les dommages et intérêts sont accordés par les cours ; si le plaignant souhaite bénéficier d'une réparation « en équité », il lui faudra apporter la preuve que les dommages et intérêts ne sont pas la solution appropriée et qu'une solution en Equity s'impose.

B. Qu'est ce que le **trust** ou la fiducie ?

L'Equity a également donné naissance à de nouveaux concepts du droit comme la fiducie/« trust ». Cette dernière est un dispositif juridique qui admet deux propriétaires : le propriétaire de droit et celui qui est reconnu par l'Equity. La fiducie ou le trust donne naissance à un système dans lequel le propriétaire originel, le constituant, confie son bien à une autre personne, le fiduciaire, qui en devient légalement le détenteur. Le fiduciaire gère alors ledit bien dans l'intérêt d'une troisième personne, le bénéficiaire qualifié de détenteur équitable. La fiducie est utilisée à des fins diverses. Prenons pour exemple le cas d'une personne souhaitant investir pour sa retraite ; dans les pays de common law, cela se fera souvent par le biais d'un fonds commun de placement (SICAV). En vertu du contrat de placement signé avec la banque, l'investisseur se trouve être à fois le constituant et le bénéficiaire, la banque étant le fiduciaire. L'investisseur confie son argent à la banque qui devient légalement le détenteur des fonds. Toutefois, en vertu du document de placement signé, la banque doit agir dans l'intérêt de l'investisseur (qui est aussi le bénéficiaire). Pour le dire autrement, la banque a une responsabilité/obligation fiduciaire envers le bénéficiaire.

C. La bataille d'Hastings

A la mort du roi d'Angleterre, Edouard le Confesseur, en 1065, Guillaume, duc de Normandie, dit Guillaume le Bâtard, fit valoir ses prétentions au trône, s'opposant ainsi à Harold, l'époux d'une des filles du défunt roi. Guillaume justifia ses prétentions par ses liens du sang avec Edouard, dont il était un lointain cousin. Il affirma en outre qu'Edouard l'avait, quelques années auparavant, officiellement désigné comme son successeur. Toutefois, à la mort d'Edouard, Harold se déclara roi. Guillaume envahit alors sans tarder l'Angleterre ; en 1066, Harold mourut lors de la bataille d'Hastings et Guillaume s'empara du trône, ce qui changea à jamais l'histoire de l'Angleterre.

A. The common law

The term common law, which has no real equivalent in French, is above all used to describe the legal system put in place by the Norman kings of England, founded on the creation of law by the courts. In the beginning this case law was developed by the royal courts established by Henry II. The term common law also refers to the legal system used in the United Kingdom and in other common law countries. However, these systems are numerous and varied. To know how the common law functions, is to understand the functioning of the legal systems of many countries in the world, the importance of which is only increasing in a world dominated by capitalism.

B. Equity

Equity was created to make up for deficiencies in the common law and resulted from people sending petitions to the King's Chancellor. Finally, equity became part of positive law, through the case law of the equity court created at the end of the fifteenth century, called the Court of Chancery. This court created remedies other than the damages that were available before the common law courts. Equity established principles to which a judge can refer, if (s)he considers that the application of the letter of the law (the common law) leads to an injustice towards the person on trial. Thus, equity created remedies such as injunctions, pursuant to which it was necessary to stop certain behavior.

C. Equity and the common law

After its creation during the 11th century, common law, as a result of the development of royal courts (*Curia regis*), gradually replaced local practices as regards the resolution of disputes. The common law, which was law created by judges and not by the law, gave primacy to judicial precedents. However, little by little, the common law became trapped in rules that were difficult to amend, with judges often too restricted by previously adopted case law. It is for this reason that the Chancellor developed equity, to establish a parallel jurisdiction. These rules, based on equitable principles, made it possible to compensate for the insufficiencies of the common law and its rigidness. Thus, the common law allowed the granting of damages to a party who suffered loss/ was harmed, as a result of the non-performance of a contract. However, if the plaintiff does not wish to receive financial compensation, but prefers instead that the co-contracting party be forced to perform the contract, (s)he can bring an action in equity and, if (s)he establishes that financial compensation is not a just remedy in the circumstances, the judge will agree.

CHAPTER 4 – THE ORGANIZATION OF POLITICAL POWER IN THE UNITED STATES OF AMERICA

Answers Chapter 4 – Part 1 – Text 1 – Exercise 1

a) Fifty, legal. b) Limited, enumerated, restricted, enumerated, defined. c) Head, in chief. d) Houses of Congress, executive. e) Two-party, liberal. f) Federal, state. g) Contract, company. h) Congress, by/pursuant to. i) Supreme Court, jurisdiction. j) Composed of/made-up of, Senate.

Answers Chapter 4 – Part 1 – Text 1 – Exercise 3

a) No, pursuant to article 6 of the US Constitution, federal law takes supremacy over state law at all times. b) No, the leading conservative party in the United States is the Republican Party. c) No, power can be expressed in the United States not only at federal and state level but also at local level. d) No, article 3 of the Constitution establishes the Supreme Court and gave Congress the power to create the federal courts of appeal and federal district courts. e) No, the two branches of government are separate and Congress elects its own leader. The President is only the head of the executive branch. f) No, only the federal government is a government of limited powers; all other powers not given to the federal government are reserved to the states.

******

Answers Chapter 4 – Part 1 – Text 2 – Exercise 3

a) Limited/enumerated, US federal Constitution. b) Checks and balances, undue. c) Effect/force, federal. d) Interest, Congress. e) Judicial review, branches.

******

Answers Chapter 4 – Part 2 – Exercise 1

a) I'll. b) We'll. c) It'll. d) She'll. e) They'll.

Answers Chapter 4 – Part 2 – Exercise 3

a) She probably won't come. b) I probably won't attend. c) We probably won't be. d) They probably won't attend. e) She probably won't go.

Answers Chapter 4 – Part 2 – Exercise 4

a) I am going to meet Jane tomorrow afternoon/I will meet Jane tomorrow afternoon/Tomorrow afternoon I am going to meet Jane/Tomorrow afternoon I will meet Jane). b) I am going to eat late tonight/I will eat late tonight. c) I am going to appear in court later today/I will appear in court later today. d) I am going to change office next year/I will change office next year. e) I am going to be promoted very soon/I will be promoted very soon.

******

Answers Chapter 4 – Part 4 – Translations

A. Contrôle juridictionnel de légalité

Le contrôle juridictionnel de légalité peut consister en un contrôle, par les cours, de la constitutionnalité des normes adoptées par les autres pouvoirs institutionnels. Il y a cependant un autre aspect de ce pouvoir de contrôle, notamment la possibilité pour les cours de juger de la légalité des actes administratifs, c'est-à-dire des décisions des autorités administratives publiques ou privées ; par exemple, une décision du Barreau de New York interdisant la pratique de la profession à un avocat. Donc, dans les pays de *Common Law*, le contrôle administratif de la légalité est réalisé par les juridictions civiles ordinaires. *A contrario*, les pays de droit civil comme la France et l'Allemagne ont établi un système de juridictions administratives dont la compétence sur ces questions-ci est exclusive.

B. Les droits des Etats

Les Etats-Unis ont été dès l'origine le théâtre d'un bras de fer constant entre les Etats et le pouvoir fédéral. Ce sont les Etats qui ont donné naissance au pouvoir fédéral, mais il est clair que, dès cette décision prise, ils doutèrent du bien fondé de cette création. C'est pourquoi ils adoptèrent immédiatement le dixième amendement, afin d'insister sur le fait que tous les pouvoirs qui n'étaient pas expressément dévolus par la constitution au gouvernement fédéral étaient réservés aux états. Ils espéraient ainsi limiter strictement le pouvoir fédéral. Toutefois, les deux cents ans qui suivirent furent marqués par la croissance du pouvoir fédéral, surtout lors de la présidence de Roosevelt. C'est avec l'élection de Ronald Reagan en 1980 que le balancier aurait rebasculé vers les Etats ; il semble cependant plus aisé de critiquer le pouvoir fédéral que de véritablement s'en débarrasser.

C. Roosevelt et la Cour Suprême

Les membres de la Cour Suprême sont nommés à vie par le Président. Seules la mort, la démission ou une procédure d'*impeachment* (mise en accusation) peuvent les amener à quitter leur fonction. L'un des plus importants pouvoirs de la Cour est celui du contrôle de la légalité, en vertu duquel elle peut décider qu'une loi adoptée par le Congrès ou un acte du Président ne sont pas constitutionnels et ne sont donc pas valides/nuls et sans effet. Lorsque le démocrate Franklin Roosevelt est arrivé au pouvoir, la Cour était dominée par les Républicains et ces juges usèrent de leur pouvoir de contrôle de légalité pour déclarer inconstitutionnelles les lois adoptées à l'initiative de Roosevelt.

Le 2 février 1937, à l'occasion d'un discours, Roosevelt s'en prit à la Cour Suprême en faisant remarquer que sept des neuf juges avaient été désignés par des présidents Républicains. Roosevelt venait tout juste d'être largement réélu et n'appréciait pas le fait que des juges non élus puissent opposer leur veto à des lois clairement approuvées par une large majorité de la population. Il menaça d'augmenter le nombre des juges de la Cour afin d'y instaurer une majorité démocrate. Ces mêmes juges républicains ont alors reculé et ont cessé de faire obstruction à l'adoption des mesures législatives souhaitées par Roosevelt.

A. Federation v confederation

The term confederation can be contrasted with that of federation and the two are not interchangeable. In a confederation, sovereignty is vested exclusively in the entities making up the confederation. In a federation, sovereignty is shared between the federal state and the federated states, although the federal government is the dominant power. There have been confederations like Switzerland, even if in reality it is now a federation and only a confederation in name; there are federations such as the United States, and there are organizations which fall somewhere between the two of them. The European Union is, for example, a political organization in which the states retain the majority of their sovereignty, although Community law takes precedence over national law. In the majority of cases, confederation is only a step towards federation.

B. Control of constitutionality

In the United States, the control of the constitutionality of a law is carried out *a posteriori*, which means that it takes place after a law has been promulgated. Thus, the control of the constitutionality of a law by the courts only occurs in the context of a real problem linked to the actual application of the law. It is thus possible that the law will be judged totally or partially unconstitutional, for external legal reasons (for example, it was adopted by an authority acting beyond its powers) or internal reasons (its content fails to respect the provisions of the Constitution, for example concerning fundamental rights). This model of constitutional control is sometimes referred to as the American model and can be contrasted with the European model. The European model is above all characterized by a centralized control, i.e. coming within the exclusive jurisdiction of an individual constitutional court.

C. Judicial review in the United States

One can define constitutional control in the United States as a system in which courts may rule on the constitutionality of any matter coming before it. This is referred to as the power of judicial review; it is not a power of revision or repeal as the judge does not change or repeal the alleged unconstitutional act. However, the court deprives it of any legal force by not applying it. Moreover, this power is not limited to laws: it extends to both legislative and executive acts. It is based on article 6 of the Constitution of 1787 establishing the supremacy of the Constitution and federal laws. The judges thus find themselves vested with a great power, to such a degree that there has been talk of a "government of judges".

<h2 style="text-align:center">CHAPTER 5 – THE COURT SYSTEM
IN THE UNITED STATES</h2>

Answers Chapter 5 – Part 1 – Text 1 – Exercise 1

a) Subject. b) Controversies. c) Instance. d) Hear. e) Pursuant. f) Municipal. g) Handed. h) Federal Supreme Court. i) Circuits.

Answers Chapter 5 – Part 1 – Text 1 – Exercise 3

a) No, the US federal Supreme Court may have jurisdiction over decisions taken by the state courts, where a question involving the interpretation of federal law is involved. b) No, the litigant normally has no choice; if a question of federal law is involved, the litigant must bring the action before the federal courts, whereas if the question involves state law, the action must be brought before the state courts. If the subject matter of the action involves an area covered by both state and federal law, the federal court can choose to exercise jurisdiction or not. c) No, decisions from the Municipal Courts are appealed to the State Court of Appeal. d) No, the United States is divided into 94 districts and twelve appellate circuits. e) No, the lowest ranking state courts are referred to as the Municipal Courts and do not have federal jurisdiction.

******

Answers Chapter 5 – Part 1 – Text 2 – Exercise 3

a) Limited, US Constitution (Article 1(8)). b) Checks and balances, undue. c) Effect/force, federal. d) Double jeopardy, offence. e) Specialist courts, customs duties.

******

Answers Chapter 5 – Part 2 – Exercise 1

a) Before I write a letter to my client, I am going to go for lunch. b) When I go to Brussels next week, I am going to eat some chips. c) Before Jane finishes writing her letter, she will have to meet her clients. d) After John goes home this evening, he will surf the Internet. e) As soon as the snow stops, John is going to go to the courthouse. f) When I call Frank tomorrow, I will ask him to attend the meeting.

Answers Chapter 5 – Part 2 – Exercise 3

a) If I do not receive a letter … b) If Frank has enough time… c) If it is sunny... d) If I study for my Bar exams… e) If I do not study ….

Answers Chapter 5 – Part 2 – Exercise 4

a) Leaves, will write. b) Goes, will take. c) Wakes up, he is going to ring. d) Arrives, will drink. e) Will meet, arrives. f) I am, will stay.

******

Answers Chapter 5 – Part 4 – Translations

A. La compétence de la Cour Suprême

La Cour ne statue en première instance que dans quelques rares cas : par exemple des affaires impliquant un des États membres de l'Union, un État étranger ou encore un diplomate étranger. Pour la plupart des affaires, la Cour possède une compétence d'appel et ses décisions ne sont pas susceptibles de recours. Seules l'intéressent les affaires impliquant les questions de droit importantes et elle choisit parmi les milliers de recours déposés chaque année ceux qu'elle souhaite examiner. Ses arrêts concernant la Constitution sont définitifs, « la Constitution est ce que la Cour Suprême dit qu'elle est » (elle définit le champ d'application de la Constitution). C'est donc la Cour Suprême qui définit, selon les normes de l'époque, la portée des droits fondamentaux des citoyens, parfois de manière extensive, parfois plus restrictivement.

B. La Juridiction des cours d'Etats

Presque toutes les affaires relevant du droit civil ou pénal des Etats débutent devant les juridictions de ces mêmes Etats ; celles-ci ont effectivement compétence pour toutes les questions relatives au divorce, à l'exercice de l'autorité parentale, aux mineurs ou encore aux affaires immobilières. Elles sont également compétentes pour juger la plupart des affaires pénales, des actions intentées en matière de contrat, des infractions routières et des requêtes visant à obtenir la réparation des préjudices personnels. En outre, certaines catégories de litiges peuvent relever de juridictions spécifiques : il existe, à titre d'exemple un tribunal spécialisé dans les affaires de succession.

C. L'organisation en circuit des cours d'appel états-uniennes

Il y a douze cours d'appel aux Etats-Unis. Tous les Etats et districts s'inscrivent dans la circonscription d'un de ces douze circuits. Chaque cour d'appel a compétence pour examiner les appels à l'encontre de décisions des tribunaux de district rattachés au circuit et leurs décisions peuvent elles-mêmes faire l'objet d'un recours en appel devant la Cour Suprême fédérale. Désormais, il existe également une cour dénommée Cour d'appel du circuit fédéral des Etats-Unis (*US Court of Appeal for the Federal Circuit*). Cette dernière traite les recours en appel formulés en matière civile à l'encontre du gouvernement des Etats-Unis mais aussi ceux concernant les affaires de brevets ou les questions de commerce international.

A. Federal and state courts

In the United States there are two independent jurisdictions: at federal and state level. In both these jurisdictions, there are first instance courts, intermediary appeal courts and courts of last resort. At both levels are found specialized courts having jurisdiction over specific matters. As with the *Cour de cassation* in France, it is not possible to apply to the US Supreme Court directly: normally, the highest court in the country can only become involved as a court of last resort, when an individual is of the opinion that his/her constitutional rights have not been respected and (s)he has already failed on appeal.

B. The Supreme Court

The US Supreme Court is the highest court in the federal system. It is made up of eight associate judges and a Chief Justice. It can only rule in law. The Supreme Court may examine the decisions of the federal circuit Courts of Appeal either: (1) by way of a request for writ of certiorari, by which the Supreme Court requests a lower jurisdiction to send it the case, or (2) by way of mandatory appeal where the Supreme Court must hear the matter on appeal, its so-called mandatory appellate jurisdiction. It may also examine decisions handed down at last resort by the highest state jurisdiction, if the constitutional validity of a law is called into question.

C. The President and the system of "checks and balances"

In reality, power in the United States is organized around a dilution of powers as opposed to a strict separation. Thus, each organ of power holds *vis-à-vis* the other organs significant control allowing for a balance of power. This is the system of "checks and balances". The President is responsible for diplomatic relations and represents the country on the international stage. (S)he appoints ambassadors and consuls, negotiates and signs international treaties, with the approval of the Senate. (S)he is the Commander in Chief of the armed forces. (S)he is responsible for developing the military policy of the United States. (S) he can decide to commit American forces abroad, without having to declare war.

CHAPTER 6 – THE NATURE OF CONSTITUTIONAL LAW IN THE UNITED STATES

Answers Chapter 6 – Part 1 – Text 1 – Exercise 1

a) Citizens, warrantless/illegal. b) Just compensation, Amendment. c) Removed, impeachment. d) Civil, ten. e) Double, provision/clause, tried. f) Right, bear. g) Supreme Court, instrumentalists. h) Grand jury, offenses. i) Pursuant/according, legislative, executive, judicial.

Answers Chapter 6 – Part 1 – Text 1 – Exercise 3

a) No, there are in fact fifty-one constitutions in the United States of America, the federal Constitution and the fifty state constitutions. b) No, since the development of the theory of selective incorporation, those rights in the Bill of Rights coming within the notion of due process, as established by the Fourteenth Amendment, also apply to the states; this is because the Fourteenth Amendment specifically applies to the states and requires states to protect citizen's due process rights.

c) No, the separation of powers in the United States is not strictly enforced as a result of the system of checks and balances, whereby the different branches of government control each other and effectively share power. d) No, the double jeopardy clause prevents someone from being tried twice for the same offence; the Fourth Amendment provides for the accused having the right to a grand jury hearing in the case of serious crimes, so as to ensure that there is sufficient evidence against him/her to justify their being sent for trial. e) No, the originalists believe that the US Constitution should be interpreted literally and should in no way be modified so as to take account of changes in society. This they believe is the role of the other powers acting in concert with the citizens of America. f) No, the President does have the power to nominate Supreme Court justices with the approval of the Senate; however, justices can only be removed by way of impeachment proceedings before the Senate.

******

Answers Chapter 6 – Part 1 – Text 2 – Exercise 3

a) Amendments, guarantees. b) Self incrimination, evidence. c) Effect/force, liberties. d) Fourth Amendment, warrantless/unauthorized. e) Standing, plaintiff.

******

Answers Chapter 6 – Part 2 – Exercise 1

a) Gone. b) Met. c) Begun. d) Had. e) Rained. f) Written. g) Ridden. h) Done. i) Known. j) Finished. k) Been. l) Eaten. m) Made. n) Seen. o) Called.

Answers Chapter 6 – Part 2 – Exercise 2

a) I have flown … b) You have stayed… c) He has finished…. d) They have gone … e) She has rung … f) We have represented ….

Answers Chapter 6 – Part 3 – Exercise 4

a) Have, have eaten, ate. b) Have, have talked, talked. c) Have visited, visited, have not been. d) Have, worked, have not worked. e) Have not, have been, have not finished.

******

Answers Chapter 6 – Part 4 – Translations

A. Les juges de la Cour suprême

La Constitution n'impose aucune restriction relative à la qualité des personnes susceptibles d'être nommées juge à la Cour suprême. Il est toutefois nécessaire que toute nomination réalisée par le Président soit approuvée par le Sénat. Généralement, ce sont d'éminents juristes, tels que Louis Brandeis ou encore Thurgood Marshall, lequel a plaidé l'affaire *Brown v Board of Education* qui permit de mettre fin à la ségrégation raciale dans les écoles, qui ont la faveur des nominations. Ces juristes aux compétences notoires ont souvent occupé des fonctions importantes dans l'appareil judiciaire : juge dans des cours fédérales inférieures, juge à la Cour suprême de leur État ou encore membre du ministère de la Justice. Earl Warren a été nommé Président de la Cour Suprême (position occupée de 1953 à 1969) après avoir été gouverneur de l'Etat de Californie. Seules trois femmes ont, jusqu'à ce jour, siégé à la Cour Suprême : Sandra Day O' Connor, Ruth Bader Ginsburg et Sonia Sotomayor. Seuls deux juges Afro-Américains ont été nommés: Thurgood Marshall, 1967, et Clarence Thomas qui lui a succédé en 1991 et siège encore à la Cour.

B. La compétence en appel de la Cour Suprême

A quelques exceptions près prévues par l'article III de la Constitution, la Cour Suprême a essentiellement une compétence d'appel qu'elle exerce de façon discrétionnaire : elle peut ainsi accepter ou refuser de délivrer une ordonnance de *certiorari*, ordonnance enjoignant la cour ayant jugé précédemment l'affaire de lui transmettre le dossier. Dans les faits, plus d'1% seulement des requêtes sont acceptées par la Cour, soit chaque année un peu plus de 100 sur 7 000. Le règlement de la Cour (article 10) précise les critères régissant l'acceptation d'un appel : il faut que l'affaire contienne une question de droit importante portant sur la Constitution ou la loi des États-Unis (une question qualifiée de fédérale) et que cette question n'ait pas été tranchée précédemment par la Cour, ou que la Cour inférieure ait statué en contradiction avec la jurisprudence antérieure.

C. Nomination des juges à la Cour suprême

Le Président a récemment confirmé qu'il était favorable à la nomination à la Cour suprême d'un juge représentatif de la « diversité » des Etats-Unis, que ce soit « par le sexe, la race, l'origine sociale ou la religion ». Interrogé par le Wall Street Journal en marge de son déplacement au Mexique, le Président a estimé que « la diversité de notre pays est une bonne chose (..) plus il y aura d'opinions et de vécus différents sur la table, meilleur sera le résultat ». Il a confirmé qu'il mènerait la procédure de désignation de façon tout aussi attentive et scrupuleuse qu'à l'occasion du choix du dernier juge nommé à la Cour Suprême.

A. The XIVth Amendment

The XIVth Amendment establishes two important rules, namely the:
- due process guarantee;
- requirement that no state shall deny to any person within its jurisdiction equal protection under the law.

The two guarantees result from the desire of the federal powers to prevent the southern states re-establishing slavery. They allow for the prevention of racial or political discrimination. The due process of law guarantee applies to all cases where an individual is the subject of an unfavourable decision. This clause allowed the Supreme Court to confer on itself a veritable criminal jurisdiction, as it not only applies to administrative and legislative acts but also to decisions from the different courts, including decisions in the area of criminal law. It is also by way of this clause that the Court developed the theory of selective incorporation.

B. The Supreme Court's discretionary power of appeal

The Court is also inclined to grant an appeal if a number of inferior courts (at federal or state level) have decided the matter in different ways. The Court can thus decide to reply to a question or choose to hear the entire matter (on appeal). The party wishing to appeal the matter to the Supreme Court lodges a written request (a petition for certiorari), asking it to hear the matter on appeal. In the request, the matter is summarized, demonstrating the federal questions at issue and the legal arguments against the decision of the lower court. The matter is accepted if four judges vote in its favour. If not, the decision of the lower court is confirmed.

C. The judges of the Supreme Court

Congress has established by law the number of judges sitting on the Supreme Court. In the beginning the number was seven, nine since 1869, one of whom presides over the other judges. The presiding judge is referred to as the Chief Justice and the remaining judges are known as Associate Justices or simply Justices. Article III governs the manner of their nomination and their privileges. They are nominated by the President with the consent of the Senate (sometimes the Senate's approval may be withheld, but few candidates are rejected in this way). They remain judges for as long as they wish and may only be removed from Office after being judged by Congress, according to the same impeachment proceedings applicable to the President of the United States, which has never happened to a Supreme Court judge.

CHAPTER 7 – THE ORGANIZATION OF POWER IN THE UNITED KINGDOM

Answers Chapter 7 – Part 1 – Text 1 – Exercise 1

a) Settlement, Protestant. b) House of Lords, House of Commons. c) Nominal, exercise. d) Executive. e) Constitution, statute. f) European Union/European Economic Community, European Union law, precedence. g) Magna Carta, limit.

Answers Chapter 7 – Part 1 – Text 1 – Exercise 3

a) No, there has been devolution of power from Westminster to Scotland, Northern Ireland and Wales. b) No, the UK does not have a codified constitution set out in one constitutional document; rather the UK Constitution is made up of a number of different sources. c) No, the Queen may only exercise this power upon the recommendation of the Prime Minister. d) No, the power of the UK judiciary is diminishing because more and more laws are being adopted in Brussels by the European Union. e) No, only people of the Protestant faith can be appointed as Monarch.

******

Answers Chapter 7 – Part 1 – Text 2 – Exercise 3

a) Constitutional, nominal. b) Westminster, regional/devolved. c) Fundamental, case law. d) Northern Ireland, Scotland. e) Ministers, Cabinet.

******

Answers Chapter 7 – Part 2 – Exercise 1

a) For; b) Since; c) Since; d) Since; e) For; f) For; g) Since; h) For.

Answers Chapter 7 – Part 2 – Exercise 3

a) Have known, have been; b) has had, has become; c) began, have had; d) have been, have lived; e) has been, was; f) began, have completed; g) have known, has been.

Answers Chapter 7 – Part 2 – Exercise 4

a) Fell, fallen b) Gave, given, c) Bit, bitten d) Wore, worn. e) Grew, grown. f) Got, got, g) Drank, drunk.

******

Answers Chapter 7 – Part 4 – Translations

A. Qu'est exactement la Magna Carta?

La *Magna Carta* fut signée en juin 1215 par les barons de l'Angleterre médiévale et le roi Jean sans Terre. *Magna Carta* est un terme latin qui signifie *Grande Charte*. Elle fut signée à Runnymede près du château de Windsor, où les membres de la famille royale anglaise continuent de résider aujourd'hui. La charte était une tentative des barons destinée à empêcher le roi d'abuser de son pouvoir, en particulier celui de lever l'impôt. En signant ce document, le roi Jean sans Terre démontra la relative faiblesse de la monarchie dans l'Angleterre médiévale. Comment un roi supposé être tout puissant dans son propre pays, a-t-il pu accepter les exigences de barons normalement placés sous son autorité ? Dans les faits, le roi n'a eu que très peu, voire pas, de choix.

B. « House of Commons » (La Chambre des communes)

La Chambre des communes s'est développée au cours du quatorzième siècle et a siégé sans discontinu depuis. Suite à l'union politique avec l'Ecosse et l'Irlande proclamée en vertu de l'Acte d'Union, les membres de la Chambre des communes provinrent de l'ensemble du Royaume-Uni et non plus seulement de l'Angleterre et du Pays de Galles. Historiquement, la Chambre des communes était bien moins puissante que la Chambre des Lords ; aujourd'hui son pouvoir législatif est bien supérieur à celui des Lords. En vertu de la loi sur le Parlement de 1911, le droit des Lords d'opposer un veto aux propositions de lois a été réduit en un simple pouvoir permettant de retarder l'adoption d'un texte. La Chambre des Lords peut désormais suspendre l'adoption de toute législation mais seulement pour une période de temps limitée. Le gouvernement du pays est responsable devant la Chambre des communes et le Premier ministre ne reste au pouvoir qu'aussi longtemps qu'il conserve la confiance de la Chambre des communes. Bien que quelques ministres du gouvernement soient issus de la Chambre des Lords, la quasi-totalité d'entre eux provient de la Chambre des communes.

C. Qu'est-ce-que l'habeas corpus?

L'habeas corpus est un ancien droit de *common law*; en d'autres termes, c'est un droit qui fut développé en premier lieu par les tribunaux. En vertu de ce droit, les tribunaux ont le pouvoir d'émettre une ordonnance extraordinaire d'habeas corpus ordonnant à la Couronne, si celle-ci restreint la liberté d'une personne, de produire sans délai le prisonnier devant la cour et de motiver les raisons expliquant la privation de liberté. En l'absence d'une motivation suffisante, la cour a le devoir de libérer l'intéressé. L'habeas corpus est au cœur des systèmes jurisprudentiels de *common law* et il est marquant que, même dans l'Angleterre médiévale, le pouvoir de la Couronne ait pu être contrôlé de cette manière.

A. The House of Lords

The House of Lords first sat as a separate chamber in the 14th century. From the beginning, the House of Lords was made up of Lords Temporal and Lords Spiritual, both appointed by the King. From the 15th century onwards Lords Temporal were also referred to as peers. Originally, the House of Lords could reject and veto legislation proposed by the House of Commons but over time this power was reduced and finally abolished. The change came about in 1909 when the House of Lords refused to pass the budget prepared by David Lloyd George. Socialist in direction, the budget laid the foundation stones for the later creation of the Welfare State. The Lords' rejection of the budget led to the adoption of the Parliament Act, 1911, under which the Lords retained a right to examine and delay the passage of bills[2] passed by the House of Commons but were deprived of their right to veto such legislation.

B. What is devolution?

Devolution essentially involves the setting up of elected regional assemblies in each of the home countries making up the United Kingdom[3]. Each area has been the subject of a Devolution Act defining the different powers granted to each by the national government. These powers guarantee a limited right of autonomy for Scotland, Wales and Northern Ireland. However, they do not include the transfer

---

[2]   The adoption of legislation goes through three stages, having a different name at each stage a(n):
  –   *bill*, the name given to a proposal for a law prior to its being accepted by both the House of Commons and the House of Lords;
  –   *Act of Parliament*, the name given to the proposal after it has passed both Houses but prior to its being given the royal assent;
  –   *statute*, the name given to the proposal once it has been signed by the Queen and published in the Statute Books.
[3]   With the exception of England.

of major powers, such as the control of the taxation, armed forces or a foreign policy role. Such issues remain under the control of the central government. In this sense, some consider devolution as having failed to deliver the degree of autonomy desired by segments of the populations living in these areas.

C. Where does Habeas Corpus come from?

Although the courts first developed habeas corpus, the Magna Carta also specifically provides for the right to make an application for habeas corpus. According to the Magna Carta: *"No free man shall be taken or imprisoned (...) or exiled except by the lawful judgment of his peers or by the law of the land"*. Indeed, the right to habeas corpus was already settled practice and part of the law at the time of the adoption of the Magna Carta, and was thus a fundamental part of the unwritten law of the land. It is an example of the medieval courts developing principles that continue to have constitutional relevance today.

CHAPTER 8 – THE COURT STRUCTURE IN THE UNITED KINGDOM

Answers Chapter 8 – Part 1 – Text 1 – Exercise 1

a) Criminal, civil. b) Instance, Magistrates'. c) Non-indictable/summary/ minor offences, Crown Court. d) Minor, summary. e) Lie, Supreme Court. f) European Court of Human Rights, European Convention on Human Rights. g) Criminal, crossover.

Answers Chapter 8 – Part 1 – Text 1 – Exercise 3

a) No, although the Magistrates' Court is predominantly a court of criminal jurisdiction, it also has limited responsibility for civil law matters, such as debt collection. b) No, the Supreme Court may only hear appeals on questions of law. c) No, only a certain number of indictable offences are capable of being tried as either indictable or non-indictable offences. d) No, the UK Supreme Court has jurisdiction over all of the United Kingdom. e) No, there is no right of appeal from the UK system to the EU system. However, the UK courts may write to the EU courts asking for advice as regards the interpretation of EU law.

******

Answers Chapter 8 – Part 1 – Text 2 – Exercise 3

a) Fast-track claims, case manager. b) Indictable, non-indictable (minor offences, summary offences, misdemeanors). c) Fact, High Court, Queen's Bench Division. d) Deter, compensate. e) Domestic, exhausted.

******

Answers Chapter 8 – Part 3 – Exercise 1

a) Frank is always …; b) Frank usually …; c) The client will probably …; d)

The client is already …; e) Frank finally …; f) Frank is finally …; g) Does Frank always …; h) Can you always…; i) When does Frank usually …; j) Frank has already; Frank occasionally ….

Answers Chapter 8 – Part 3 – Exercise 2

A. i) Jack often …; ii) Jack frequently …; iii) Jack generally …; iv) Jack never arrives; v) Jack rarely arrives ….

B. i) I generally …; ii) I hardly ever draft …; iii) I occasionally…; iv) I never draft …; v) I seldom draft ….

C. i) Jack usually …; ii) Jack generally …; iii) Is Jack ever ….; iv) Jack is seldom in …; v) Jack is frequently; vi) Jack is always ….

Answers Chapter 8 – Part III – Exercise 3

a) The office is often …; b) Frank usually …; c) I do not always …; d) Frank never takes.

******

Answers Chapter 8 – Part 4 – Translations

A. Qu'est-ce que la procédure de l'article 267 du traité sur le fonctionnement de l'Union européenne?

La procédure du renvoi préjudiciel est mise en œuvre lorsqu'un procès devant une juridiction nationale soulève une question de droit de l'Union européenne. Si la juridiction nationale n'est pas certaine de l'interprétation ou de la validité d'une norme européenne, elle peut soumettre une question sur ce point à la Cour de justice. La juridiction nationale saisit ainsi la Cour de justice d'une demande de renvoi préjudiciel, afin de lui permettre d'appliquer correctement les dispositions pertinentes du droit de l'UE dans le cadre de l'affaire au principal. La fonction de la procédure de renvois préjudiciels est de garantir l'application effective et uniforme du droit de l'UE dans l'ensemble des Etats membres.

B. L'indépendance judiciaire

Le pouvoir judiciaire joue un rôle essentiel dans la société britannique. Pour le mener à bien, il se doit d'être indépendant. Les décisions et jugements adoptés doivent l'être sans parti-pris politique. En effet, l'indépendance judiciaire est vue par beaucoup comme constituant la partie la plus importante/pierre angulaire du système de Westminster. Mais qu'est-ce que l'indépendance judiciaire ? Les juridictions de Grande-Bretagne sont connues sous le nom de cours de la Couronne dans la mesure où leur compétence dérive du pouvoir exécutif de la Couronne. Cependant, bien qu'étant gérées par le pouvoir exécutif, les cours ont l'obligation d'être indépendantes à la fois du pouvoir exécutif et du pouvoir législatif. Ainsi, le pouvoir exécutif ne peut retarder ou détourner/obstruer le cours de la justice. En outre, le pouvoir exécutif ne doit jamais forcer les juges à agir d'une manière qui ne serait pas impartiale. Enfin, les juges ont la sécurité de l'emploi : ils ne peuvent être révoqués que s'ils se rendent coupables d'un manquement grave.

C. Actions civiles portant sur un montant modique et juridictions du Royaume-Uni

Si le montant d'une demande est égal ou inferieure à 5000£, celle-ci sera généralement jugée en vertu de la procédure de règlement des litiges ne dépassant pas une somme modique. Cependant, si la demande est relative à une réclamation pour préjudice personnel, elle ne relèvera que de ladite procédure si la valeur de la demande ne dépasse pas 1000£. Dans certains cas, même si le montant de l'affaire est supérieur à 5,000£, en cas d'accord entre les parties le tribunal peut accepter de se prononcer en vertu de la procédure de règlement des litiges, ne dépassant pas une somme modique, afin d'autoriser une résolution rapide de l'affaire. Les demandes portant sur des sommes modiques sont normalement soumises aux juges de district et les décisions sont prises par un juge unique et sans jury.

A. Organization of the High Court

The High Court is organized into three separate divisions. The first is known as the Queen's Bench Division and has jurisdiction over disputes in common law, for example contracts, torts or land law. The Queen's Bench Division also has courts that act as specialist sub-divisions, including a Commercial Court and an Admiralty Court (dealing with shipping matters). The next division is called the Chancery Division and has jurisdiction over wills, settlements, trusts, bankruptcy, land law, intellectual property (copyright and patents) and corporate law. Many company law cases are dealt with in a specialist sub-division of the Chancery Division, referred to as the Companies Court. Finally, there is a Family Division dealing with divorce and child welfare matters and also the administration of wills.

B. The Court of Appeal

The Court of Appeal of England and Wales is the second most senior court in the UK legal system. The Court of Appeal hears criminal appeals in the Criminal Division and civil appeals in the Civil Division, led by the Lord Chief Justice and Master of the Rolls respectively. The Criminal Division hears appeals from the Crown Court, while the Civil Division hears appeals from the County Courts and High Court of Justice. The right to appeal is not automatic and prior permission to appeal is required, from either the lower court or from the Court of Appeal itself. An appeal must have a *real prospect of success*, or there must be *some other compelling reason why the appeal should be heard*, in order for an application to be accepted.

C. The Supreme Court

The Supreme Court of the United Kingdom hears appeals for all matters arising under the jurisdictions of England & Wales, Northern Ireland and Scotland. It is the court of last resort and highest appellate court in the United Kingdom. The Supreme Court also has jurisdiction to resolve disputes relating to devolution. Established by the Constitutional Reform Act 2005, the Supreme Court has replaced the former final appellate jurisdiction, the House of Lords[4]. Prior to the Constitutional Reform Act, the House of Lords was made up of a legislative and a judicial branch. Indeed, one of the reasons behind the creation of the Supreme Court was to clearly separate power between the judicial and legislative branch, even if in reality such links were symbolic.

CHAPTER 9 – THE CREATION OF THE EUROPEAN UNION

Answers Chapter 9 – Part 1 – Text 1 – Exercise 1

a) European Economic Community (EEC), Treaty on European Union/Maastricht Treaty (TEU). b) European Commission, European Union. c) European Coal and Steel Treaty, sowed. d) European Council, member states. e) Audit, finances. f) Treaty on European Union/Maastricht Treaty, police, judicial.

Answers Chapter 9 – Part 1 – Text 1 – Exercise 3

a) No, the European Coal and Steel Treaty is no longer in force and came to an end in 2002, after 50 years. b) No, it is the European Council that is made up of the Heads of State of each of the member states; the Council of the European Union is comprised of relevant government ministers. c) No, the Maastricht Treaty incorporated the European Community (EC) (previously the European Economic Community) into the European Union and the EC ceased to exist after the adoption of the Lisbon Treaty. d) No, the Euro is made up of nineteen of the twenty-eight EU member states; it is an example of a two-speed European Union.

******

Answers Chapter 9 – Part 1 – Text 2 – Exercise 3

a) Common Agricultural Policy (CAP), agricultural. b) Executive, Council of the European Union. c) Transfer, member states. d) Council of Europe, 1952. e) Monopoly, abusing, power.

******

Answers Chapter 4 – Part 2 – Exercise 1

a) Have already finished. b) Had already finished. c) Had already started. d) Has already started. e) Had already left.

Answers Chapter 4 – Part 2 – Exercise 2

a) Was raining. b) Had stopped. c) Had finished. d) Had washed. e) Was washing.

---

[4] Although primarily a legislative body, the House of Lords prior to the Constitutional Reform Act (2005) also included the final appellate jurisdiction for the UK, staffed by Law Lords appointed by the executive for this purpose.

Answers Chapter 4 – Part 2 – Exercise 3

a) Did you see, was, had not seen. b) Do you recognize, have not seen, have not spoken. c) Did you go, arrived, had already made. d) Was, had, was eating. e) Did you do, wanted, had already seen.

******

Answers Chapter 9 – Part 4 – Translations

A. Le Parlement européen

Le Parlement européen est élu par les citoyens de l'Union européenne pour représenter leurs intérêts. Institué dès les années cinquante par les traités fondateurs, ses membres ne sont élus au suffrage universel direct que depuis 1979. Des élections sont organisées tous les cinq ans et chaque citoyen de l'UE possède le droit de vote et d'éligibilité. Le Parlement européen exprime ainsi la volonté démocratique des citoyens de l'Union, soit plus de 490 millions de personnes, et représente leurs intérêts quand il négocie avec les autres institutions de l'Union. Aujourd'hui, il compte 736 membres qui proviennent des 28 Etats membres de l'Union. Ses membres (députés européens) ne siègent pas par nationalité mais au sein de sept groupes politiques européens qui représentent l'ensemble des idéologies politiques, de droite comme de gauche.

B. Le Conseil de l'Union européenne

Le Conseil est le principal organe décisionnel de l'Union européenne. Il a été institué par les traités fondateurs dans les années cinquante. Il représente les Etats membres et un ministre de chaque Etat assiste à ses réunions. Si l'ordre du jour est relatif à la politique économique, seront présents les ministres des finances de chaque Etat membre et la formation du Conseil est alors communément dénommée « ECOFIN ». De la même manière, si le Conseil doit évoquer des questions environnementales, ce sont les ministres de l'environnement qui seront présents et c'est le « Conseil environnement » qui se réunira. Les relations de l'UE avec le reste du monde sont gérées par le Conseil des affaires étrangères.

C. La Commission européenne

La Commission est l'institution de l'Union européenne qui est la plus indépendante des gouvernements des Etats membres. Sa mission est de représenter et de défendre les intérêts de l'Union dans son ensemble. Elle rédige des propositions de nouvelles lois européennes qu'elle transmet au Parlement européen et au Conseil. La Commission représente également le pouvoir exécutif de l'Union et est responsable de la mise en œuvre des lois adoptées par le Parlement et le Conseil. Comme le Conseil, la Commission a été instituée dans les années cinquante en vertu des traités fondateurs.

Le terme « Commission européenne » peut revêtir deux sens :
-    il peut signifier l'équipe de Commissaires européens – un pour chaque

Etat membre – nommés pour diriger l'institution et la représenter dans ses relations avec les autres institutions ;
-   deuxièmement, le terme peut signifier l'institution elle-même et l'ensemble de son personnel.

A. The Court of Justice of the European Union

The Court of Justice of the European Union is made up of three separate courts: the General Court, the Civil Service Tribunal and the Court of Justice. The function of the Court of Justice of the European Union is to ensure that in the interpretation and application of the EU Treaties the law is observed. As part of that mission, the Court of Justice of the European Union:
-   reviews the legality of the acts of the institutions of the European Union;
-   ensures that the member states comply with their obligations under the Treaties; and
-   interprets European Union law at the request of the national courts and tribunals.

B. The budget of the European Union and Court of Auditors

The European Union has a budget of approximately 120 billion euro, around 1% of the gross national income (GNI) of its 28 member states. Compared to the national budgets of its member states, this amount is relatively small. However, for some poorer member states, funds from the EU play an important role in financing public activities such as the development of infrastructure. The revenue of the European Union mainly consists of contributions from members states based on their GNI and on a measurement connected to value added tax collected by the different member states. Both the Council and the European Parliament working together decide on the budget annually. The role of the Court of Auditors is to ensure that the money is being spent correctly and that EU citizens are getting good value for their hard earned Euros.

C. What is qualified majority voting?

In some particularly sensitive areas such as common foreign and security policy, taxation, asylum and immigration policy, Council decisions have to be unanimous. In other words, each member state has the power of veto in these areas. On most issues, however, the Council takes decisions by way of qualified majority voting. The system works in the following way. Between 1 December 2009 and 1 November 2014, a qualified majority is achieved once a proposal receives 255 votes out of 345, representing at least 50% of the member states. From 2014 onwards, the rules concerning qualified majority voting will change to put in place a system based on a double majority. According to the new rules of the Lisbon Treaty applicable from 2014, to be adopted a legislative proposal will have to receive 55% of member state votes representing at least 65% of the Union's population. This system guarantees that the most populated member states will not dominate or block the legislative process.

CHAPTER 10 – THE NOTION OF FREE MOVEMENT IN THE EUROPEAN UNION

Answers Chapter 10 – Part 1 – Text 1 – Exercise 1

a) Internal market, common market. b) Capital, exchange controls. c) Free movement, goods, workers, services and establishment. d) Single market, barriers e) Establishment, legal. f) Suppression/removal, quantitative. g) Mutual recognition, harmonization. h) Authorized, member state.

Answers Chapter 10 – Part 1 – Text 1 – Exercise 3

a) No, the creation of the single market required a limited harmonization of essential rules dealing with issues such as consumer protection. b) No, member states are expressly prohibited from applying quantitative restrictions to goods coming from other member states. c) No, the notion of the single market applies to the four factors of production, namely the free movement of goods, workers, services, establishment and capital. d) No, the requirement of free movement of workers set out in the Treaty on the Functioning of the European Union prevents member states from discriminating between workers. e) No, mutual recognition means that member states agree to recognize on the basis of reciprocity the regulatory rules applicable in other member states. f) No, the phrase single market passport refers to the fact that under the principle of mutual recognition, a firm authorized to do business in one member state, may then rely on that authorization to offer its services or to establish in any other member state.

******

Answers Chapter 10 – Part 1 – Text 2 – Exercise 3

a) Schengen Accord, two-speed Europe. b) Free, factors of production. c) Goods, equivalent effect. d) Mutual recognition, harmonization. e) Established/authorized, single market/European Union.

******

Answers Chapter 10 – Part 2 – Exercise 1

a) Waiting, waited. b) Quitting, quit. c) Writing, wrote. d) Shouting, shouted. e) Swimming, swam. f) Aiming, aimed. g) Opening, opened. h) Helping, helped. i) Sleeping, slept. j) Taping, taped. k) Beginning, began. l) Occurring/occurred. m) Happening, happened. n) Referring, referred. o) Raining, rained. p) Running, ran. q) Winning, won. r) Explaining, explained. s) Burning, burnt. t) Charming, charmed. u) Buying, bought. v) Trying, tried. w) Tying, tied. x) Dying, died. y) Choosing, chose. z) Riding, rode.

******

Answers Chapter 10 – Part 4 – Translations

A. Qu'est ce que signifie l'expression « Europe à deux vitesses »?

Des notions telles que cercles concentriques, coopération renforcée ou Europe à deux vitesses renvoient toutes au même processus : l'intégration au sein de l'UE s'effectue à des vitesses variables. Cette situation est provoquée par la réunion d'un nombre limité d'Etats membres de l'Union qui choisissent d'approfondir leur coopération sans que les autres Etats membres y participent. Parmi les exemples de coopération renforcée, l'Euro. Bien que l'Euro soit la monnaie officielle de l'UE, tous les Etats membres ne sont pas membres de la zone Euro. Le recours à de telles coopérations permet d'affirmer que l'UE est divisée en plusieurs cercles concentriques :

- le premier cercle comprend l'ensemble des Etats membres ;
- le second cercle comprendrait les pays qui ont décidé d'intégrer davantage leurs économies.

B. Que sont les Accords de Schengen?

Les Accords de Schengen constituent un exemple parfait d'Europe à deux vitesses : un nombre d'Etats membres de l'UE se sont entendus afin de permettre la libre circulation des personnes et la suppression des contrôles aux frontières entre eux. La zone sans frontières créée par les Accords de Schengen, aussi dénommée l'espace Schengen, comprend les 25 Etats membres, une population de 500 millions de personnes et une superficie de 4,316,099 km². Tous les Etats membres, à l'exception du Royaume-Uni et de l'Irlande, ont signé le traité de Schengen. Les nouveaux Etats membres n'ont pas à signer le traité de Schengen car il fait désormais partie de l'acquis communautaire.[5]

C. Reconnaissance mutuelle des qualifications professionnelles entre les Etats membres

La question de savoir comment évaluer les qualifications obtenues dans des pays tiers se pose lorsque l'on envisage la question de la libre circulation des travailleurs. En effet, il serait inutile de disposer d'un droit à la libre circulation des travailleurs si les Etats membres étaient autorisés à utiliser des questions secondaires comme la non-reconnaissance des diplômes étrangers afin de protéger leur marché de l'emploi. L'approche de l'UE n'a pas été d'essayer d'harmoniser l'ensemble des règles relatives aux formations aboutissant à l'obtention d'un diplôme. Ceci aurait été trop compliqué à accomplir. L'Union a plutôt introduit le principe de la reconnaissance mutuelle dans chaque domaine particulier en harmonisant, lorsque nécessaire, de manière limitée certains points clés.

---

[5] L'acquis communautaire correspond au socle commun de droits et d'obligations qui lie l'ensemble des États membres au titre de l'Union européenne. Ainsi, le traité de Schengen forme une partie intégrale du droit de l'UE, même si deux Etats membres ne l'ont pas signé.

A. The free movement of goods

Member states may only restrict the free movement of goods in exceptional cases; for example when there is a risk under the heading of public health, environment or consumer protection. In order to minimize risk and at the same time provide for the free movement of goods, EU legislation harmonizing important member state technical regulations has been introduced in the case of sectors manufacturing dangerous goods. However, lower-risk sectors have not in general been the subject of legislation on a European level. Trade in *non-harmonized* sectors relies on the principle of mutual recognition, under which products legally manufactured in one member state should, in principle, be able to move freely throughout the EU single market.

B. The free movement of capital

Not so long ago Europeans were obliged to manage and invest their savings in the country where they lived. Now, as a result of the liberalization of capital movements and payments, EU citizens can conduct most financial operations in any of the twenty-eight EU member states; for example, opening a bank account, buying shares in non-domestic companies or purchasing real estate. Free movement of capital is an essential condition for the proper functioning of the single market. It enables a better allocation of resources within the EU, facilitates trade across borders, promotes workers' mobility and makes it easier for businesses to raise the money they need.

C. The Single Market in financial services and the rest of the world

The creation of a more integrated market for banks and financial conglomerates is a core ambition of EU policy in the area of financial services. However, Union activity in this field is not just inward in its effect, it also has external permutations. In fact, the external dimension of EU financial services policy plays an essential role in its actual development. For example, policy is normally developed in the context of its *regulatory dialogue* with members of the Basle Committee. EU financial services policy also has an external aspect when negotiating the preparation of accession countries' transposition of financial services legislation[6].

---

[6] *Transposition of legislation* refers to the legislation a country has to adopt in order to bring its body of national legislation, in line with EU legislation at the moment of its accession to the organization.

www.ingramcontent.com/pod-product-compliance
Lightning Source LLC
Chambersburg PA
CBHW061155240326

R18026400001B/R180264PG41519CBX00002B/3